THE
GEORGIAN COUNTRY HOUSE

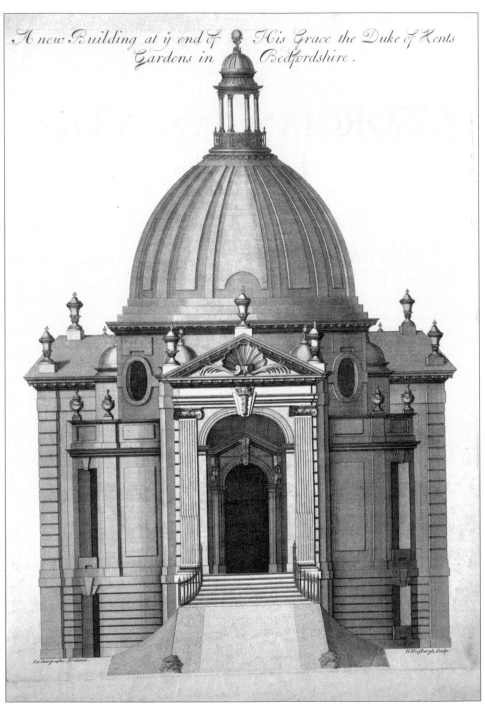

Henry Hulsbergh after Thomas Archer, A New Building at ye end of His Grace the Duke of Kent's Garden in Bedfordshire, *privately published, 1711. Worcester College, Oxford.*

THE
GEORGIAN COUNTRY HOUSE

Architecture, Landscape and Society

DANA ARNOLD

WITH CONTRIBUTIONS FROM
TIM CLAYTON, STEPHEN BENDING,
M.H. PORT, PHILIPPA TRISTRAM AND
ANDREW BALLANTYNE

SUTTON PUBLISHING

First published in the United Kingdom in 1998 by
Sutton Publishing Limited · Phoenix Mill
Thrupp · Stroud · Gloucestershire · GL5 2BU

British Library Cataloguing in Publication Data
A catalogue record for this book is available from the British Library

ISBN 0 7509 1590 0

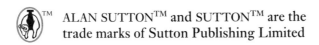

ALAN SUTTON™ and SUTTON™ are the
trade marks of Sutton Publishing Limited

Typeset in 11/12 pt Ehrhardt
Typesetting and origination by
Sutton Publishing Limited
Printed in Great Britain by
Butler & Tanner, Frome, Somerset.

Contents

Contributors

Dr Andrew Ballantyne is Senior Lecturer and Director of Postgraduate Studies in Architecture at the University of Bath. He is the author of *Richard Payne Knight, Architecture, Landscape and Liberty* and is compiling a book of essays on contemporary architecture, *The Nest and the Pillar of Fire*.

Dr Stephen Bending is a Lecturer in the English Department at the University of Southampton and has been a visiting fellow at Harvard, UCLA and the Huntingdon Library, California. He is co-editor of a forthcoming anthology, *The Writing of Rural England, 1500–1800*.

Tim Clayton was the Bromberg Fellow in the Study of Prints at Worcester College, Oxford and is currently cataloguing the George Clarke (1661–1736) collection there. He is the author of *The English Print 1688–1802*.

Professor M.H. Port is Professor Emeritus of Modern History at Queen Mary and Westfield College, University of London. He is the author of *Imperial London. Civil Government Building in London, 1851–1915*.

Philippa Tristram is Reader Emeritus in English at the University of York. She has published on a range of subjects, including medieval art and literature, nineteenth- and twentieth-century literature and politics. Her most recent book, *Living Space in Fact and Fiction*, explored the use made by novelists of architecture and interior design. She is at present writing on the portrayal of China in England prior to the Macartney Embassy of 1793.

List of Illustrations

Acknowledgements

This book began as a course outline for the MA degree in Country House Studies which I teach at the University of Leeds. The process of constructing a programme of postgraduate study around the country house revealed the complexities of its histories. This was nowhere more apparent than in my own period of specialization, 1700–1840. The purpose of the course and of this book is to place the country house centre stage in the Georgian era, to reveal its pivotal role for any exploration of the social and cultural map of the period. This aim is founded on the belief that if we look at architecture through the other end of the telescope we can learn ever-expanding amounts about a given point in time, and about ourselves.

The preparation and launch of the course, now in its third year, and the writing of this book have been a huge undertaking. Looking back it seems more daunting than when I began and there are many people to thank for their help and encouragement. My colleagues in the Department of Fine Art have been unfailingly supportive and helpful, not least in enabling me to have a sabbatical term to write this book. Without their generosity, and understanding of the intellectual premise of this project neither the MA nor this volume would have been possible. I am particularly grateful to Professor Adrian Rifkin who commented on the draft of my text and as my co-editor of *Art History* assumed extra responsibilities in order that I could complete this book. I must also mention Dr Barbara Engh whose critique of my theoretical ideas, together with our lengthy discussions of what we both see as 'the temporal sublime', was invaluable.

Collaborative work and interdisciplinarity are important aspects of present-day academic research. And I would like to thank the authors of the invited essays whose contributions greatly enrich the book through their undoubted expertise and the breadth their chapters add to the survey. Any shortcomings in the book are my own.

The collation of the illustrations has been a major undertaking in its own right and I would like to thank the following for supplying or helping me locate the illustrations for this book: Dr Brian Allen and the staff of the Paul Mellon Centre for Studies in British Art; Rosemary Baird, Curator of Goodwood House; David Griffin and the staff at the Irish Architectural Archive; Jane Sellars, Principal Curator at Harewood House; Gemma Milburn and Janet Pell of the Department of Fine Art at the University of Leeds; Ed Gibbons of the National Trust Photographic Library, who has kindly granted me permission to use a range of images of National Trust properties; Susan Palmer and Stephen Astley of Sir John Soane's Museum; and Frank Salmon.I would also like to thank Dr Mary Cosh for the references she gave me for American travellers in Georgian Britain.

I am indebted to Sarah Moore, the editor and designer, who has worked tirelessly and enthusiastically on this book. My special thanks go to my research student, Abigail Moore, who compiled the excellent index with her customary efficiency and good humour.

Finally, I would like to acknowledge how important the support of my family and friends has been during this extended period of research. Thank you Devra, Jos, Yvonne but most of all Jose. My interest in the country house and its landscape was encouraged from an early age by my grandparents, Democritus and Lily, who took me on regular outings to Chatsworth and the Peak District. Their love of the landscape and awareness of social history was truly infectious and has informed my thinking ever since. I hope they are pleased with the result. And, yet again, Ken Haynes has shown exemplary patience throughout, and that *is* a fact.

Dana Arnold
London SW13
August 1998

Preface

The country house is more than just a building. It remains an essential feature of the countryside; a bench-mark of architectural production and an emblem of a distinctive social system. The country house differs from a work of art which can be displayed in different settings while the subject matter, form and intrinsic meaning remain unchanged. The physical structure of a country house is continually altered over time as additions and alterations are made. Moreover, the country house can change its function as it meets the different demands of its occupants although its exterior appearance may be superficially unaltered. And its meaning may change depending on the nature of the context.

Considered against this backdrop of flux and change it is useful to view the country house as a text that can be read and which is in turn a cultural artefact. There are many readings of this text, each revealing new insights and explanations. The country house cannot then be interpreted merely in terms of itself or its internal structure. To determine the meaning of a country house in the long eighteenth century[1] it is necessary to relate it to the specific social, political, economic and cultural milieu within which it existed and functioned. The process of locating it within its appropriate contexts is not merely to provide historical background it is to begin the process of interpretation.

This approach underlines the importance of treating the architecture of the eighteenth and early nineteenth century not as a limited body of design which reflected certain social values. Instead country houses were an essential instrument of the development and dissemination of these ideas. By reading the country house as a text we can, despite stylistic differences, identify similar ideological debates and issues that emerge in an interdisciplinary study through which we can understand the relationships between cultural practices and artefacts. Indeed it underlines the point that to consider a building in isolation as a total history in itself and to concentrate solely on form or appearance is to denude it of much of its meaning.

The purpose of this book is to locate the country house at certain moments of its evolution in the long eighteenth century and to examine the interaction of aristocratic and bourgeois ideals which together with an agrarian economy created a vision of class unity bound together in the notions of patriotism, national prosperity and happiness. The country house and its estate was the fulcrum of this cultural hegemony and this is explored through its appearance in literature, the relationship of town house and country house, the importance of antiquity and the public consumption of the aesthetic improvements to the architecture but more importantly the landscape of country estates. This approach demonstrates that the sum of the parts of the country house is greater than the whole, that is to say the architectural form of the building itself.

This book is an interdisciplinary study and it explores the relationship between different approaches to the country house not only in the topics discussed but also in the interaction between the main body of the text and the invited essays. These bring in a range of expertise which gives a broader understanding and a more diverse interpretation of the country house. The opening essay maps out the intellectual framework for this study and signals the variety of ways of looking at the country house taken in the subsequent chapters.[2] Each of these chapters acts as a signpost offering a route through a specific area of country house history. As with any set of signposts, it marks out only one pathway and there are alternatives.[3] The principal focus of study is the country house in England but examples from other parts of the British Isles are not excluded. Moreover, it is part of the intention of this volume to propose a way of examining the country house through its architectural and social significance as well as its cultural contexts. This method of interpretation is not confined to the country house. It is a way of revealing the meaning of all kinds of architectural production.

1 The Country House: Form, Function and Meaning

Dana Arnold

The country house has been the subject of many different studies from a range of disciplines. Each reveals a new layer of meaning or significance in this most enduring of cultural icons. This book presents a social and cultural history of the country house by focusing on certain moments of its evolution in the eighteenth century. The chapters explore specific instances of the interaction of the architectural form of the country house with its differing social functions and cultural meanings. By using the country house as a lens through which to explore a range of interpretations from a variety of disciplines the country house is shown to be a matrix in which fundamental aspects of the history of the Georgian period are held. This new approach of positioning the architecture and landscaping of the country house within different social and cultural contexts builds on and benefits from preceding studies.[1]

It is important first of all to draw together previous ways of writing about architectural history to show how this study complements them. Of particular interest here is the use of biography, stylistic analysis and social history and their influence on our understanding of the country house.

The attraction of exploring a country house through the life of either its architect or patron – or indeed the interaction of both – is a significant force in the construction of its history. This is particularly the case when the architect or patron has been identified as a major figure in the evolution of the country house, for instance, Colen Campbell's Stourhead, Wiltshire (1720–4) (fig. 1.1) or Horace Walpole's Strawberry Hill, Twickenham (1748 onwards) (fig. 1.2). But there is a divergence within the biographical approach to country house history that has consequences for the way in which the building is presented. The biographical approach is limited by the life of the architect and how the country house corresponds to his architectural practice and whether it comes at the beginning, middle or end of his career. In this way architecture is mapped against the personal development of the designer which implies some kind of progress; this offers a tidy way of bundling together the disparate strands of the evolution of the country house into a neat, coherent and progressive history. And part of the aim

Fig. 1.1   Stourhead, Wiltshire, main elevation from Vitruvius Britannicus, *vol. III, plate 41.*

of this book is to unravel these strands in order to explore the discontinuities and contradictions of the country house. If the architect is presented as the principal figure involved in the design it can take on his or her characteristics. For instance Robert Adam's work in the field of country house design is often referred to as 'Adam's country houses'. This implies that architecture can be explained solely through the architect, that is through what he said and did. But many architects left no manifesto or statement of intent or any kind of comprehensive archive. In the case of Adam the *Works in Architecture* (vol. I, 1773, vol. II 1779, and vol. III published posthumously, 1822), published with his brother James, reveal little of their approach to design and does not discuss all their major commissions.[2] The biographical way of looking at buildings can present further difficulties. Often a period of extension or renovation or a new project was worked on by more than one architect. If we stay with Robert Adam and consider Kedleston (pl. 5), the Derbyshire seat of Lord Scarsdale and surely one of his finest country houses, the difficulties become apparent.[3] Robert Adam was not the first architect to be involved with the project. Rather, shortly after his return from Italy in 1758 he replaced Matthew Brettingham and James Paine who had produced the initial designs and begun work on the central block and quadrants.[4] Adam worked on the house between *c.* 1760–70 and was responsible for the south front, saloon,

Fig. 1.2   Strawberry Hill, Twickenham, c. 1748, designed by a committee which included the patron Horace Walpole. Photograph by Dana Arnold.

interior decoration and features in the grounds including the bridge and the fishing house. But George Richardson, a member of Adam's architectural office, produced several important designs including some for the ceilings of the principal rooms.[5] Richardson is tied more closely to the designs as he dedicated his *A Book of Ceilings composed in the Stile of the Antique Grotesque* (1774–6 and 1793) to Lord Scarsdale. Is Kedleston then an Adam building? And by locating it within the framework of Adam's œuvre are other interpretations and meanings of Kedleston obscured? Houses were often worked on and developed over considerable periods of time. Again Adam's work at Osterley, Middlesex (1763–80) for Robert Child, comprising the portico and interior remodelling, is only one of a series of architectural interventions in the house which dates back to the sixteenth century (figs 1.3 and 1.4).[6] Can these interventions comprise the subject matter of architectural history? Moreover, the tendency here is towards description either of what the architect did or the broader perception of the stylistic consequences of the architect concerned. This separates the function of the building, the theory of the processes of architecture and the broader social and cultural significance. To this end the country house is presented in a kind of historical cul-de-sac divorced from any contemporary or theoretical meaning it may have.

Fig. 1.3   Osterley, Middlesex, 1761–80, the entrance front. Robert Adam's magnificent portico and interior remodelling are later additions to the house. Photograph by Dana Arnold.

The construction of histories of the country house around biographies of patrons also places a distinct perimeter around the level of meaning given to the building. There is no doubt that the patron was an essential factor – s/he initiated the project, imposed personal preferences and not least paid for it. New money often prompted new building projects. For instance, the Child banking family at Wanstead (1714–20) (fig. 1.5)[7] created a country seat made possible only through their splendid wealth. Robert Walpole's Houghton, Norfolk (1722–35) makes a distinct statement about the patron's status and ambitions but emphasis on this underplays the relationship between the different architects involved, particularly Colen Campbell and James Gibbs, and the innovations in planning.[8] Moreover, some of the most eminent patrons of the arts in the eighteenth century might be under represented in such a history of the country house. Lord Burlington is a prime example of this. Burlington's country seat Londesborough in Yorkshire underwent only minor interventions in its architecture and landscape (fig 1.6),[9] although it must be recognized that the design for his own villa at Chiswick on the outskirts of London was considered one of the most startling innovations of the time (fig. 1.7). Yet Londesborough remained outside this tide of architectural development. The role of the patron also raises the question of who was

Fig. 1.4 Osterley, Middlesex, detail of the portico. Photograph by Dana Arnold.

responsible for the design. And here again Lord Burlington takes centre stage in the discussion about the design of Holkham, Norfolk (pl. 7), almost eclipsing the important role played by the patron Thomas Coke, created Earl of Leicester. (pl. 1)[10] The interaction of Coke, Burlington and William Kent, all of whom have been attributed with the design alongside Matthew Brettingham the elder, remains unresolved.[11] The triumvirate of the Earl of Carlisle, John Vanbrugh and Nicholas Hawksmoor, who were involved, in varying capacities, with the conception, design and construction of Castle Howard, Yorkshire, presents a similar case in point (fig. 1.8).[12] Both these houses demonstrate the complexities of the production of a design, the constraints on the certainty of firm attributions and the historian's difficult task in chronicling and equating these. These two ways of constructing country house histories through biography move attention away from the building itself. But a preoccupation with style moves the pendulum completely the other way.

The definition of style is a vital problem in architectural history. Architecture and style are interlinked to the point that style can be believed to contain the essence of architecture. But if this were the case style would constitute the subject of architectural history. Style is rather the specific organization of form. But the characteristics of a style consist of a repertory of ornamental components which

Fig. 1.5   Wanstead, Essex, 1714–20, designed by Colen Campbell for the Child banking family. It was demolished in 1824.

cannot be confined to a single period – many appear again and again in different configurations. So a style is characterized by the manner in which form is interpreted. What changes form? Is there a kind of spontaneous development? Or does the historian trace lines of change which are only possible to construct with the benefit of hindsight? One way of doing this is to use the Hegelian notion of a spirit of the age. This means every epoch has a distinctive set of characteristics which manifest themselves in all aspects of culture and society. Continuity and progress are identified in this model as each epoch reacts against the preceding one but certain elements are retained and subsumed in the new era. Hegel identified this as thesis–antithesis–synthesis or dialectical approach to the processes of history. Architectural style can be seen as a manifestation of the spirit of the age and Hegel's way of explaining development and change has proved attractive to architectural historians who have been concerned principally with classical architecture. Hegelian dialectic transposes itself well to the juxtaposition of the severity of early eighteenth-century Palladianism and the mid-century frivolity of the rococo which can be seen to result in the neo-classical style at the end of the century. But throughout the eighteenth century different styles coexisted and their apparent dominance or otherwise can be as much a product of the historian's aims and interests as any quantification of contemporary

Fig. 1.6   Londesborough, Yorkshire, from an estate map of 1739. One of the few country seats which underwent only minor architectural intervention in the eighteenth century, it was demolished in 1818.

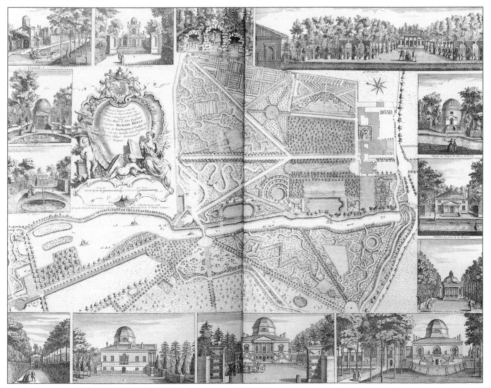

Fig. 1.7   Map of Chiswick Villa and gardens by Jean Rocque, 1736. The design for the villa for Lord Burlington was one of the most innovative of the time.

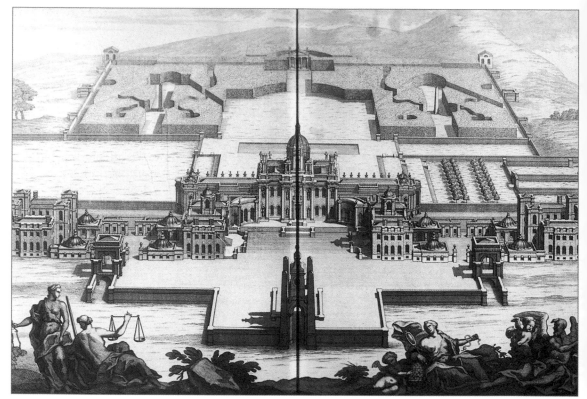

Fig. 1.8   Castle Howard, Vitruvius Britannicus, *vol. III, plates 5 and 6. The house cannot be attributed to one architect or designer but was the product of complex collaboration.*

preference or historical truth.[13] This is made more complicated when it is remembered that architects sometimes worked in different styles and some of these styles are more closely identified with particular architectural credos than others. Moreover, the emphasis on the classical – in the broadest sense – and its dominance in the period has resulted in the sidelining of other kinds of architectural production, for instance gothic, chinoiserie and the primitive, all of which manifested themselves in significant ways in country house architecture and are discussed in subsequent chapters of this book. What is important here is that disparate styles in the same period indicate a lack of unanimity in public taste which implies that different formal elements represent the distinct ideologies of social classes. Thus a style can become representative of a class ideology.[14] This has direct relevance for a study of the styles of country house building, especially for a consideration of the classical country house.

The map of the history of British architecture which encompasses the Georgian period is still identified as that drawn up by Sir John Summerson in his seminal work *Architecture in Britain 1530–1830.* It is important to consider how this canonical text has shaped subsequent views of country house architecture in the eighteenth and early nineteenth centuries with particular reference to style. The choice of examples made by Summerson as a set of stepping stones through the architecture of the Georgian period has become the bench-mark of greatness. But he presents development of architecture in the period as some kind of spontaneous series of changes where a repertory of ornamental components reappears. Summerson is concerned principally with classicism and it is the classical country house which dominates – the 'purer' the style the better. This approach constructs categories of quality determined only by twentieth-century criteria based on a knowledge of what we know to have happened later and our fuller understanding of classical systems of design. It results in architects like James Gibbs[15] being positioned outside the canon of architectural production and anomalous buildings like Strawberry Hill being ascribed to an amateur[16] rather than an architect and hence put out of the main loop of architectural production.[17] Palladianism becomes defined by default rather than by any clear contemporary treatise or manifesto. And Summerson even admits that the name Palladianism is an inaccurate but nevertheless a useful taxonomic tool.[18] Yet as the architecture of the Georgian country house is undeniably predominantly classical, the use of the ornamental motifs which comprise this system of design must have some relevance to the system of ideas and beliefs of the society which built them.

Fig. 1.9   Grimsthorpe, Lincolnshire, 1722–6, as illustrated in a watercolour drawing for one of Sir John Soane's Royal Academy Lectures. Courtesy of the Trustees of Sir John Soane's Museum.

This system must embody political, economic, cultural and philosophical beliefs of the dominant ruling class. The deviations in styles,whether Palladian, neo-classical or baroque, matter less than the persistent use of this repertory of classical elements. And on closer inspection the distinctiveness of these categories is further eroded. This is exemplified in the debates around the shift in attitudes towards classical architecture in the opening decades of the eighteenth century. The 'baroque' of John Vanbrugh and the 'Palladianism' of Colen Campbell and Lord Burlington are usually placed in opposition to demonstrate a binary approach to architectural style at that time. But in fact similar elements appear in their buildings as seen in the corner towers at Vanbrugh's Grimsthorpe (1722) (fig. 1.9) and Campbell's design for Houghton (fig. 1.10) which appeared with rusticated embellishments and to which James Gibbs added cupolas (1725–8). These also appear in Campbell's third unrealized version of Wanstead (fig. 1.11) which, significantly, Summerson likens to Vanbrugh's Castle Howard:

> Wanstead was a key building of its age. It looked back to Castle Howard, but by virtue of its purity of detail superseded that house as a model . . . [Wanstead I has] as many rooms *en suite* as there are at Castle Howard . . . The elevation is an unbroken rectangle and there is an obvious revulsion from the mobile and plastic character of Castle Howard . . . [Wanstead II] approaches a little nearer to Castle Howard . . . [the] cupola over the hall an equivalent in silhouette to the dome of Castle Howard . . . [In Wanstead III] Campbell added towers (never built) to this elevation thus reproducing the Castle Howard composition pretty completely.[19]

Summerson contests that Wanstead I, II and III remained influential sources for country house design for the next fifty years. Although he acknowledges the importance of Castle Howard and Vanbrugh, this has to be distilled into a stylistic formula to suit his argument about the dominance of Palladianism.

The purpose here is not to replace Wanstead with Castle Howard as the fount of eighteenth-century country house design. Rather it is to demonstrate the diversity of classical formulae which appeared in architectural design in the opening years of the century. Indeed subsequent chapters in this book examine the use of these classical motifs which were dislocated from their original context in antique or Italian Renaissance architecture. Looking at classical architecture in the eighteenth century as a repertory of forms rather than statements of specific design credos challenges our teleological construction of stylistic histories. This opens the way for other interpretations and histories of the country house, some of which are explored in this book. The method of grouping the architecture from given periods of time under general stylistic labels has, without doubt, been the backbone of the discipline of architectural history.[20] And when used skilfully and carefully it can provide useful punctuation marks in the lengthy and complex narrative that is the subject matter of the history of Western building. But it is only one of many tools with which to explore social and cultural contexts.

It is not only Summerson's stylistic preoccupations which have coloured our view of the country house but also his choice of examples. The Anglocentric focus

Fig. 1.10   Houghton, 1722–35, detail of corner tower, the final form is a combination of the work of Colen Campbell and James Gibbs. Photograph by Dana Arnold.

of Summerson's survey results in the architecture of Scotland and Ireland being marginalized.[21] This runs contrary to and distorts the stylistic preoccupations of the survey because architects like William Adam[22] and Edward Lovett Pearce perhaps showed a greater architectural sensitivity to the ideas of Andrea Palladio and the baroque than some of those more fully discussed by Summerson. But the purpose here is not to criticize Summerson; any survey presents fundamental choices of inclusion and exclusion of material. Nor is the aim to provide a supplement to the examples Summerson discusses or to reconfigure his material or arguments. It is more to present and prompt an awareness of the consequences of this seminal and pioneering work for architectural history as a whole and here specifically for our understanding and interpretation of the country house.

The usefulness of style labels to architectural history is not in dispute but it is difficult to see how they correlate with contemporary views of architecture. Returning again to Palladianism we find that the word is little used in the eighteenth and early nineteenth centuries to describe a particular style of building. The most notable use is when specific buildings are referred to, especially the Palladian bridges at Wilton, Wiltshire and at Stowe, Buckinghamshire (pl. 8). Indeed Horace Walpole who discussed the interiors of country houses and their contents in considerable detail makes little remark about the various styles of their exterior architecture; he appears to be more

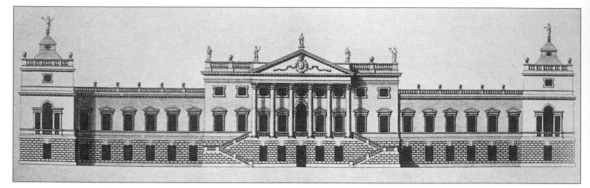

Fig. 1.11   Wanstead III, Essex, Vitruvius Britannicus, *vol III, plates 39–41, unrealized design.*

preoccupied with height. His remarks on Stourhead, Wiltshire, usually seen as a bench-mark of English Palladianism, are typical:

> The Shell of the present Stone-house was built by the Father of the present Mr Henry Hoare, the Banker, but He has finished it, added the skylight room, turned the chapel into a great Salon, and made the fine wood, water and ornamental buildings. The rooms of the house are in general too low, but are richly furnished.[23]

Questions of contemporary attitudes towards style and taste are difficult to quantify. And it is not unusual to find references to classically designed country houses as simply 'modern'. After all, Georgian country houses were modern to contemporary society and representative of their own time. The classical and historical associations have been emphasized by twentieth-century architectural historians. Once commentary is freed from the preconceived assumptions about classicism new interpretations are revealed which centre on the issue of national identity. Lord Shaftesbury's letter from Italy in 1712 is taken to herald the beginning of Palladianism[24] and the following passage is frequently cited:

> Thro' several reigns we have patiently seen the noblest publick Buildings perish (if I may say so) under the Hand of one single Court-Architect; who, if he had been able to profit by Experience, wou'd long since, at our expence, have prov'd the greatest Master in the World . . . But, I question whether our Patience is like to hold much longer . . . Hardly . . . as the Publick now stands, shou'd we bear to see a Whitehall treated like a Hampton-Court, or even a new Cathedral like St Paul's.[25]

The architecture of Wren was objected to on account of its perceived stylistic licentiousness and lack of rigour which resulted in a most unpatriotic style of building. But notably here Shaftesbury is criticizing public architecture, perhaps the most obvious face of a nationalistic style.

These comments are usually linked to two important texts which appeared shortly after Shaftesbury's letter. Campbell's *Vitruvius Britannicus* (vol. I, 1715) and Giacomi Leoni's English translation of Palladio's *I Quattro Libri dell'Architettura* (1715–16) were dedicated to George I. Together with the comments made by Shaftesbury, they are seen to signal a new approach to architecture which centred on Palladianism. Moreover, Leoni included a frontispiece prepared by Sebastiano Ricci showing Father Time unveiling a bust of Palladio underneath which is a winged figure of fame. Above this scene is Britannia with two putti holding the royal coat of arms. The message is clear: under the new royal house Palladio's principles flourish once more. Moreover, the image of Palladio himself was even made to fit. The portrait of Palladio which follows the title page is often taken at face value but it bears no relation to the portrait of the architect by his contemporary Paolo Veronese. The typical Renaissance Venetian appearance of Palladio has been changed to a clean shaven eighteenth-century face dressed in soft cap and open shirt making it more accessible and acceptable to Leoni's audience. While Leoni provided an inaccurate but nationalistically orientated guide to classical architecture through the eyes of Palladio, Campbell made a quite different contribution. The first volume of *Vitruvius Britannicus* mapped out the classical architecture of the British Isles. It was not an architectural treatise but an assemblage of images which created a new and important archive of British classicism, that is to say the use of the repertory of classical forms in a variety of configurations. And it included the work of Wren and Vanbrugh. The opening statement by Campbell makes his purpose clear:

> The general esteem that travellers have for things foreign, is in nothing more conspicuous than with regard to building. We travel for the most part, at an Age more apt to be imposed upon us by the ignorance or partiality of others, than to judge truly of the merit of things by the strength of reason. It is owing to this mistake in education that so many of the British quality have so mean an opinion of what is performed in our own country; though perhaps in most we equal, and in some things we surpass our neighbours.

He later continues:

> And here I cannot but reflect on the happiness of the British nation, that at present abounds with so many learned and ingenious gentlemen as Sir Christopher Wren, Sir William Bruce, Sir John Vanbrugh, Mr Archer, Mr Wren, Mr Wynne, Mr Talman, Mr Hawksmoore, Mr James etc., who have all greatly contributed to adorn our island with their curious labours, and are daily embellishing it more.[26]

Here Campbell turns the sights of the standards of architectural production inwards to concentrate on the qualities of indigenous architects, none of whom produced pure classical designs, and he endorses their merits. At this moment of introspection it is useful to consider how British architecture appeared to foreign eyes – a theme which recurs in subsequent chapters of this book.

The observations of a Frenchman in the mid-eighteenth century may be helpful in unravelling these attitudes towards style. Jean Bernard le Blanc, known as the Abbé le Blanc, who visited England in 1737–8 sent many letters home and these were published a decade later. Le Blanc was a sensitive architectural commentator. The following remarks were made in a letter to the antiquarian and collector le Comte de Caylus to whom he had sent *Vitruvius Britannicus* as a guide to British architecture:

Architecture is one of those things which most particularly indicate the magnificence of a nation; and from magnificence, we easily conclude grandeur. . . . Italy is the country of Europe that has produced the most masterpieces of modern architecture. The English have yet only the merit of having copied some of them. The architect who built their most famous church of St Paul at London has only reduced the plan of St Peter's at Rome, to two thirds of its size; . . . [and] wherever he deviates from his models, he has committed the greatest errors.

The greatest part of the country houses, for there are few in London, that deserve to be spoken of, are also in the Italian taste; but it has not been justly applied . . . A pleasure-house for a vigna in Rome is not a model for a country house in the neighbourhood of London.

He goes on to praise Inigo Jones and to mention the efforts of Lord Burlington through his buildings and publications to promote Italianate taste. But notes:

These models have not made the English architects more expert; for whenever they attempt to do anything more than barely to copy, they erect nothing but heavy masses of stone, like of Blenheim-Palace, the plan and front of which you will find in the *Vitruvius Britannicus*.[27]

Le Blanc is also critical of the English use of ornament which he considers at times to be 'perfectly childish'. His example is Merlin's Cave in Richmond Park by William Kent which housed the Queen's country library and also contained wax figures of Merlin and others: 'It is impossible to conceive of anything of a worst taste' (fig. 1.12). The Abbé is using the yardstick of Italian architecture to judge English architecture and, unsurprisingly, it is found wanting. Similarly, if we look for a whole-hearted and accurate adoption of classical architecture, let alone Palladianism, we will not find it in the architecture of the English country house. The architectural form can, like the adoption of Italianate manners, be viewed either as undigested and uncomfortable or a selective reuse of other traditions to express cultural distinctiveness. Le Blanc's recognition of the use of a repertory of classical elements in a variety of configurations exemplifies this dilemma. English classicism was displeasing to le Blanc through its failure to adhere to Italianate formulae. But at the same time he recognizes it as nationally distinctive.

The idea of a national style based on a variety of configurations of classical elements helps to explain the architectural production of the opening decades of

Fig. 1.12   Merlin's Cave, Richmond Park, 1735. It was built for Queen Caroline to house her library and shows the diverse range of William Kent's designs. It was demolished in 1766.

the eighteenth century. Classical forms, whether in architecture, painting sculpture, garden design or literature enabled the expression of the fundamental ideology of a culture which aligned itself with Augustan Rome. And the use of classicism as a primary expression of English culture helped to underpin the imperialist nature of early eighteenth-century British society.[28]

This gives some kind of rationale to the diversity of classical formulae rather than picking one strand as the progressive element. Indeed stylistic histories which offer an evolutionary view of architecture, impose a notion of continuity and progress on country house design which might not necessarily be there. But discontinuity is not a problem if the historian recognizes the limitations of teleological methodologies. Palladianism might appear to be the inevitable style for the Augustan era but is this really the case? Does something become Palladian in this era because it is no longer baroque? And can the baroque of architects like Vanbrugh be seen as part of the repertory of classical elements rather than a break with the Palladian tradition? Furthermore, in the absence of large numbers of replica Palladian buildings is it possible that the classical style is telling a different story which remains partly unread?[29] This seems likely when it is remembered that the importance of classicism as an expression of cultural ideologies has been recognised in other fields of cultural production – most notably literature.[30]

The introduction of social history as a method of analysing architecture has signalled an important move away from biographical or stylistic surveys. The social approach was pioneered by Mark Girouard in his ground breaking study *Life in the English Country House*. Here social life is used as a way of examining a building. More recently kitchens and patterns of eating and drinking have come under scrutiny.[31] But the interaction of social activity and architecture is problematical: is the social history a context or an explanation? And does this approach give us any kind of broader cultural meaning as it pins down the function of a building to the notion of how it was used by different social groups and to the range of social activities which took place in and around it. This understanding of function is doubtlessly an essential part of the history of the country house but it ignores an essential feature of the meaning of the country house – its metaphorical function.

The metaphorical function of the country house can be identified as its status as a symbol of the power and wealth of the landowner and more broadly the social, cultural and political hegemony of the ruling classes. In no way is this metaphorical function opposed to the physical function of the country house. Rather it reinforces the physical function of the building. The house was at once the focal point of the estate and the primary residence of the landowner – the family seat. The house was a place of business, whether political or estate, and it provided a backdrop both to the extensive collections of fine and decorative art owned by every member of the aristocracy and to the social rituals the aristocracy performed.

Metaphorical and physical aspects combined to make an embodiment and reinforcement of a distinctive social system enhanced by a set of cultural values, some of which were based on indigenous traditions and others borrowed from antiquity. In this way the country house functioned as a symbol of social control and the supremacy of the ruling class. This control was according to E.P. Thompson 'located primarily in the cultural hegemony and only secondarily in an expression of economic or physical (military) power'.[32] Moreover, Thompson recognizes that defining control in terms of cultural hegemony does not signify an abandonment of any kind of analysis. Rather it allows analysis to be made at the point where power and authority manifest themselves to create a mentality of subordination within the populace.[33] In other words, the country house's role as a symbol of patrician authority is paramount in this context. This is seen in the relationship between the style of architecture and the style of politics, and in the rhetoric of the gentry, and in country house interiors and collections. All these proclaimed the stability and self-confidence of the aristocracy in the face of threats to their pre-eminence.

The value of the country house is then greater than the intrinsic meaning of an individual building. Every house was a microcosm of the social, political and cultural trends in Britain and had a crucial role in maintaining the status quo in the face of increasing adversity. The ruling class maintained a resounding influence on the lives and expectations of the lower orders. To this end the country house functioned as a stage for the performance of highly visible paternalistic displays. During the eighteenth century the pomp and ceremony of

Fig. 1.13   William Hogarth, The Rake's Progress II: The Rake's Levée, *engraving after a series of of paintings, 1733–4. Hogarth is parodying the social rituals of the ruling élite.*

social rituals and the symbolic use of ornamental dress – including the wearing of wigs and powder – grew in importance. And the country house was a backdrop to this as well as being the site of rituals like the hunt, the celebration of marriages or national festivals. All these elements were used to exact deference from the lower orders and reinforce the social system (fig. 1.13). Parallel to this was the formidable presence of the country house in the rural environment as both a representation of the ruling class and the linchpin of country life. The country house functioned to moderate, preserve and represent the status quo.

The notion that country house architecture is the physical embodiment of governmental and social systems is evident in the important role country houses played in the architectural production of the period. The eighteenth century is noted for these private mansions, including those in urban settings, rather than public buildings or even royal palaces. The country house and its estate were therefore an ordered physical structure that acted as a metonym for other inherited structures – this encompasses the make-up of society as a whole, a code of morality, a body of manners, a system of language and the way in which an individual relates to their cultural inheritance. Through this we can reveal much about the period's dominant culture and ideology. Raymond Williams identified this as 'a lived hegemony is always in process . . . [it] does not passively exist as a form of dominance. It has continually to be renewed, recreated, defended and modified. It is also continually resisted, limited, altered, challenged by pressures not all its own.'[34] The changing relationship between the aristocratic and bourgeois classes is part of this; as the *nouveau riche* were included in the aristocracy so it became a more exclusive club and other lower orders were in turn denied the feudalistic and paternalistic rights and privileges they had previously enjoyed. Patterns of land ownership go some way towards illuminating this point. But defining who owned what is not easy and the statistics that do exist have been gathered using different sets of measurements and criteria.[35] Moreover, the only two major land surveys which took place before the twentieth century were the Domesday Book of 1086 and the Returns of Landowners of 1873 referred to as the new Domesday.[36] In 1688 15–20 per cent of usable land was held by the great landowners, that is those with an estate of more than 10,000 acres. By the end of the eighteenth century the amount of land owned by this social group had increased to 20–25 per cent. This is discussed by G.E. Mingay who recognizes a 'practical monopoly of the land held in the hands of the few';[37] by 1876 the *Spectator* noted that 'Seven hundred and ten individuals own more than one quarter of the soil of England and Wales'.[38] This figure was made up of those who owned more than 5,000 acres in any one county. Towards the end of the eighteenth century the change from a morally based to an economically based country society was expressed in William Cobbett's distinction between a resident 'native gentry attached to the soil and known to every farmer' and a gentry which was hardly resident 'looking to the soil for its rents, viewing it as a mere object of speculation . . . and relying for influence not upon the good will of the vicarage, but upon the dread of their power'. This aspect of the significance of land ownership and its impact on class consciousness results in a shift in attitude towards the land – 'limited and not always saleable rights *in* things were being replaced by virtually unlimited and saleable rights *to* things'.[39] This change in social make-up of landowners and their gentry tenant farmers redefined the social meaning of the country house and placed different emphasis on its contemporary cultural significance.

The politics of exclusion and privilege were used to galvanize different facets of society. It is possible to go beyond this to see how the house and its estate became part of the increasing cultural consumption of the period and, therefore, a bench-mark of cultural values. The growth of a consumer society resulted in the 'packaging' and 'selling . . . of the English countryside as a privately owned but nonetheless publicly consumable product – the embodiment of a way of life one could buy *into* (on psychological and ideological levels) if not actually buy'.[40]

This can be called the culture industry, part of the newly emergent consumer society, and the role this kind of consumerism played in the creation of a socially stabilizing consensus among different classes via an amalgam of traditional and non-traditional values.[41] This is seen in the proliferation of collections fed partly by the wish to own objects relating to the culture of antiquity – or good copies of the same – which sprang from Grand Tourism and a growing passion for British manufactures. The value of the country house as a site of display and conspicuous consumption is seen in new styles of architecture and the owner's ability to outshine rival estates and project an appropriate symbol of status and socio-economic power. Consumption of the country house took place on different levels. The house and estate could be viewed from afar by the lower orders and farm workers or close up by the tourist classes, usually middle class and lower gentry. The opening of the great estate to the public underlined the idea that property, authority and the idea of virtue were all bound up in the meaning of the country house. Opening it to the public helped to engender the feeling of a seamless society at once excluding and including different social groups but reflecting the cultural hegemony built on rapprochement between different social classes. This is seen in the increasingly popular phenomenon of home tourism and the proliferation of printed material concerning the country house which gave the lower social orders glimpses of a world to which they would never belong. Yet at the same time these acts engendered a sense of communality with the landowners.

All of this extends the meaning of the house beyond a set of architectural forms or styles to something more intrinsic to the national consciousness and shows it played a crucial part in the maintenance of a distinct social system against a background of upheaval and change. In this way the country house helped to define and promote a cohesive national identity throughout the long eighteenth century.

2 The Country House and its Publics

Dana Arnold

The public consumption of private property[1] in the Georgian period has been the subject of social history and histories of taste.[2] And some of the more lucid accounts, for instance the writings of Celia Fiennes[3] and Daniel Defoe,[4] have been published as chronicles of the time and still make a lively and entertaining read. This chapter positions the phenomenon of country house visiting within the broader paradigms of home tourism and the social structure of the long eighteenth century. It also examines how the country house was 'consumed' at both first and second hand during the period. The study falls into two main parts: the process of visiting and recording; and a consideration of the range of materials that gave the country house a broader public. Underlying these two main elements is the theme of architectural awareness in the period and how this pervaded the experience of the country house. It was, after all, the largest and most impressive building many would ever see – albeit frequently only from a distance. And the limited number of public buildings in major cities made the country house all the more noteworthy. In tandem with this aspect of the country house the proliferation of publications concerning architecture in general and the country house in particular are considered in this chapter as one way in which architecture entered the realms of polite society and intellectual discourse in the long eighteenth century; this also addresses the wider issue of the consumption of the country house by a broad range of publics at second hand through printed sources.

Domestic tourism[5] and within it the practice of country house visiting was not just the preserve of the upper classes.[6] It operated on many different levels from the poorest members of society glimpsing the country house from a distance to members of the upper ranks taking stock of their peers' economic and cultural worth. This chapter concentrates on the middle- and upper-class visitor to country houses and gardens. Moreover, the impressions of visitors from both America and Europe are considered both as a foil to indigenous responses and as an example of the consumption of British culture by foreigners. This makes an important contribution to our knowledge of the different kinds of tourists in the

Fig. 2.1   Eastbury, Dorset, gateway to stableyard by Sir John Vanbrugh. The house was begun in 1718 for George Dodington. Roger Morris completed it for Dodington's nephew Lord Melcombe in 1733–8. It was demolished in 1775 except for this gateway and one wing. Photograph by Frank Salmon.

eighteenth and early nineteenth centuries and informs us about how the country house was seen as a symbol of the nation.

The term visiting is here taken to mean both the invited and uninvited act of touring a country house and/or its estate. One of the questions raised is what impact did these different kinds of visits have on the concept of the country house and its perceived values. In answering this, present-day theories on the cultural significance of tourism may be helpful. Modern tourism has been identified as 'the ceremonial ratification of authentic attractions as objects of ultimate value . . . The actual act of communion between the tourist and attraction is less important than the *image* or the *idea* of society that the collective act generates.'[7] As such the act of visiting attractions functions as a confirmation of an entire body of social, economic and aesthetic values that reinforce the dominant assumptions and the existing structure of society. This chapter reveals that this interpretation is relevant to country houses in the Georgian period. The country house played an active role in perpetuating the cultural hegemony of the ruling élite through the practice of visiting. It became a signifier of the social order and so a bench-mark of class difference.[8] This goes some way towards answering the question why public access was granted at all.

The language of the house and park was one of exclusion. High walls often surrounded the demesne – in the case of Blenheim, Oxfordshire (fig. 2.2), constructed at the vast expense of over £1,000 per mile. The landscaped garden stood apart from the rest of the estate usually separated by a ha-ha. But for the country house to be effective as a statement of authority and rank it had to be seen. Long distance vistas were therefore important and can be seen in the work of portraitists of country houses who, together with landscape painters, played a significant role in making private property appear accessible.[9] Moreover, admission for the viewing public into the gardens or the house itself, gave a closer glimpse of the ultimate symbol of social and economic power. There is no doubt that one of the functions of domestic tourism was to give the illusion of inclusion in an increasingly exclusionary society. In this context tourism facilitated limited access for the many to the country house and its estate. But perhaps the most important category of visitor was the social or near social equal. Here the house, collections and parkland represented the taste of the owner. This was an innate quality born of class. Allowing taste to be seen – or putting it on display – both endorsed the cultural superiority of the nobility and reinforced their position among their peers. This distinction demonstrates the most obvious differentiation between the kinds of publics which consumed the country house – between tourist and guest/invitee.

Hospitality

The starting point for this consideration of visiting must then be the terms on which houses were available and to whom. The roots of country house visiting – when considered objectively, the peculiar practice of letting strangers tour around one's house – lie in the concept of hospitality. This is a central plank of the social stratification of English society that predates the period under discussion. Within the house itself the communal dining table in the great hall where master and servants ate echoed the unquestioned obligation to provide not only for social inferiors but also for visitors. This is seen in the dining hall at Hardwick, Yorkshire, built in about 1580.

During the latter years of the seventeenth century as the daily lives of the nobility became more private and the planning of houses changed to incorporate this shift the emphasis on hospitality did not go away. Indeed, the provision of guest apartments was a fundamental part of country house planning throughout the eighteenth and early nineteenth centuries. Moreover, as the enthusiasm for home tourism developed so did the volume of those wishing to encroach on the privacy of the occupants of country houses.

However, in spite of the fact that guest accommodation was available, there was a decline in the amount of time spent in and the volume of guests invited to the country house during the course of the eighteenth century. This trend is largely ascribed to the growing importance of the city and the time spent there. The attraction of the season and then the spa towns and the racecourse meant that families were infrequently present at their country seats. Periods of residence varied but the country was generally seen as dull. Stays there were to perpetuate the notion of hospitality by inviting guests, holding perhaps one party and bestowing enough 'benevolence' on the labouring classes to keep them going until the next visit. The decline of the country seat as a site of hospitality was noted even by the mid–eighteenth century; as *The World* remarked in December 1754, 'the most fatal revolution, and what principally concerns this season, is the too general desertion of the county, that great scene of hospitality'.[10] Nevertheless those guests who were invited were well cared for; what changed was the status of the uninvited guest.

An American traveller at the beginning of the period gives a flavour of the generous reception given to uninvited visitors of an appropriate social rank.[11] William Byrd's *London Diary* recorded his stay in Britain from 1717 to 1720 and his return in 1721.[12] This period was the beginning of the boom in country house building. Indeed, Defoe commented only a few years later in his preface to the first edition of *A Tour Through the Whole Island of Great Britain* (1724) that:

> Even while the sheets are in the press, new beauties appear in several places, and almost to every part we are obliged to add appendices, and supplemental accounts of fine houses, new undertakings, buildings &c.

Byrd was well connected with the upper echelons of English society. As a plantation owner and government official in the colony he kept company with both the Walpoles – Horace was then Surveyor and Auditor General of plantations – and the Earl of Orrery. Most of his time was spent in London where he enjoyed the full benefits of the city's entertainments. His visits to country houses, usually in the summer, were sometimes unannounced and not usually accompanied by any of his aristocratic acquaintances. But the hospitality was always generous. In May 1718 Byrd and a Colonel Cecil called unannounced on the Duke of Argyll at Sudbrooke, Petersham. The Duke, who was going out for the day, instructed his servants 'to entertain us with all the house afforded'.

Byrd's party did extremely well in the Duke's absence staying until 6 p.m. eating strawberries and beef and drinking burgundy and champagne.[13]

This tradition of hospitality to those of appropriate rank continued into the nineteenth century and is amply documented. Indeed, this level of welcome in the English country house was confirmed by two further American visitors both touring Britain after the American Revolution/War of Independence. The naturalist Benjamin Silliman[14] remarked when he arrived at Wilton in 1805:

> I was without introduction or recommendation, and my appearance, on account of my recent fall, was rather against me, but a fee to the servants gained me ready admission, and every attention which I desired.[15]

The attention paid to invited guests was even more impressive. Henry Colman, an agricultural writer, toured the British Isles in the middle years of the nineteenth century and many noble farmers were keen to welcome him.[16] On his visit to Goodwood (pl. 2) the Duke of Richmond showed Colman round personally.[17] And while on a stay at Wentworth Woodhouse, at the invitation of the Earl of Fitzwilliam, Colman remarked that the level of hospitality was as high as he had become accustomed to and:

> There was likewise what is always to be found in an English House, a writing-table, letter-paper, note-paper, and a letter box is kept in the house, and notice given to the guest always as to what hour the post will leave.[18]

Colman was endlessly impressed by the standard of housekeeping and the attention he received from servants. His clothes were brushed and laid out for him and fires kept lit in his room – both luxuries in his opinion.

Not all visitors were quite so overawed by this tradition of hospitality. Two European travellers viewed the practice of welcoming strangers of appropriate rank and the social rituals which it embodied in a very different light. A perceptive, if not cynical view, of the hospitality of country house owners to their social equals is expressed by the German aristocrat Prince Pückler-Muskau. He travelled Britain between 1826 and 1828 and his candid observations were recorded in his letters home:

> It requires a considerable fortune here to keep up a country-house; for custom demands many luxuries, and according to the aspiring and imitative manners of the country, as much (in the main things) at a shopkeeper's house as at the Duke's; a handsomely fitted up house, with elegant furniture, plate, servants in new and handsome liveries, a profusion of dishes and foreign wines, rare and expensive dessert, and in all things the appearance of superfluity, – 'plenty' as the English call it. As long as there are visitors in the house, this way of life goes on; but many a family atones for it by meagre fare when alone: for which reason nobody here ventures to pay a visit to the country without being invited, and these invitations usually fix the day and hour. The acquaintances are generally numerous: and as both room and time allotted to the guests are small,

one must give place to another. True hospitality this can hardly be called; it is rather the display of one's own possessions, for the purpose of dazzling as many as possible.[19]

The Prince went on to remark that after this open house, which lasted for a month or two, families spent the rest of their time in the country visiting others so, presumably, perpetuating the trend he identifies. Perhaps here Pückler-Muskau was discussing those who aspire to belong to the upper echelons of society. Indeed by the time he was writing, this class of wealthy gentry had increased substantially and frequently emulated the patterns of living of their social superiors. However, the uncomfortableness of the assumed manners and social rituals which surrounded the receiving of guests was identified earlier in the period by the Abbé le Blanc. He made some interesting remarks about cultural attitudes and the Italianate taste when he went on to discuss the interaction of English and Italian patterns of living:

Those Englishmen who want to pass for men of taste have to do many things against the grain; they are forced in every thing to constrain their own taste for a foreign one. They pay very dear, they say, or hear musick that displeases them; their tables are covered with meats to which they cannot accustom their palates; they wear cloaths that are troublesome to them, and live in houses where they are not at their ease. This is not the only country where we find men who are the dupes of this sort of madness, who sacrifice their ease to the fashions of a real pleasure to what is only a shadow of it. How must this folly make true philosophers laugh.[20]

The display of hospitality and wealth experienced by Byrd, Colman and Prince Pückler-Muskau together with le Blanc's comments demonstrate the role of the country house as a site for the display of rituals which underlined the social and cultural hegemony of the ruling élite. And in the case of Pückler-Muskau variations in the make-up of that class are identified.

This hospitality was not, and indeed could not, be extended to all-comers. But provisions were made for the comfort of visitors both inside and outside the estate. There is no doubt that the increasing fashion for country house visiting gave an important boost to local economies on a variety of levels. Clusters of inns and hostelries in the estate village or immediate vicinity provided food and lodgings for visitors as well as selling small guidebooks.[21] William Byrd's remarks on his visit to Blenheim (figs 2.2 and 2.3) show that some aspects of country house visitinghave hardly changed for the present-day tourist:

about twelve we got there and saw the house and garden which were extremely fine. We then saw the bridge which was also fine and remarkable. Stayed till 6 p.m. breaking only for lunch at the Bear Inn.[22]

The Bear is still providing refreshment for visitors to the house and grounds. Perhaps an even greater prefiguration of current trends in country house visiting

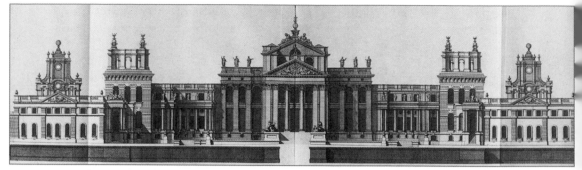

Fig. 2.2   Blenheim Palace, Oxfordshire, 1705–16, entrance front, Vitruvius Britannicus, *vol. I, plates 57–8. Sir John Vanbrugh's work was finished off by Nicholas Hawksmoor, 1722–5. As early as 1718 Blenheim was attracting large numbers of visitors.*

is evident at Rokeby, Yorkshire, where, according to Arthur Young, a tearoom was provided in the grounds by the owner Sir Thomas Robinson.[23]

The terms of admission

The terms on which houses were available to visitors varied according to the social class of the visitor and the disposition of the occupants and the housekeeper. Generalizations are always risky, but there appears to be some consensus among writers about conditions of access and the payment of fees.

This chapter has already shown that entry into country houses could be gained by the casual visitor of the appropriate class without appointment. The amount seen by the visitor depended to some extent on whether they came with a letter of recommendation and on the cooperation of the housekeeper who would usually expect a fee. Horace Walpole was one of the most up-market tourists to record their travels in detail. His *Journals of Visits to Country Seats* include his reactions to country houses formed during regular tours from July 1751 to September 1784.[24] The purpose of these notebooks is unclear; they may have been *aide-mémoires* for Walpole as to the possessions of his peers or he may have intended some kind of publication. Descriptions of the collections sometimes comprised simply a list. For instance the cabinet room at Stourhead is recorded thus:

> *In the Cabinet-room.*
> Three views of Venice, by Caneletti.
> The prodigal Son, by Sebastian Ricci.
> Holy Family, after Raphael.
> Flight into Egypt, by Carlo Maratti.
> Rape of the Sabines, by Nicolo Poussin.
> Marriage of St Catherine, by Baroccio.
> Holy Family, after the Raphael at Versailles.
> Ruins of Rome, over doors by Paoli Anesi.[25]

Fig. 2.3   Blenheim Palace, garden front. Photograph by Frank Salmon.

Walpole was not, however, afraid of the occasional adjective. Of the interiors of Kedleston he noted 'Magdalen, Annibale Caracci, good. very bad large History, D°. pretty little Polenbrugh. Sleeping Cupid, Elizabeth Sirani. fine Claud.'[26] But some of his comments were of a distinctly personal nature – especially his remarks about Boughton, home to the Montagu family:

> . . . a vast house in the French Style of Architecture, stands in a hole. . . . What is most striking, is the prodigious quantity of pedigrees heaped all over the House, along friezes of whole galleries, over chimnies, & even at the end of every step of the stairs, with no meaning that I can conceive, unless the late Duke, by whose order they were put up, & who was a humourist, intended it for the *Descent* of the Montagus.[27]

The amount of attention Walpole paid to the collections held in country houses makes a useful pendant piece to a later cultural tourist. The German art historian Dr Gustav Waagen had already published *Art and Artefacts of England* when his *Treasures of Art in Great Britain* emerged in 1852 based on his first visit in 1835 and amendments made as a result of two subsequent stays.[28] It covered most of the major private art collections in Britain, many of which were held in country houses. Waagen's text is more sophisticated and doubtless benefits from the development of art criticism in the years separating him and Walpole. Yet, Waagen was aware of Walpole's travels and mentions them in his text.[29] Like Walpole, Waagen's serious interest in collections and artefacts underlines the role

Fig. 2.4   Temple Newsam House, Leeds, West Yorkshire. As at other major houses, visitors were often admitted by the housekeeper to see the wealth of treasures without the owner ever being involved. Photograph by Dana Arnold.

of country houses as repositories and sites of display representing notions of patronage and taste. Moreover, Waagen's tours of Britain demonstrate how important an introduction to the owner of the house and/or a compliant housekeeper were – especially to someone passionately interested in the art treasures of the houses. Even his best laid plans could be scuppered. Waagen's visit to Wentworth Woodhouse, Yorkshire, caused him to remark:

> I had reckoned on a leisurely inspection of all the objects of art, as Lord Landsdown, at my request, had kindly promised to recommend my wishes to Lord Fitzwilliam. I was therefore unpleasantly surprised on hearing that his lordship was absent at his Irish estates, and had left no orders with the housekeeper respecting me. I was therefore obliged to content myself with a very superficial view, while a sight of the garden, of which I had heard much, was not to be thought of.[30]

Admission could be gained to houses without letters of recommendation. Waagen remarked that at Temple Newsam, Yorkshire (fig. 2.4):

> The housekeeper assured me that there were more pictures in the other rooms of the house; but as these apartments were 'engaged' and as I had been unable to obtain any letter of introduction to Mr Ingram, I was obliged to relinquish the hope of seeing them.[31]

He had a similar experience at Nostell Priory, Yorkshire, and did not attempt to see the collections at Duncombe Park, Yorkshire, as he had no letter of introduction to Lord Feversham.[32]

The gap between visitor expectations and what the house owner was prepared to offer, or perhaps endure, widened as the period progressed. The increased volume of tourists, including those of sufficient rank to expect hospitality, resulted in an inevitable loss of privacy during the diminishing time spent in the country and increased visitor wear and tear. Indeed the sense of *noblesse oblige* which underpinned the opening of a country house to the casual visitor was stretched to its limits. Walpole perhaps summed up the frustration at the invading hoards or 'the plague' as he calls them in a letter to Sir Horace Mann on 30 July 1783: 'I am tormented all day and every day by people that come to see my house, and I have no enjoyment of it in summer.'[33] Given Walpole's own extensive travels and detailed inspections of his peers' houses and collections it is hard to feel much sympathy for him. But he took steps to remedy the situation the following year as alongside the personally signed admission ticket (1784) Walpole introduced a 'page of rules for admission to see my House'.[34]

But these *ad hoc* arrangements for the upper end of the visiting classes who could expect to see the inside of the house were only one aspect of country house visiting. As the practice of visiting country houses and/or their landscapes grew in popularity, restrictive admission rules and fees were introduced. These were not always clearly publicized and led to frustrating journeys by eager prospective visitors. On being turned away from Sherbourne, Dorset the Honourable John Byng exclaimed thus: 'Let people proclaim that their great houses are not to be view'd, and then travellers will not ride out of their way in false hopes.' Perhaps unsurprisingly the experience coloured his opinion of the house which he described as 'ugly . . . melancholy and tasteless'.[35]

Opening times and entrance fees are also referred to by Henry Colman but he expresses a quite different point of view to Byng:

> I have often heard it complained of, that fees are to be given for visiting these places, but in my opinion wholly without reason. At Blenheim and Studely Parks the fees are fixed, at Chatsworth and most places, they are left optional with the visitor, though as confidently expected as in the former cases. . . . I see no reason why the public should claim to be admitted to the private residence of any gentleman, and it seems to me an act of great courtesy, on his part, to admit them upon any terms. The public have so long enjoyed the privilege of admission, that they seem to claim it as a right.

Colman thought that the factor of fees whether compulsory or voluntary kept down numbers and remarked:

> A liberal and just mind will feel grateful that he is permitted to see these things.[36]

These are telling comments as they indicate how visiting helped engender the illusion of inclusion into an exclusionary society which bound together different classes through a feeling of unity. Indeed, Byng's comments imply that admission

*Fig. 2.5   A river god (the Tiber),
Stourhead. A lifesize figure by John
Cheere which is part of a set of
complex references to Roman
antiquity in the grounds of the house.
Photograph by Dana Arnold.*

to houses was the expected norm. Moreover, some aspects of the house and its estate, particularly the gardens, were meant to be seen and provisions were made to enable this.

In the first half of the eighteenth century garden landscapes attracted most visitors and this was the intention of the owners.[37] Most notable among these are Hagley, The Leasowes, Stowe and Stourhead. The experience of these landscapes was carefully directed and controlled. First guidebooks and plans offered written and visual explanations of the design and symbolism. In addition, there was often only one route through the garden which ensured the sights were seen and in the right order and from the correct viewpoint. Many landscapes had associative values and consciously evoked antique and contemporary literature and philosophical ideas. Some of these references were more subtle than others. For instance at Stourhead Henry Hoare made reference to the Aeneid and Roman antiquity (pl. 10). The river god (fig. 2.5), whose cave faces the grotto, represents the Tiber. Just as Tiber directs Aeneas, here he guides the visitor with a dramatic gesture towards the Pantheon.[38] At Stowe the Temple of Ancient Virtue delivered a distinct moral message – when compared with the ruined Temple of Modern Virtue it made a critical judgement on contemporary society (fig. 2.6).[39] But at both Stourhead and Stowe British history and past greatness were not forgotten. The Temple of the British Worthies at Stowe celebrated past British culture and

Fig. 2.6   The Temple of Ancient Virtue, Stowe, Buckinghamshire, 1735–7, by William Kent. When compared with the ruined Temple of Modern Virtue, this design made a clear comment on the decline of morals. Photograph by Dana Arnold.

intellectual production through portrait busts of the likes of Shakespeare and Bacon set into an Italianate architectural framework (pl. 9). The triangular Gothic form of Alfred's Tower at Stourhead (fig 4.4) commemorates peace with France and the succession of George III (regarded like Alfred as a truly English king) in 1760.[40]

It is impossible to estimate how much of the subtler or more esoteric meaning of these landscapes was absorbed by the visiting public. But the potency of the country house and its parkland, simply through their magnificence and scale as images of a ruling élite, is not in doubt. Just as the country house established the nobility as leaders in taste so the landscape garden functioned as a more publicly accessible advert of their cultural and social superiority.[41]

The literature of country house visiting

Reference has already been made to a variety of accounts of the country house, the various ways in which it was recorded and how ideas about it were disseminated. It is important to distil these different kinds of written account to form an idea of the range of publics for the country house and of the array of social and cultural meanings inherent in it. As the eighteenth century progressed, tour books and guidebooks developed along with the fashion for home tourism and, within this, country house visiting. The diverse literature of domestic tourism in the eighteenth century, including travel journals, guidebooks, recorded tours and poems, gives some idea of the wide-ranging interest in and influence of this activity. This body of literature reveals that country house visiting was only one part of the social convention of travel and tourism which engendered an appreciation of national treasures whether they were architecture, contrived or natural landscape,[42] or the antiquities of the British Isles – including both Roman and Gothic remains.[43]

The texts which discuss country house visiting can be divided into three principal categories:[44] private diaries, travel accounts often intended for publication, and guidebooks.[45] Accounts of visits to country houses, and tours of the countryside recorded in personal diaries were often not intended for a general audience of the writer's contemporaries let alone the critical and analytical eye of the present-day historian or social theorist. Of those which have subsequently appeared in print the writings of Celia Fiennes, Horace Walpole and the Honourable John Byng now have perhaps the widest currency.

Travel accounts intended for publication proliferated during the eighteenth century. The most well-known early example here is Defoe. His journalistic style of writing and obvious interest in the whole of the British landscape – both country and city – positions the country house within the social and economic context of the time. Indeed, Defoe vividly describes the amount of development and change taking place across the country. His remark on the improvements to the infrastructure, carried out in part by the landowning classes – ' 'tis more than probable, that our Posterity may see the Roads all over England restor'd in their Time to such a Perfection, that Travelling and Carriage of Goods will be much more easy both to Man and Horse' – shows how easier access and travel faciliated home tourism. Moreover, Defoe recognizes the pace of these changes by stating if an account such as his were written every year 'every New View . . . would require a New Description; the Improvements that encrease, the New Buildings erected, the Old Buildings taken down'. Most notably, Defoe ties these developments to notions of national identity: 'in a Nation, pushing and improving things as we are: These Things open new Scenes every Day, and make *England* especially shew a new and differing Face in many Places, on every Occasion of Surveying it.' A similar journalistic approach, with special emphasis on agricultural developments in the countryside was taken by Arthur Young who wrote several tours later in the century including *A Six Weeks Tour through the Southern Counties of England and Wales* (1768) and *A Six Months Tour through the North of England* (1770).[46] Alongside specialist surveys, more general panegyrics appeared in substantial quantities. These took the form of county histories or tours of specific areas such as the Revd Gilpin's *Observations on the River Wye, and Several parts of South Wales, etc. relative chiefly to Picturesque Beauty; made in the Summer of the Year 1770* (1782).[47]

The third category of guidebooks to the country house is possibly the most diverse. They ranged from ephemeral, simply printed 'guides' available from local innkeepers and aimed principally at the casual visitor to elaborate

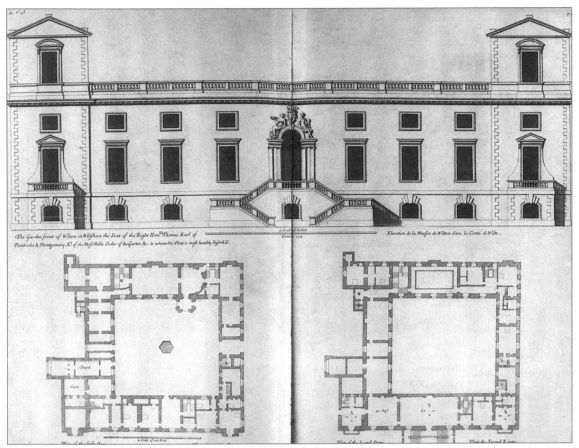

Fig. 2.7   Wilton House, Wiltshire, garden front by Inigo Jones, c. 1640, Vitruvius
Britannicus, vol. II, plates 61–2. Visitors came to see both the house and its collection.

publications celebrating the house and gardens and even catalogues of
collections. For instance Wilton (figs 2.7 and 2.8) was renowned for its fine
collection and the publication of *The copious and Comprehensive catalogue of the
Curiosities of Wilton-House* ran to 150 pages. Guidebooks proliferated as the
fashion for home tourism developed. It is here that the most complicated
relationship between middle-class consumption of the country house and the
marketing of it by a variety of publications comes to the fore. The most popular
sights such as Blenheim and Stowe had the biggest selection of guidebooks. But
did these make them more popular with the tourists? This problem was picked
up on by the Honourable John Byng who commented:

> I must think that it is from writing they [Hagley and The Leasowes] become so
> celebrated, for penmanship has the power of puffing inferior places and
> rendering them visitable by the curious and admired by the ignorant.[48]

Fig. 2.8   Wilton House, section of the great dining room, Vitruvius Britannicus, *vol. II, plates 61–2.*

The country house and architectural discourse

The proliferation of published material and the development of a print culture made the country house available to an ever-expanding range of publics. But this more general appreciation and interest in architecture ran parallel to the practice of visiting or home tourism; the visual or written discussions of the country house replaced rather than accompanied the building itself. The verbal appreciation of the abstract qualities of architecture related instead to the concerns of moral and aesthetic theorists who saw their social and cultural ideals as intrinsic to the principles of design.[49] This body of literature reveals how architecture entered the realms of polite discourse so taking on a different set of cultural meanings to those displayed to visitors and tourists. Early manifestations of the role played by architecture, especially the country house, in intellectual debate can be seen in poetry, particularly the work of Alexander Pope. It is seen to embody much that Pope both admires and scorns about contemporary society. This is nowhere more apparent than in his *Epistle to Lord Burlington*, (1730–1). Here Pope links architectural design to taste:

> You show us Rome was glorious, not profuse
> And pompous buildings once were things of use.
> Yet shall (my lord) your just and noble rules
> Fill half the land with imitating fools;
> Who random drawings from your sheets shall make;
> Load some vain church with old theatric state,
> Turn arcs of triumph to a garden-gate;
> Reverse your ornaments, and hang them all
> On some patched dog-hole eked with ends of wall;
> Then clap four slices of pilaster on't,
> That, laced with bits of rustic, makes a front;
> Or call the winds through long arcades to roar,
> Proud to catch cold at a Venetian door;
> Conscious they act a true Palladian part,
> And, if they starve, they starve by rules of art. (23–38)

Pope's attitude towards the adoption of Italianate architecture has resonance with those expressed by the Abbé le Blanc discussed in this and the preceding chapter. Indeed, he identifies a divergence between the unquestioning use of this architectural system, the profligate spending of certain patrons, and taste – the very thing this explosion of building was meant to display:

> At Timon's villa let us pass a day
> Where all cry out, 'What sums are thrown away!'
> So proud, so grand: of that stupendous air,
> Soft and agreeable come never there.
> Greatness with Timon, dwells in such a draught
> As brings all Brobdignag before your thought. (99-104)

Pope's references to architecture and landscape in his *Epistle* epitomize attitudes towards the country house and its estate in the early eighteenth century. Furthermore, the importance of the working land is emphasized:

> His father's acres who enjoys in peace,
> Or makes his neighbours glad if he increase:
> Whose cheerful tenants bless their yearly toil,
> Yet to their lord owe more than to the soil:
> Whose ample lawns are not ashamed to feed
> The milky heifer and deserving steed;
> Whose rising forests, not for pride or show,
> But future buildings, future navies grow:
> Let his plantations stretch from down to down,
> First shade a country, and then raise a town. (181–90)

At this time the language and vocabulary of architectural criticism was undeveloped – as exemplified in the comments of Defoe, Walpole and even le Blanc. Consequently the absence of precise and accurate terminology was a stumbling block to discussing architecture *per se* and its symbolic meaning. Removing the discussion of the aesthetic and moral qualities of architecture to the realms of poetry helped to overcome these problems of taxonomy. The language of poetry provided a system of classification of ideas necessary to discuss architecture in conceptual terms. This is important because early in the eighteenth century architecture began to be represented and understood as an abstract entity embodying social and cultural values.

The implications of Pope's literary discourse on the status and meaning of architecture were manifested in two distinctive trends in visual representations of the country house. The work of Kip and Knyff as published in *Britannia Illustrata* (1707) and their later volumes *Nouveau Théâtre de la Grande Bretagne* (1716 onwards) and Colen Campbell's three volumes of *Vitruvius Britannicus* (1715, 1717 and 1725) stand distinct from the literature of the country house discussed so far in several ways. Firstly the size and weight of these volumes confined them for use in the library, drawing-room or cabinet of curiosities. As such they were not guidebooks, nor were they treatises. Instead they provided visual surveys of British architecture including churches, public buildings but most of all country houses. Kip and Knyff and Campbell's texts are secondary to

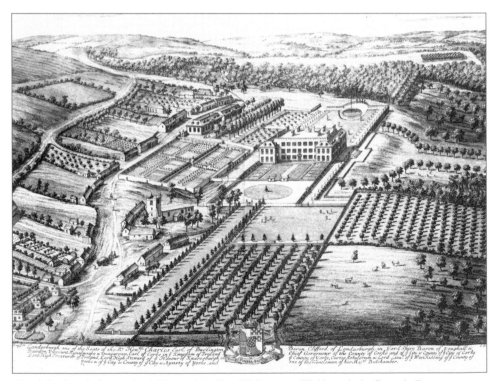

Fig. 2.9   Londesborough. J. Kip and L. Knyff, Nouveau Théâtre de la Grande Bretagne, *vol. (1716) Kip and Knyff's work put the country house in its topographical setting.*

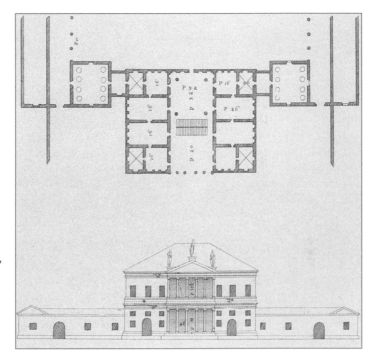

Fig. 2.10 The Villa Mocenigo, A. Palladio, I Quattro Libri dell'Architettura, *Book II, plate 37. Palladio provided detailed surveys of buildings.*

the images and offer little analysis of the plates. Kip and Knyff's volumes contain bird's-eye views which contextualized the country house within its geographical setting with the figures in the illustrations providing a pictorial narrative (fig. 2.9).[50] Indeed the method and conventions of representation in these volumes subjugated the architecture of the country house in favour of the detailed and accurate representation of the gardens and the estate. The recognition of the importance of the landscape to the social and cultural meaning of the house has resonance with Pope's discourse in the *Epistle*. Moreover, this tradition of representation continued and developed throughout the eighteenth century.[51]

The assumption has frequently been made that Campbell's three volumes of *Vitruvius Britannicus* acted as a kind of manifesto for Palladianism. But the sparse nature of the text and absence of any clear instructions or opinions on the art of design makes this unlikely. Even a brief comparison with Palladio's *I Quattro Libri dell' Architettura* reveals more differences than similarities. Palladio's treatise provides detailed and measured drawings of his own buildings and reconstructions of ancient ones (fig. 2.10) often in plan elevation and section. There is always a scale and the dimensions of individual ornamental elements and the orders are provided (fig. 2.11). A technical section on how to build and design elements like staircases gives Palladio's work a practical edge. Its size meant the volume was portable and usable on site as a guide and as an easy way of recording personal responses to buildings. It was used in this way by Inigo Jones, Lord

Fig. 2.11   The Temple of Peace (Basilica of Maxentius), A. Palladio, I Quattro Libri dell'Architettura, *Book IV, plate II.*

Burlington and Robert Adam (fig. 2.12).[52] Campbell's text is quite different. It lacks the formal organization of Palladio, provides only an arbitrary scale with which to judge the length of a building's façade, and includes only limited architectural details.

Campbell's method of recording the most notable British buildings became a mainstay of the whole period. John Woolf and James Gandon published volumes four and five of *Vitruvius Britannicus*, in 1767 and 1771 respectively, and republished Campbell's initial three volumes.[53] The series was later revivified by George Richardson as the *New Vitruvius Britannicus* which appeared in two volumes between 1802 and 1808 and between 1808 and 1810.[54] If we consider the tradition established by *Vitruvius Britannicus* its distinctiveness and significance becomes apparent. The techniques of making visual representations of architecture are relevant here as the plates in *Vitruvius Britannicus* divorce architecture from any background or setting (fig. 2.13). The anti-pictorial nature of the plates is further emphasized as elevations are drawn in orthogonal perspective (fig. 2.14).[55] This way of recording an elevation or section on a flat spatial plane denied the illusion of space or volume seen in paintings or the work of Kip and Knyff. But this kind of two-dimensional image allowed a more accurate recording of architectural elements. Groundplans provide the only guide to the three-dimensional form of the building (fig. 2.15). The result is a more abstract

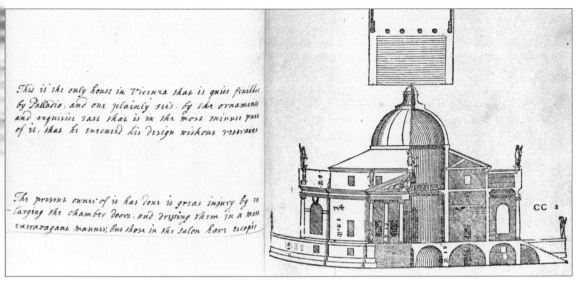

Fig. 2.12   A. Palladio, I Quattro Libri Dell'Architettura, *a page from Lord Burlington's copy showing the Villa Rotonda annotated in Burlington's hand. Courtesy of the Trustees of the Chatsworth Settlement.*

representation and concept of architectural design. For the country house this meant that the reductive images of plans and elevations could be appreciated for their composition and rhythm and even their classical references – the same kind of critical apparatus that could be used for Pope's poetry. The appreciation of these abstract principles of design was an expression of class and taste. But this taste was not a blind following of Palladio's principles. Instead it came from an indigenous tradition of literature and aesthetics which drew in part on the classical examples. This difference between English architectural production and Palladian or strictly classical design is identified and vilified by le Blanc on the grounds of an absence of taste.

> You are acquainted with *Vitruvius Britannicus* and as you are not only a master of the rules of all the arts, but have that exquisite taste which is much superior to the rules themselves, because it is the hidden principle of them: don't you think the author of that work has had all the remarkable buildings in England designed and engraved on purpose to shew us, that architecture is a science, which is not yet naturalised here? It is one of those that depend on taste, and therefore may still be a long time foreign in this island. It is not that architecture is void of known principles and certain rules, some of them founded on nature; . . . and others successively established and unanimously agreed to, as the result of the experience of our predecessors; but the most difficult and most extensive part of it, that of decoration, and the ornaments it is capable of receiving, taste alone must give; and taste gives nothing in this country.[56]

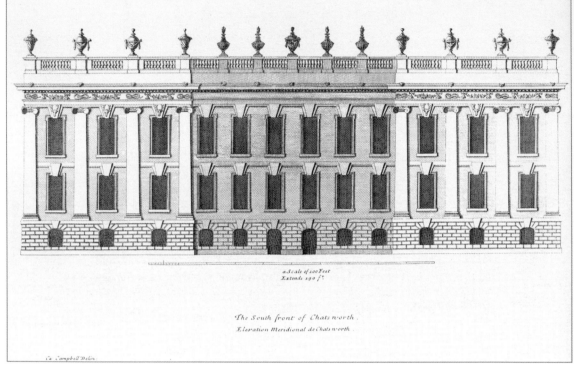

Fig. 2.13   Chatsworth, Derbyshire, south front, Vitruvius Britannicus, *vol. I (1715), plate 76. Colen Campbell's representations of buildings contrast with those supplied by Palladio.*

The process of distancing architecture from its physical context and making it part of intellectual debate in the opening years of the eighteenth century had important consequences. Firstly, architecture became the concern of the patrician élite. Their aesthetic and moral values were expressed by Pope and codified into a visual language by Campbell. Secondly, the codification of architecture into a distinct, recognizable and readable system ultimately placed architectural discourse in the wider public domain; once the language which codified architecture was established the principles could be grasped by the literate classes. This led to the democratization of the appreciation of country house design. Just as literary accounts of and pictorial guides to Britain and the country house proliferated in the eighteenth century so did the abstract discussions of architectural design. In this way *Vitruvius Britannicus* helped to establish the widespread appreciation of architectural design. As the visual language of architecture became more widely understood so ideas were spread. This is particularly relevant for the country house as books of designs for it proliferated towards the end of the eighteenth and beginning of the nineteenth century. It is in these texts that the democratizing principles of the appreciation of architecture through inexpensive publications can be seen to be at work.

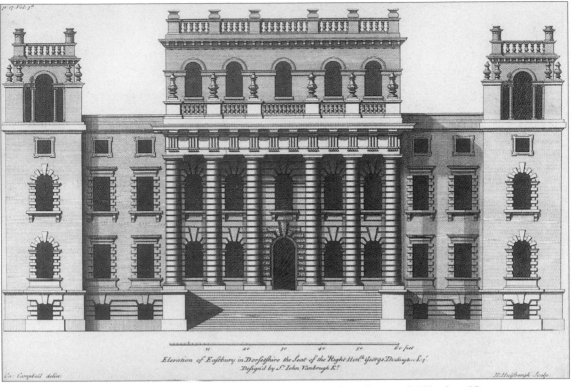

Fig. 2.14 Eastbury, Dorset, principal façade, Vitruvius Britannicus, vol. III, plate 17.

In the period 1780 to 1815 over thirty books of country house designs were published.[57] These were produced mostly by architects of the second rung, a notable exception being Sir John Soane's *Plans, Elevations and Sections of Buildings* (1788) and *Sketches in Architecture* (1793). The plates were mostly of extant works and are a useful guide to the range of styles which were fashionable at the time. Architects such as John Plaw who published *Rural Architecture* (1802) or Robert Lugar whose *Architectural Sketches* appeared in 1805 saw these texts as a means of self-advertisement. Plaw stated that he 'begs leave to inform his Friends and the Public, that he furnishes designs, and working drawings, and will advise or attend to their execution (if required), at the usual commission. Letters post-free will be duly attended to.' Lugar offered similar services. But the importance of these publications in this context is that they indicate a desire to spread the qualities of country house design across a broader social group. The relatively inexpensive texts were purchased and read by a wide-ranging public, some of whom commissioned buildings in the hope of emulating their social superiors. But underlying this was also a growing interest in country house architecture and these books of designs helped the process of democratizing the appreciation of it.[58]

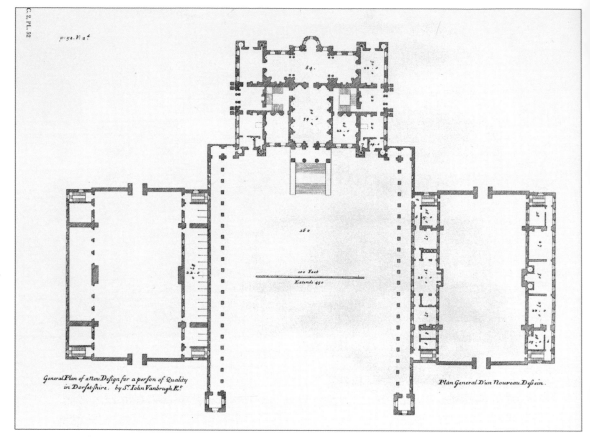

Fig. 2.15   Eastbury, groundplan, Vitruvius Britannicus, *vol. III, plate 52.*

There is no doubt that the country house was exposed to an ever-expanding public during the eighteenth century. This symbol of the cultural hegemony of the ruling élite was consumed in a range of ways, each adding a further layer of meaning to it. Moreover, the increase in home tourism coupled with a growing interest in architecture meant the country house permeated many levels of society and became a bench-mark of class difference, social aspirations and architectural criticism. As such the country house represented notions of national identity which were understood and interpreted by its foreign and British publics.

3 Publishing Houses: Prints of Country Seats

Tim Clayton

'Great Britain may justly boast her decided superiority over every other state in Europe, in the grand display of its numerous Country Seats', affirmed J.P. Neale's introduction to his six-volume *Views of the Seats of the Noblemen and Gentlemen in England, Wales, Scotland and Ireland* (1818–23). Within the period of this study Neale's was a late if important contribution to a thriving branch of print publishing. By 1830 there were perhaps a thousand different plates of country houses – a quite remarkable competitive celebration of the architecture and grounds of the country seat.

Yet little attention has been paid to them beyond their potential as illustrations. A print has supplied the place of a lost drawing where a plan or an elevation was required or has retrieved the appearance of a house that has ceased to exist. Historians have not discussed the published record of Britain's country seats as a phenomenon in its own right or considered how and why the prints themselves came into existence.[1] What motivated their publication? What were they intended to communicate about the building or garden that was, through publication, brought to the attention of a wider public? What was the market for such prints and what influence did they have? Prints were much more widely seen than paintings. Volumes of them, perused in the library, constituted a visual record that could be studied. Publication defined a canon of familiar material and this role in assigning status alone deserves attention.

Some architectural prints have already received close scrutiny in Eileen Harris's *British Architectural Books and Writers 1556–1785*. As part of a wider study of architectural texts, Harris considered collections of prints that were sold as volumes, providing exemplary accounts, for instance, of *Vitruvius Britannicus* and James Gibbs's *Book of Architecture*. However, books of topographical views were excluded as of peripheral relevance and although small sets of architectural prints sometimes came within Harris's purview, individually published prints did not. This chapter attempts a preliminary survey of separately published prints and books of views and tries to develop some approaches to their interpretation. There is not space here for a complete survey and I have insufficient evidence for conclusive analysis but I hope that by suggesting the potential of printed pictures as primary sources the chapter may stimulate further enquiry.

I have already indicated a distinction that can be drawn between two kinds of prints of country houses – plans and elevations, and the view. Views of houses and gardens were decorative, invited admiration, and provided souvenirs for tourists. Architectural elevations and plans, on the other hand, had a more specialized purpose in documenting developments in design for an international community of architects and connoisseurs and also in providing practical patterns for other builders to copy. They were educational: in 1699 it was argued that 'fine Books of Architecture have made a great many Good Architects; who without going to Italy, where are the fine Relicks of Antiquity, have formed a true and good Manner, and perfected their Studies in this Art by the Help of Graving, which faithfully represents the Plans, Profils, the Elevations and Measures of the finest Buildings'.[2] Plans and elevations were sometimes also produced for private circulation among friends or members of a committee in order to gain approval for a projected design or funds for a building project.

The two types of print were to be found in combination. Sets of views of châteaux published in France in the seventeenth century had contained plans in order to explain the spatial context of the whole garden. Series with a more precisely architectural orientation contained views in order to show the architecture in its final setting. This applied equally to Israel Silvestre's views of Versailles, etched between 1664 and 1684, and to William Chambers's *Plans, Elevations, Sections, and Perspective Views of the Gardens and Buildings at Kew in Surrey* (1763). The tradition of treating house and garden (or even park) as a unity enjoyed similar longevity. Suites of views of one property would cover many aspects of the house and of its gardens. Sometimes there might be more emphasis on the house, sometimes more on the garden, but the two were treated as an organic whole.[3]

French artists and publishers set the tone and defined approaches to the depiction of houses and gardens with suites of views of particular properties, such as Israel Silvestre's *Liancourt* (1655–6) and *Fontainebleau* (1649–50 and 1658). An alternative model, developing from the *plan relevé* to the 'bird's-eye view' in France and in Holland allowed most features of an estate to be revealed in a single print. Two hundred or more small but detailed views of houses around Paris and of provincial châteaux, principally by Adam Pérelle, were gathered into *recueils* by Nicolas Langlois and Jean Mariette. Records of gardens in other countries were published in their shadow. Giovanni Battista Falda's views of villas and gardens around Rome were influential. Views of Swedish palaces were published in Stockholm during the 1690s and there were numerous views of Dutch houses and gardens, but the largest and most modern imitated the increasingly sophisticated example of Versailles.[4] The link to tourism was clear in the text accompanying prints. A new set of views of Versailles published by Gilles Demortain in 1716 explicitly followed the recommended route round the gardens. France – especially Versailles – was the established model for emulation.[5]

England made a stuttering start to its contribution with isolated publications such as De Caux's *Wilton Gardens* (*c.* 1644). Henry Winstanley's Audley End suite (1676) followed this in combining plans and elevations with views in the French manner.[6] In about 1680 he projected the earliest attempt at a large-scale series, issuing an etched advertisement showing his own house at Littlebury. This most helpful document reveals a series of enduring motives for producing prints of houses:

> The undertaker of this great work can not be thought to designe extraordinary profitt to himselfe, considering ye. charge of Copper Plates, ye. expences of journeys, especially to places farr remote to take designes &c.: But that he hath seen most of ye famosest Houses in France, Italy & Germany, & have been drawn to ye: expence & trouble of travalling by sight of some Prints done after them in this kinde; And haveing likewise observed many most worthy houses in England, not onely of Noble men but likewise of Gentlemen, that have bestowed great charges in beautifieing their Fronts with good Architccture & Symmetry, which is for ornament, more than convenientcy. And notwithstanding these great expences, their houses are not only unknown to all forreigners that come not into England, but likewise to all people that travaile not about, and not heard of by many people of ye same County. I have proposed this way to shew my endeavour to serve my Country, by letting forreigne Nations have a sight & small prospect, of what is as much deserveing as in any Kingdome, & an easy way for all my Country men, to turne from leafe to leafe, & soe to have a sight of as many houses in few minutes, as would cost many days & weeks to travaile to them.

First, Winstanley invoked patriotic rivalry just as Neale was to do over a century later. Winstanley had seen prints of other nations' houses and felt that foreigners should be made aware that this country also could boast façades with 'good Architecture and Symmetry'. Winstanley was not yet so confident as Joseph Smith who, some thirty years later, declared his intention 'to expose to the Eyes of the World . . . the Grandeur of this Nation'.[7] Secondly, publication would bring local prestige. Winstanley argued that there was little point making houses beautiful if the improvements were not seen and it was especially important that the gentry of the owner's own county should appreciate his tasteful expenditure. Finally, Winstanley deployed a common argument in favour of printed pictures – that they were potent instruments of enlightenment. Prints enabled people to view and compare many houses in minutes with little expense and no trouble. On the other hand they encouraged some, like Winstanley himself, to travel to see the architecture in person.

Winstanley's proposal reveals that although an entrepreneur lay behind the scheme the selection of houses to be included would depend on the initiative of their owners:

> All Noble men and Gentlemen that please to have their Mansion Houses design'd on Copper Plates, to be printed for composeing a volume of ye Prospects of ye Principall Houses of England: May have them done by Mr. Hen: Winstanley by way of subscription, yt. is to say subscribing to pay

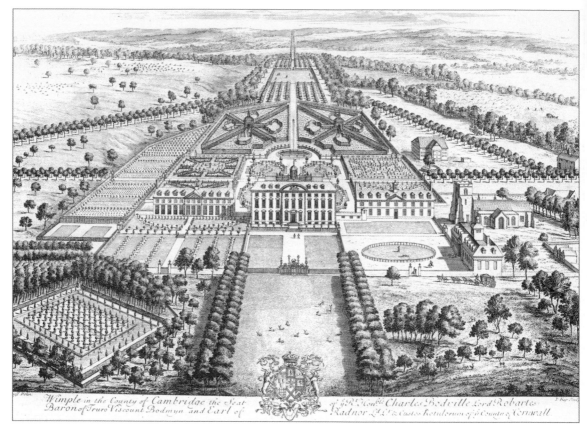

Fig. 3.1   J. Kip after L. Knyff, Wimple in the County of Cambridge, *published by Knyff,*
c. *1701, engraving with etching. Norman Blackburn, antiquarian printseller, London.*

five pounds at ye delivering of a fair Coppy of their respective houses as large as
this Plate; or Ten pounds for one as large as Royall paper will contain: He
likewise obligeing himselfe to furnish as many Prints of all sorts, att 4*d*: and 6*d*:
a Print as any that subscribe shall require, & to deliver one fair sticht Book of as
many houses as shall be done when it is demanded without further charge.[8]

Each owner was to pay for the view of his own property, rather as if he had
commissioned a private plate.

Winstanley's plan seems not to have progressed to his satisfaction. Around
1700 a similar scheme was proposed by Leonard Knyff who invited owners to
sponsor a series of much larger plates of '100 Noblemen and Gentlemens Seats'.
This was not a complete success either. Having failed to reach his target of 100
subscribers, Knyff sold his plates. But his prints were soon selling well on the
open market (fig. 3.1). The eighty completed plates were first published as
Britannia Illustrata by the print and bookseller David Mortier in 1707 but

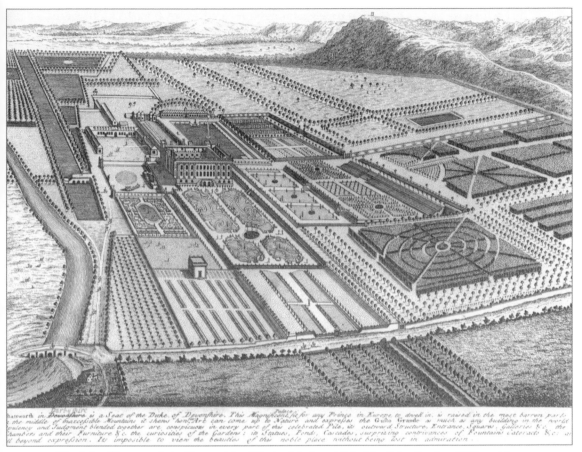

Fig. 3.2 Chatsworth in Devonshire [Derbyshire], *published by John Bowles, 1724, etching.
British Museum, London.*

Mortier, the printseller Joseph Smith, the bookseller Daniel Midwinter and the
printseller Henry Overton apparently each owned a share in Knyff's plates and
reissued them in combination with suitable additions from their own stock.[9] John
Kip and others advertised their willingness to draw and engrave houses for
English patricians who would present prints of them to friends and clients as
evidence of their *virtù*, as Lord Salisbury did to George Clarke.[10] The plates were
then sometimes sold to printsellers (fig. 3.2). Smith's *Britannia Illustrata* volumes
II and IV added up to ninety more country houses to Knyff's record.[11] Mortier
and Smith combined these prints with others in French–language export editions
entitled *Nouveau Théâtre de la Grande Bretagne*.

This was effectively the first large collection of views of English houses (some
Scottish houses were added to Smith's fifth volume) and it was specifically
presented as a statement of national affluence and architectural taste. It is worth
noting a striking difference between these views and those published in France.

French views had at first been overwhelmingly devoted to royal palaces and were later dominated by the town houses and suburban retreats of the new financial élite, whereas in England, despite some attention to royal palaces, far greater emphasis was placed on the provincial possessions of both great nobles and county gentry.

The enthusiasm for architecture that provided a favourable climate for *Britannia Illustrata* also nurtured a demand for elevations of fronts and plans of the new layout of rooms with symmetrical suites of chambers and cabinets. Here too publication was driven by newly confident rivalry with France. During the seventeenth century a long series of plans and elevations by Jean Marot recorded the developing sophistication of French building, an initiative continued by Pierre and Jean Mariette. In England *Vitruvius Britannicus* (1715) was the first collection of views to show houses as architecture. Its publication narrowly preceded, or possibly interrupted, a similarly fine series of views of contemporary French architecture published by Jean Mariette. These were eventually published as a book, *L'Architecture Française*, in 1727, but they had originally been issued over a number of years in little stitched sets of six or so prints each devoted to a particular house. To judge from the dedications, *Vitruvius* was originally undertaken with the backing of prominent Tories who had already adopted Inigo Jones as a national architectural hero, although its aim of celebrating the finest new British architecture made a welcome for a broad range of stylistic approaches obligatory.[12] The collection continued to be developed as a gallery of British architecture but with increasing Palladian emphasis in a second volume in 1717 and a third, containing some views and garden plans, in 1725. A poor 'fourth volume' was issued in 1739 by the booksellers George Foster, John Wilcox and Henry Chapelle, incorporating recent surveys and Watteauesque views by Jean Rocque, together with old plates acquired from Joseph Smith (some intended for continuations of *Britannia Illustrata* or *Vitruvius Britannicus* and some which had already been included in the *Nouveau Théâtre*).[13] A nobler continuation was initiated by John Woolfe and James Gandon in 1764. Styling their collection volumes four and five, they disowned the fourth volume of 1739 and returned to the approach of the first three volumes with apparently precise plans and elevations of recent buildings.[14]

A third context for the production of views of country houses was the county history. Views of seats had been a feature of Robert Plot's *The Natural History of Stafford-shire* (1686) and were prominent in Sir Robert Atkyns's *The Ancient and Present state of Gloucestershire* (1712) and the Revd John Harris's *The History of Kent* (1719). In county histories particular pressure was placed upon owners to defend both their status in local society and the prestige of their county, for authors relied upon the pride or goodwill of owners for illustrations of the fine properties that the county might boast. Histories emphasized the continuing importance of the county structure and of the families within it. In this context new money could show off acquired good taste in architecture while old money could assert its pedigree by displaying its ancient seat. It became conventional for a section of such a history to be devoted to the touristic sights within it. Thus the Revd John Collinson's 1781 proposal for *The History and Antiquities of the County of Somerset*, devoted section three to 'Descriptions of Gentlemen's Seats, Public Buildings, Romantic Prospects, and picturesque Ruins, with the Arms and Genealogies of illustrious Families'. Collinson's conditions for publication presented the case plainly:

> Plates of Gentlemen's Seats and Public Edifices are great and necessary Embellishments to a Work of this Nature: But as the Expence of these would be too heavy for the Editors, they hope those Gentlemen, who wish to have Views of their Seats inserted, will be at the Charge of the Engravings, which will remain a public Record of their Families to Posterity.

Houses were to be drawn on summer tours by the illustrator Thomas Bonnor and a further announcement encouraged recalcitrant owners to forward their orders before Bonnor's final tour. Like potential subscribers to prints in London, local householders were invited to judge the standard of what had been done by inspecting finished proofs 'at Mr Cruttwel's, printer, Bath; and at the Rev Mr Collinson's Long-Ashton Somerset'.

That this procedure became standard is confirmed by the 1793 proposals for the Revd Stebbing Shaw's *The History and Antiquities of Staffordshire*: 'Noblemen and Gentlemen will, he trusts, as usual, contribute the plates of their own mansions . . .'. Proposals in 1801 for the *History of the County of Suffolk* provided a cunning, but understandable, rationale for the practice:

> no seat, as such, of any Nobleman or Gentleman, can be introduced to increase the expense of the Work. And the reason is obvious: it will be impossible to draw the line. If an engraving of one seat be given, the owner of another, perhaps equally interesting and beautiful, may reasonably be offended by the omission of his. It is however, unjust to the Public, that all such should be omitted. In one way only (and it has been done in other counties) can this difficulty be surmounted: if any Nobleman or Gentleman be desirous of enriching the Work with a view of his place, and will have a drawing engraved, or commission the Author to get one executed, he will be proud to insert it.[15]

Individual prints of distinguished houses adding lustre to a particular region were now sometimes published locally. A view of the architecturally distinguished Tudor mansion of Hengrave Hall, Suffolk, for instance, was published by subscription in 1775 for *2s 6d* and dedicated to its owner Sir Thomas Gage by the printseller John Kendall of St Edmondsbury. Its publisher claimed that Hengrave 'was Built in the Reign of King Henry VIII and is a singular and most noble edifice'.[16]

Most of the prints that have been discussed so far had been sponsored by the owner of the property. By the mid–eighteenth century commercial speculation yielded further views of houses and their contents and gardens. Certain major houses were already becoming centres for tourism on some scale, notably Blenheim, Wilton, Houghton and Stowe. Wilton's associations with Inigo Jones, the champion of British architecture, gave it national significance for connoisseurs. James Kennedy's *The Antiquities and Curiosities at Wilton House* (1768), itself 'enriched with 25 engravings of the Capital Statues', quoted Horace Walpole's assertion that Wilton was 'one of the principal Objects in the History of the Arts and Belles Lettres', an early defence of the country house as an art object of national historical importance. Such a status was already argued by the published record. Six plates of Jones's architecture at Wilton appeared in the second volume of *Vitruvius Britannicus* (1717) and another view was added in 1725. Sixty of its statues were published by Cary Creed in 1731 and four of the most important paintings were engraved about 1732. Others were added later.[17] The elevation of Roger Morris's Palladian bridge, built in 1736, was engraved by Paul Fourdrinier in 1740. John Rocque published a survey of the house and gardens with views of buildings about 1750 and the house and bridge were shown in Luke Sullivan's view of 1759.

The Plans, Elevations and Sections, Chimney Pieces and Ceilings of Houghton in Norfolk were published in 1735 although publication of the picture collection did not really get under way until after Robert Walpole's death. However, about a dozen paintings had already been published before John Boydell undertook a full-scale record of the collection in 1775 with sale to Catherine the Great impending.

Wilton and Houghton fascinated connoisseurs but Blenheim always had a wider appeal. Blenheim enjoyed the symbolic military and political significance of a house built with money granted by Parliament as a reward for the Duke of

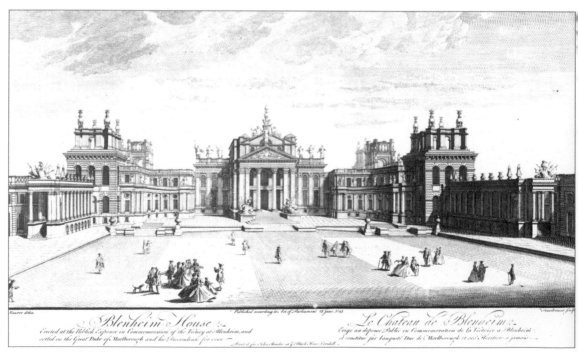

Fig. 3.3 Paul Fourdrinier after J. Maurer, Blenheim House, *published 1745, engraving with etching. British Museum, London.*

Marlborough's achievement in saving the empire, preserving European liberty and humiliating Louis XIV. The prints that represented the house and its gardens rarely allowed foreigners to forget these points and invited British natives to glory in Marlborough's victories. A first set of huge plans and elevations, distributed by Jacob Tonson and advertised in the *Spectator* in 1711, bore inscriptions in English, Latin, Italian and French to ensure that their message was understood.[18] Further two- or three-sheet views were soon published more cheaply by Thomas Bowles, Joseph Smith, Thomas Taylor and Henry Overton. Smith's was incorporated in *Britannia Illustrata* and Tonson's were copied for *Vitruvius Britannicus* with a plan of the park being added in 1725. From Bowles one could also buy three views and a plan on one imperial sheet. The statue of Queen Anne in the library was published. A new perspective view after Maurer by Fourdrinier was issued by Bowles in 1745 (fig. 3.3) and in 1752 John Boydell published four views, two of which showed the new canal in the park. Blenheim also displayed an unusually fine collection of paintings, some of which were published. When *Time Cutting Cupid's Wings* by Van Dyck and Rubens's self-portrait with his wife and child (1758) were engraved by Macardell their location at Blenheim was mentioned on the print.

Stowe was, like Blenheim, an extension of the Oxford tour. Here the house, though newly built and richly appointed, contained little of exceptional interest, but the gardens were unmissable. 'Enfin j'ai vû Stow', wrote the anonymous author of the French language guide published in 1748, 'cette petite merveille de nos jours, & le lieu le plus enchanté de toute l'Angleterre! Il n'est point de Voïageur tant soit peu Connoisseur & Curieux, qui venant à Londres n'aille voir Blenheim, & surtout Stow, comme étant tout ce que ce riche Pays a de plus brillant & de plus magnifique.' Its description as 'an enchanted place' recalls earlier descriptions of Versailles: it was remarked, for instance, on the first of a series of views published in 1693, that 'il faut voir ce lieu enchanté pour en juger'.[19] The first guidebook to Stowe, Benton Seeley's *A Description of the Gardens of Lord Viscount Cobham* (1744) was preceded by some years by the first set of views. In 1739 Sarah Bridgeman, widow of the designer of the garden, had published a plan and fifteen views of Stowe gardens that Charles Bridgeman had commissioned from the leading illustrator of French gardens, Jacques Rigaud. In 1746 the Bridgeman views were remaindered for 2 guineas, half the original price, by a consortium of printsellers including the powerful Bowles brothers and they were reprinted in 1752.[20] In 1750 Seeley added to his guide a set of thirty-eight thumbnail views of garden buildings on ten plates by George Vertue and Gerard Vandergucht to be sold not only by Seeley in Buckingham but also by the leading printseller Robert Sayer in London. In the same year Seeley's idea was plagiarized by the London printseller George Bickham. The thirty small souvenir views that accompanied Bickham's guide were advertised as available framed and glazed for the closet at 3*s* plain and 6*s* coloured – a marked contrast with the 4 guineas originally demanded for Bridgeman's fine prints. Like Seeley's, Bickham's views were sold at the New Inn built for tourists at the entrance to Stowe gardens, in the two Buckingham bookshops and in London. In 1753 Bickham published an updated set of sixteen views and a plan, with the backing of

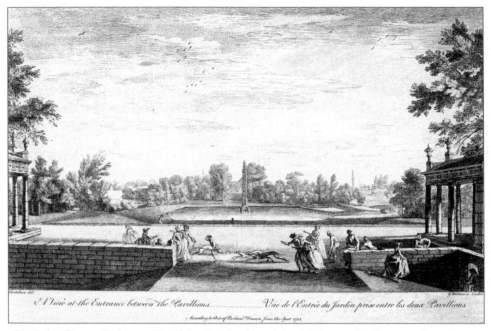

A View at the Entrance between the Pavillions................Vûe de l'Entrée du Jardin prise entre les deux Pavillions.
According to Act of Parliament Drawn from the Spot 1753.

Fig. 3.4   George Bickham after John Baptist Chatelain, A View at the Entrance between the Pavilions, Stowe, *published by Bickham*, 1753, *engraving with etching. Grosvenor Prints, London.*

Sayer and the Bowles brothers (who later acquired the plates) (fig. 3.4). These showed improvements made to Stowe since Bridgeman's day. Later Bickham added a further six large views. Bickham's 1753 set was sold for 1 guinea plain and 2 coloured. In 1759 his guide was '1s without the Plan, 1s 6d with the Plan, with the Views of all the Temples and Ornamental Buildings in the said Gardens, 6s bound'.[21] The cheapest set of twelve 6 × 4 in views was available from Sayer for 1s 6d. Such extensive coverage of a single garden in a series of prints recalled the treatment of Versailles. Jacques Rigaud had revived the practice in France with sets of St Cloud, for instance, in 1730 and Charles Bridgeman's original undertaking (that of a designer, not an owner) put Stowe into direct competition with the best gardens of France.

A large majority of the other houses that were published in the mid-century were situated in 'the Campagna of London', links in the chain of elegant villas and pleasure gardens that encircled the metropolis. Most attention was paid to the royal palaces (fig. 3.5) and gardens of Kensington, Hampton Court, Richmond, Kew and Windsor (fig. 3.8) and to the Earl of Burlington's villa and garden at Chiswick (fig. 3.6).[22] Claremont yielded a survey (1750) and two views (1750, 1754) by Jean Rocque. Of the other Pelham houses, both Henry Pelham's Esher and the Earl of Lincoln's Oatlands were surveyed by Rocque in 1737 and engraved by Sullivan in 1759 while Oatlands was also the subject of a pair of views by

Fig. 3.5　William Woollett, A View of the Garden &c at Carlton House in Pall Mall, *published by John Tinney et al 1760, as revised by Henry Parker, Robert Sayer, John Bowles, Carrington Bowles and John Boydell, c. 1765, engraving with etching.*

William Elliott after Jean Pillement published in 1762. John Tinney became the principal entrepreneur behind such projects, issuing a pair of views of Cliveden (1753), a pair of Sir Jeremy Sambrook's Gubbins (1748), four of West Wycombe (1757), two of Whitton (1757), two of Hall Barn (1760), and views of Foots Cray, Combe Bank and Painshill (1760). Bowles and Sayer published views of Oatlands, Esher, Woburn, Cliveden (1759) and two of Mereworth (*c.* 1765).

The attractions offered by these villas varied. Gubbins had pleasure gardens and history (as Sir Thomas More's dwelling). Painshill, Hall Barn and West Wycombe also boasted attractive pleasure gardens while Whitton was 'famous for the compleatest collection of exoticks then extant in England'. Admission to view the Palladian architecture and fine paintings at Foots Cray was by ticket on Thursdays. Combe Bank and Mereworth were also Palladian villas of acknowledged beauty. The appeal of elegant houses within easy reach of London was confirmed in the six volumes of *London and its Environs Described* (1761) which discussed the principal villas, listed their contents, and illustrated them in small but attractive prints.[23]

Fig. 3.6 John Tinney after John Donowell, A View of the Back Part of the Cassina & part of the Serpentine river terminated by the Cascade in the Garden of the Earl of Burlington at Chiswick, *published by Tinney, 1754, engraving with etching. Norman Blackburn, antiquarian printseller, London.*

Other houses that were published were situated in close proximity to watering spots. The gardens of Studley Royal near Harrogate were shown in four views by Anthony Walker published by Sayer in 1758 together with views of Chatsworth and Castle Howard. Chatsworth (also published by Thomas Smith in 1744) was a compulsory excursion on any tour to the much visited spas and picturesque scenery of the Peak District. At Bath, Prior Park, Ralph Allen's seat, was engraved in 1752. As roads and coaches improved the *New Bath Guide* recommended excursions to more distant properties. Stourhead, a suggested destination in the 1784 edition, had been published by Francis Vivares in 1775 in two views by Copplestone Warre Bampfylde. These celebrated the famous gardens and their architecture, but the house was also noted for its paintings and some of these had also been published.[24]

Many of these designs obtained wider exposure through the copies that illustrated the cheap folios published by J. Cooke, *The Complete English Traveller* (1771–2) and *The Modern Universal British Traveller* (*c.* 1777). *The Complete English Traveller* was issued in sixty sixpenny weekly numbers each of which included one cheaply engraved and anonymous print. Nearly all plagiarized earlier engravings and eight showed country houses.[25] The volume proceeded by county in imitation of more erudite county histories. Palaces and gardens of the nobility and gentry were a special feature of this confident guide which commenced with the announcement that 'England, or Great Britain considered as one of the European states, exceeds them all in power, riches, learning and grandeur', and then assured readers that 'Learning is so diffused through all ranks of beings that even a common Plebeian knows more than some Spanish dons'. Cheapish publications such as this were, indeed, a vehicle by which information originally presented through relatively expensive media was reassembled for more widespread distribution. *The Complete English Traveller* contained an allegedly half-complete list of over 500 subscribers 'printed exactly as they were delivered by the Hawkers and others'. In contrast to the knights and esquires of more distinguished subscription lists, nearly all these subscribers were designated plain mister. In the suspiciously similar *Modern Universal British Traveller* the number of plates was increased. Eleven of the twenty additional plates showed houses or gardens. *A New Display of the Beauties of England* (3rd edn, 1776) contained similar information but in a portable, two-volume octavo format. Its publisher, Robert Goadby, 'presumed, that this Work will be found an agreeable companion for those who may occasionally visit different parts of England, in order to take a view of the many fine palaces and seats with which this kingdom abounds'. The prints were all copies of others (including Woollett's Foots Cray, fig. 3.7), and showed picturesque landscape and ruins as well as views of houses. But seats were *A New Display*'s speciality and an index to some 250 that it described was printed at the end.

Fig. 3.7 William Woollett, A View of Foots Cray Place in Kent, the Seat of Bourchier Cleeve Esqr, *published by John Tinney, Thomas Bowles, John Bowles & Son and Robert Sayer, 1760, engraving with etching. British Museum, London.*

The improvement of roads and coaches and the consequent expansion in travel and tourism surely inspired these volumes as well as an extraordinary proliferation of small but finely engraved views of country houses that occurred from the later 1770s. These were parts-publications with monthly groups of plates accompanied by short letterpress descriptions. The pioneering publication was George Kearsly's *The Copper Plate Magazine* which combined views of seats with picturesque ruins and landscapes. But in 1779 William Watts who had engraved for Kearsly launched a subscription for *The Seats of the Nobility and Gentry, In a Collection of the most interesting and Picturesque Views.* He found about 600 subscribers, including 27 peers, but also many plain misters and many with provincial addresses. A number of provincial (especially Liverpudlian) booksellers and printsellers subscribed and twenty sets were ordered by Messrs Bennett and Hake, booksellers at Rotterdam. The prints were issued in 'numbers' containing four views for 4s between 1779 and 1786, by which time Watts was suffering from serious illness and financial embarrassment. He intended to engrave a further five numbers to make 100 houses, and appealed to his subscribers to allow a rise in price to 6s each number, 'in consequence of the great Advance in the Price of Paper and indeed of almost every other Article since its Commencement'. Although the subscribers were understanding, illness confined the set to eighty-four prints.[26]

Watts's designs were either drawn by one of a team of draftsmen (some, like Ralph Beilby, regionally based) or copied from existing paintings like Halswell House, Somerset, which was taken from a painting that John Inigo Richards had exhibited with the Society of Artists in 1764.[27] Watts himself drew houses near London and in Norfolk. He did not necessarily work with the encouragement, or even the permission, of the owners, fewer than half of whom were subscribers and when Watts attempted to sketch Chiswick, ignorant of a rule forbidding visitors to make drawings of the house, he 'met with very disagreeable Treatment'. Publishers were now selecting from the range of houses those that they thought would be most interesting to the public.

In January 1787 William Angus announced his intention to continue Watts's work in *The Seats of the Nobility and Gentry in Great Britain and Wales* (1787 onwards). By 1804 he had added fifty-seven plates.[28] The booksellers Harrison & Co. had already launched a series of 100 *Picturesque Views of the Principal Seats of the Nobility and Gentry in England and Wales* (1786-8). These were not engraved to quite such a high standard of delicacy as Watts's, but they were far from crude and good printmakers were employed. Thomas Milton's *Collection of Select Views from the different Seats of the Nobility and Gentry in Ireland*, launched in 1782 with the help of William Watts, had meanwhile extended coverage to Ireland.

Despite all this activity artists continued to publish individual prints and sets and patrons continued to commission private plates. The mixture of houses, antiquities and natural scenes that was characteristic of county histories tended to become standard in short series of aquatint views. These also often took the form of a tour of a certain district or along a certain route, reflecting both the manner in which the artist came by the views and their role as souvenir or guide for travellers. Thus Charles Tomkins advertised 'The most interesting views in the Isle of Wight

. . . comprehending the most remarkable ANTIQUITIES, GENTLEMEN'S SEATS and VIEWS OF NATURE, either sublime or beautiful.' Tomkins's tour, published in 1796, contained eighty aquatints, chiefly devoted to picturesque landscapes and antiquities with three of Netley Abbey and four of Carisbrook Castle, but it still featured such houses as Norton Lodge, the seat of Mr Binstead, Fairlee, the seat of John White Esq. and Westover the seat of L.T. Holmes Esq. The set also included views of such small, picturesque properties then in vogue as Norton Cottage the retreat of Sir A.S. Hammond. Archibald Robertson's *The Great Road from London to Bath and Bristol* (1792) covered a similar mixture of picturesque antiquities (Stonehenge, Farley Castle) and landscapes (St Vincent's Rocks) with seats including Park Place, Donnington Grove, Bowood and Corsham House.

Aquatint, giving the appearance of watercolour, became a popular medium for views about 1780. Aquatints looked good hand-coloured and gave the impression of facsimiles of drawings made by artists on tour – spontaneous reactions to inspiring sights. Engraving, on the other hand, was monumental, capable of a much longer print run and also of fine and precise detail. But engravings were expensive and this is why they became smaller. At just over 4 guineas to subscribers (increased to 6 guineas bound by 1803 when sold by Boydell) Watts's series was affordable, but a long series of large engravings for which a guinea each might have to be charged would have been prohibitively expensive.[29] Where aquatint was used the print run would be restricted, probably to a few hundred, and this made it a less suitable medium where more extensive sales might be anticipated. Series of houses in aquatint on the model of Watts's were rare. Richard Havell's *Noblemen's and Gentlemen's Seats* (1814–23) was an unusual

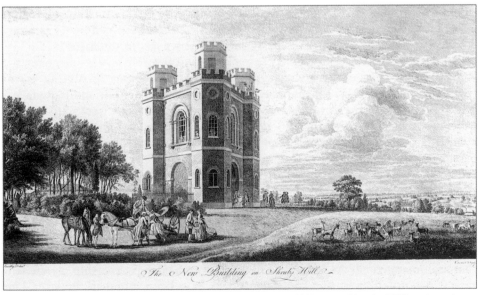

Fig. 3.8 Peter Canot after Thomas Sandby, The New Building on Shrubs Hill, *privately published 1754, engraving with etching. Grosvenor Prints, London.*

collection of twenty large prints showing most of the principal attractions of the south of England. But the trend with aquatint views, as time went by, was for houses to take third place behind natural landscape and antiquities. To a degree this was related to the vogue for the wild landscape of the Celtic fringes, of mountainous Wales and Scotland, and the relative scarcity of fine houses and gardens in these inaccessible regions. One exception was Thomas Johnes's Hafod, set amid the mountains of mid-Wales. This was one of very few gardens to be the subject of a suite of prints. James Edward Smith's *A Tour to Hafod in Cardiganshire, the seat of Thomas Johnes* (1810) consisted of twenty-three pages of letterpress and fifteen large and coloured aquatints created by J.C. Stadler after John Warwick Smith.

Between 1700 and 1830 new printmaking processes were developed and drawing and engraving improved drastically. Content altered less. Architecture remained as central to Neale in 1820 as it had been to Winstanley around 1680. Naturally, prints reflected changing fashion: Gothic piles and picturesque cottages mingled with classical villas and palaces and letterpress advertised the suitability of Gothic as a modernizing style for a very ancient seat. Pleasure gardens were giving way to parks as a setting for views by 1760 when Woollett drew the simple and unadorned turf of Foots Cray. Grass swept to the front door in almost all the views of Watts, Harrison and Angus.

The staffage of figures is revealing although it would be naive to suppose it naturalistic. Rigaud's Stowe is almost as heavily populated as his Paris châteaux, but although Stowe probably did become quite crowded soon after its gardens were publicized, Rigaud's numerous figures surely reflect compositional requirements and Bridgeman's aspirations rather than observed reality. No doubt artists continued to use figures to make attractive compositions but the more modest companies to be seen in Woollett's views may not be unrealistic. Lybbe Powys noted that 2,324 people signed the Wilton visitor's book in 1775 from which one might well deduce fifteen or more visitors a day in summer.[30]

What such figures are doing may be more significant. Kip's views demonstrate the amenities afforded by his seats. Tiny figures are hunting or playing bowls (there is a bowling green in almost every view). Servants are few and tourists are only prominent in the royal palaces. By contrast mid-century views are heavily populated both with tourists and with parties of pleasure. Some point out the beauties of the architecture or admire the closure of a vista, others, as at Foots Cray, ignore the house in favour of surveying the extensive natural landscape with the aid of one of those scientific instruments for which British craftsmanship was renowned. Many figures simply enjoy themselves in couples or in small groups. They converse politely. Their dress and deportment is of exemplary elegance. Gesture, behaviour and manners might safely be imitated by the viewer. Accessories, such as the telescope or musical instruments, suggest ways in which parties of pleasure might amuse themselves. Several views show pleasure boats that are documented. At West Wycombe, Buckinghamshire, the ship completely rigged was noted by Young and cannon balls have been found in the lake. The huge swan shown by Woollett at Kew was the *Augusta*, launched for the birthday of the Prince of Wales in 1755 and 'formed in an entirely new Taste, and made to imitate a Swan swimming . . . The Neck and Head rise to the height of 18 Feet; the Body forms a commodious Cabbin, neatly decorated, and large enough to accommodate 10 Persons, and the Feet are so artfully contrived as to supply the Place of Oars. . .'.[31] Troops of gardeners mow, brush and roll the grass. The figures shown in the prints are commendable, helping the prints to announce country house gardens – or at least the touristic gardens shown in these views – as proper arenas for polite display, another newly introduced facility for leisure.

As Mark Girouard has pointed out, late eighteenth-century views differ in that their landscapes are relatively deserted. Admittedly some later views show secluded private houses, but Girouard's emphasis on the new attractiveness of solitude, a new desire to escape the crowd, is also valid.[32] Conventionally a couple, perhaps with children, are shown in each view. Enjoying the house becomes an individual rather than a social experience, privacy and seclusion are valued. Servants are rarely seen, although the occasional gardener may still brush leaves from the lawn. Nevertheless, the letterpress accompanying each print continues to emphasize the attractions of the houses for visitors. There have been changes. Old master paintings are no longer the only pictures worth seeing. In Angus's description of Brocket Hall, Hertfordshire, *British* paintings took pride of place. He drew attention first to the portrait of the Prince of Wales by Reynolds and the ceiling by John Mortimer and Francis Wheatley, then to a large Teniers, and the Chinese boat on the lake. At Wentworth House Watts picked out West's paintings *Cymon and Iphigenia* and *Diana and Endymion*, mentioning also the statues, garden and garden architecture.

Views treated the country house as an aesthetic object but one that was indicative of wealth and affluence. Sometimes the views themselves or accompanying letterpress celebrated enclosure or the fertility of the surrounding land but the views were generally neutral on social issues and reticent on the economy of game and oaks (even if the bountiful and useful landscape could hardly be missed and deer were ubiquitous).[33] The effect of the series around 1800 was to celebrate primarily the sheer number of fine houses in well-kept parks. They appealed to an audience sympathetic to the aspirations of landowners and they were designed to impress, making a patriotic statement about wealth and taste to foreign as well as domestic consumers. For foreigners the prints showing the new 'naturalistic' gardens of the 1740s and 1750s and the later parks provided further evidence to confirm their opinion that a regard for nature and liberty was a fixed part of the Englishman's character. Englishmen were quite happy to cultivate this view and views reflected their passion for touring the grounds of their neighbours or betters.

Who bought these views and what did they do with them? We need more research to be sure. Views of houses were never more than moderately priced and were copied to serve a lower stratum of buyers. The audience was certainly not confined to those who might aspire even to a very modest seat. The large prints sold for about 3s 6d uncoloured, or in sets of six for a guinea. The fact that the principal wholesale distributors, John Boydell, Robert Sayer, the Bowleses and even Cluer Dicey, made an effort to acquire views of seats and gardens suggests that they sold well. Through these printsellers they would have reached the widest possible market in the provinces, in Europe and in the colonies. Some were certainly exported to America. In 1772 John Overlove, a Virginian correspondent of the tobacco merchant John Norton, was charged £6 16s 6d for '12 Large Prints of Gentlemens Seats in Peartree frames'.[34] Both Sayer and Bowles extended the exposure of the views in their stock by duplicating large prints in smaller, much cheaper format. John Bowles's *British Views*, published in the late 1720s, contained a selection of the most celebrated houses published thus far, with engraved commentary suitable for the non-connoisseur. Later Bowles and Sayer published a set of twelve small copies of designs by Woollett, Sullivan and Walker for 1s 6d along with similar sets of Stowe, and of royal gardens. Dicey copied these. They must have retailed as decoration for poorer homes as the printsellers' catalogues suggest ('sets of small prints very saleable and cheap') but they might also have been pasted in albums by wealthier people.

Most individually published views were intended to be framed for home decoration. Their suitability for this purpose was enhanced by presentation in pairs or sets so that a wall or a staircase could be decorated with matching prints. Similarly the invitation to buy such sets coloured indicated use as decoration. When colour really came into vogue around 1780 printsellers presented coloured aquatints in gold frames. Country houses were pasted to the wall by ladies decorating print-rooms. At Blickling in Norfolk Bampfylde's views of Stourhead were incorporated into the decoration of the print-room and at Enville views of celebrated houses and gardens decorated a garden building. They were used as toys. In 1747 William Henry Toms advertised the 'surprising Appearance' of his large views by Rigaud of Claremont and Castle Hill when 'view'd in a Concave Glass' and other views of houses will also have been looked at through these amusing instruments which produced a three-dimensional optical illusion.[35] Kip's views, *Vitruvius Britannicus*, and the 'magazines' and 'collections' of Watts, Angus and Harrison were usually bound and were intended for perusal at a reader's leisure in the library.

For publishers country houses were among the remarkable objects that a country might boast. Their publications stimulated tourism. In England publishers were inspired by the success of views of foreign houses as well as the admiration felt for foreign houses by travellers. It was argued both textually and visually that British houses might match those of the continent. Later in the century, with the stock of fine houses substantially reinforced by new building, it could be claimed that Britain had outstripped the continent. The pattern of publication reflected an appeal at first directed to connoisseurs, to foreign visitors and to the polite world gathered in London. Individual local enterprises, notably the publication of county histories, began to promote fine houses on a regional basis. But gradually an appreciation for fine architecture and painting, for elegant pleasure grounds and picturesque landscape, became an article of polite culture across the country. Prints promoted this development, serving both as advertisements and as models, extending awareness of the country house as a theatre of expression for both owner and visitor. Ultimately it became possible to publish views of houses on a national scale with the support of a national network of subscribers.

4 One Among the Many: Popular Aesthetics, Polite Culture and the Country House Landscape

Stephen Bending

Later eighteenth-century landscape gardens have been linked both with the mass-produced aesthetic of a commercial culture and the class exclusions of a patrician élite.[1] They stand in a peculiar relation to a culture of commodities, speaking of a world of landowning and a set of values apparently distinct from commercial capitalism while nevertheless being immersed in that very culture. In this chapter I will suggest that polite culture's response to such gardens represents a strangely fragmented body of writing, insisting on difference while laying claim to cultural unity.

One account of landowning and aesthetics which has become increasingly influential in the last few years is John Barrell's use of civic humanism as a means of explaining élite culture's self-representations and self-justifications.[2] In brief, Barrell suggests that the high culture of the landed élite draws on a distinction between the ideal and the particular, the general and the specific, both in aesthetics and politics. And that it is the ability of the independent landowner to see the ideal, the general (the big picture) – rather than having a limited vision caught up in their own concerns (profession, trade, etc.) – which gives him the right to legislate for the nation. In these terms, we can then understand gardens as one of the ways in which élite culture represents itself to the wider world. From such a perspective the landscape garden is well suited to the needs of the landowner: in creating an idealized landscape the landowner demonstrates his clarity of view and therefore his fitness to govern.

While earlier historians of the landscape garden suggested that later eighteenth-century designs allowed the individual to indulge in feeling and the subjective pleasures of sensibility,[3] recent work has pointed to the ability of such landscapes to bar the vast majority of polite society from personal engagement, to demonstrate in physical terms the owner's membership of an élite club and the visitor's inability to engage in the central polite activity of social emulation.[4] They

Fig. 4.1   Bowood, Wiltshire, laid out by Lancelot 'Capability' Brown between 1761 and 1786. Photograph by Stephen Bending.

are said to be landscapes of exclusion, physically demonstrating the owner's élite status while preventing the non-landowner from laying claims upon them as social or aesthetic space. In this account, later eighteenth-century gardens represent not a space in which to emote, not a concern with personal expression, but are one of the means by which a propertied élite buy into a shared polite culture which excludes all those without land. The lack of iconography, the lack of local detail, becomes a way of denying the non-landowner any kind of personal engagement or contact with the owner. According to this account, in these huge park landscapes the visitor is set adrift in a big empty space: there is nothing with which to engage (fig. 4.1). In the words of Edward Harwood, 'Far from privileging the self, the Brown landscape swamped it in a sea of gently undulating grassland and clumps of trees'. Moreover, buying a landscape from 'Capability' Brown denied the personality of the owner and provided only a 'class identification masquerading as taste'; and as a result the nature of the landscape shifted entirely from the personal to the generic.[5]

   This is an attractive and in some ways compelling model which no doubt works when exploring the garden from the perspective of the landowner; but it ignores the ways of seeing that visitors bring with them to a garden, the assumptions and perspectives which allow them to see.[6] What I will suggest is that, far from being dominated by the landowning aesthetic suggested by recent commentators, country house visitors were trying to find ways of asserting their own cultural status through a demonstration of socio-aesthetic competence. Thus, while civic humanism has been much vaunted in recent years as a key to eighteenth-century aesthetics, its own engagement in relation to the broader democratization of aesthetics taking place in the second half of the century needs to be more fully recognized.[7] Beyond the aesthetics of the patrician élite we should be aware of a whole range of discourses for which such a classically freighted theory has only the most limited relevance. And outside the broad consolidation of class interests lies a series of battles for control over socio-aesthetic space, where 'aesthetic' texts are an expression of cultural formation and the tensions within that formation. That is, by concentrating on the formal tracts and discourses of the traditional élite – with their stress on the ideology of civic humanism – one fails to encounter the vast amount of aesthetic writing produced by a wider polite culture, the social engagement and fluidity of which makes it quite distinct from, but nevertheless engaged with, élite writing. What I am arguing is that the sense of both inclusion and exclusion is central to the experience of the garden in the later eighteenth century. Gardens could not only accommodate but were accommodated to a wide range of concerns. Visitors of substantially different social and political standing were encouraged in the belief that the garden catered for their own needs and that in so doing it signalled their membership of polite culture even as it marked out their difference from social inferiors or political enemies. Thus in later eighteenth-century gardens we can explore the contest between an élite culture, which may indeed choose to justify itself in terms of a classical socio-aesthetics of civic humanism and the liberal arts, and a far broader polite culture with which it is engaged but from which it seeks to differentiate itself. Indeed, the garden is one of the foremost sites in which that 'polite' clash takes place: it acts as a shared space in which a series of differentiations are enacted. As a central object of politeness it is recognized as a physical meeting place for polite society but as a site also generated out of the meeting of the discourses of polite culture. While certainly able to articulate the fairly narrow aesthetics of the élite, the garden also felt the effects of what we might call the increasing democratization of the aesthetic as the élite language of connoisseurship starts to be challenged by a broader and rather vaguer language of taste.

It is worth stressing that this range of responses remains possible throughout the century and that one should therefore be wary of any grand claims about a shift from public to private as the century progresses. In 1793, for example, Edward Clarke is still able to claim both travel and in particular the garden as the preserve of the educated élite. On reaching Wilton, during his *Tour through the South of England, Wales, and part of Ireland*, Clarke sets about describing the grounds of the estate.[8] After listing the 'objects' (river, Palladian bridge, waterfall, piazza, etc.) he despairs of the inadequacy of his own language: 'From this paltry insignificant outline, I leave the peruser of these pages to form his own opinion, as to the wonders of Wilton. I am neither willing nor able to give him a better' (pp. 31–3). For a 'just idea' a man must not only visit for himself, but must be 'possessed of taste, learning, and ingenuity. He must be master of his own time, and permitted to examine it at his leisure.' Only then can a 'true representation' be achieved. Emphasis, that is, falls not simply upon a list of objects, but upon the viewer of those objects. Most obviously male, the viewer must be also a gentleman and a master of his own time. Clarity of vision is here dependent on social class and yet is also claimed as a universal rather than a personal response. The goal of objectivity, the creation of the 'just idea', is only possible for the educated gentleman. The values of patrician culture here claim normative status.

If few could live up to such demands, many were happy to proffer their views nevertheless. And one way of making sense of the vast increase in travel and travel writing in the eighteenth century is in terms of a polite culture attempting to represent its communal concerns. As Paul Langford has pointed out, the term 'polite' is itself ambiguous. If it was associated with 'the trappings of propertied life', it was also concerned with aping the manners and morals of social superiors, with aesthetic and intellectual taste and, notably in the later eighteenth century, with sentiment and the language of 'feeling'. As Langford writes, 'The essence of politeness was often said to be that *je ne sais quoi* which distinguished the innate gentleman's understanding of what made for civilized conduct, but this did not inhibit others from seeking more artificial means of acquiring it.'[9] Inevitably this meant also the constant application of double standards: to rise in society one aped the manners of one's social superiors but sneered at those lower on the social ladder attempting the same thing. This accounted in part for the bickering in travel writing over how one should describe a given scene. Indeed, in these terms the assertions of a writer such as Clarke can be seen as just another attempt to exclude perceived social inferiors from polite culture. But if the large-scale landowner used the 'natural' garden to imply an equal naturalness in his social and political position, others were to use that same space to assert their own membership of the polite world.

A crucial aid to the widening of polite society was the increasing emphasis on feeling and sentiment as the century progressed: an emotional response in the language of feeling became a means of asserting one's place within a substantially broadened élite of the propertied classes.[10] Clarke attempts to define aesthetic language in terms narrow enough to exclude all but the educated and wealthy élite. But part of the success of polite culture as a broad culture of the propertied comes from an increasing confidence in an equally broad language of taste; a language which remains very much in use today. In words such as *beautiful*, *lovely*, *grand*, and *pretty* we see an aesthetic language which is broad enough to include a wide range of responses and speakers within a narrow range of terms: if that language seems inadequate to the term 'aesthetic', we should perhaps question our notion of such a term's relevance to society at large. Whatever else it may be, such a language seems inherently non-exclusive; it throws emphasis on a shared – if by definition banal – social response. Indeed this very lack of complication itself becomes a means of cementing the ties of polite culture: this is not the language of an élite connoisseurship, nor is it concerned with being overly precise. The interest of such language lies exactly in its quotidian nature, and my interest in turn lies in the kind of scenes it is appropriate to use these terms about, but also therefore in the sense of the aesthetic as a shared social space. While the leisure activity of travel itself excluded the majority of eighteenth-century society outside the propertied classes, within its own terms this language of taste became one of the means by which members of 'respectable' society could demonstrate such membership: one may not *own* a landscape garden, but if one can appreciate its value then one can also make some claim to being a part of the culture which produces it. Terms such as *lovely* and *beautiful* and the emphasis on nebulous private feeling allowed that claim to be made by a substantial section of society. In so doing they inherently challenged the claims of patrician culture to the singular control of aesthetic meaning. In the widespread use of this language we see an increasing democratization of aesthetic space, for the range of people claiming the garden as their own is massively broadened. As Ann Bermingham has argued more specifically in terms of the picturesque, 'In aestheticising the natural and often commonplace scenery of Britain, the Picturesque awakened a large segment of the population to the realisation that aesthetic judgement was not the gift of the privileged few but could be learned by anyone and applied to just about anything.'[11]

It is to some of the applications of this democratized language of taste that I now wish to turn. In the 1790s a traveller such as Lady Anne Hadaway, a member of the powerful Grenville family, can write in the style of the confident aristocrat, at home with the owners of the gardens and houses she visits, willing to quiz a pompous inventor on the details of his new carding machine, or judging the relative merits of different towns.[12] When she comes to describe a garden, however, the aristocratic advantages of education and leisure become more difficult to assert in an aesthetic terminology she shares with most travellers. Thus, at Longleat (landscaped by Brown from 1757) she writes, 'The Grounds . . . are particularly beautiful, and the Water very fine'. While at Stourhead, if she demonstrates her ability to translate the Latin inscriptions, she nevertheless describes the gardens in terms of the 'curious', the 'pleasing' and the 'beautiful'. The grotto with the statues of a sleeping nymph and the god of the River Stour are described, the journey from here to the Pantheon with its further statues is made, and the Bristol cross and Temple of the Sun are all mentioned, but no attempt is made to 'read' the iconography of the design (fig. 4.2). Even at Alfred's Tower – where we might expect some notice of the name and historical associations – we are told of the 'charming' ride round it, its height (130 feet), and the fine view across seven counties which it provides. If we turn to the *New Bath Guide*, a work published for day-trippers from the city most famous for its mixing of social groups, the language is strikingly similar. At Corsham Court (landscaped by Brown from 1759 and altered by Repton in the 1790s) we are told that 'The park and gardens afford a variety of picturesque and beautiful prospects. . . . Genteel company have permission to view the house and pictures, on Tuesday and Friday.' And at the grotto in Stourhead (fig. 4.3), visited by Lady Anne, we are told, 'The figure of the nymph herself is elegantly formed, and the waters tinkling round her, with the gloom and stillness of the place, have an effect that is pleasingly melancholy to the imagination. Quitting this grotto, which is in the truest style of rural simplicity, you next ascend a flight of steps into the shrubbery

*Fig. 4.2   Stourhead, Wiltshire, the Temple of Apollo / Temple of the Sun, from the lake.
Photograph by Stephen Bending.*

Fig. 4.3   Stourhead, Wiltshire, the Nymph of the Grotto. In front of the statue an inscription from Pope reads:

*Nymph of the Grot these Sacred springs I keep
And to the murmur of these waters sleep;
Ah! spare my slumbers, gently tread the cave,
And drink in silence or in silence lave.*

Photograph by Stephen Bending.

which, leading along the borders of the river, brings you to the Pantheon. . . .' Here too we are told of the number of steps in Alfred's tower (321 apparently) and of the fine views having climbed them: 'Nothing can be conceived more striking than the prospects from every side of this structure, round one turret of which, for the benefit of the view, a gallery has been railed in, in the securest manner.'[13] No attempt is made to read an iconographic programme (fig. 4.4). Instead we find the same generalized language of taste, the same concern for odd – almost domestic – detail.

Such travellers are precisely *polite* and therefore are both recognized and accepted as members of society; accepted, that is, because they implicitly upheld the values of landed culture. But if the discourse of garden visiting – whereby the lowly gentleman could comment upon the estate of a lord – suggested some sense of equality, such equality was frequently contested: there remained an acute and quite palpable awareness of social distinction in a polite world which nominally ignored such divisions. And we can see some of the ways in which this works if we consider visitors' accounts of one particular garden, Piercefield in Gwent, south Wales.

Close to Tintern Abbey and looking down on the River Wye, Piercefield was laid out by Valentine Morris in the middle of the eighteenth century. Morris's father had made a vast fortune from slavery and cattle on his estates in Antigua,

*Fig. 4.4 Stourhead, Wiltshire,
Alfred's Tower. The inscription
beneath the statue of Alfred reads:*

*Alfred the Great. A.D. 879 on this
    summit
Erected his standard against the
    Danish Invaders
To him we owe
The origins of Juries
The Establishment of a Militia
the Creation of a Naval Force
Alfred the light of a benighted age
was a Philosopher and a Christian
The Father of his People
The Founder of the English
Monarchy and Liberty.*

Photograph by Stephen Bending.

and if we would characterize this money as new commercial wealth, Morris himself attempted to transform it by recreating the mythic life of medieval hospitality, opening his cellars to all and sundry, feeding every passer-by, and lavishly entertaining guests of any sort. And it is to the responses of some of those guests that I now turn. Piercefield was visited by many of those writers whose responses we would now place in the aesthetic 'mainstream', from George Mason and Thomas Whately to the famous picturesque traveller William Gilpin. Unlike Mason (a Member of Parliament) or Whately (who worked at the Treasury for some years), Gilpin was not a substantial landowner. But in his tour of Piercefield he offers confident judgements of its picturesque and sublime scenes, and is happy to judge its defects and offer advice to its owner. He addresses an audience of aesthetic equals in a manner which suggests a confidence in the shared values of a broad social class. At the same time, it is important to recognize that the judgements in Gilpin's tours were to be toned down substantially between the manuscripts first circulated and the accounts finally published. Even after editing there remains a sense that the aesthetic offers a shared cultural space for the enormously wealthy Morris and the relatively impecunious Gilpin, but those acts of self-censorship also articulate Gilpin's recognition of the kinds of social and aesthetic compromise which becomes necessary in the shift from private experience to polite public representation.

Given Gilpin's characteristically critical response to 'made scenery', Piercefield gets off very lightly. By contrast, at William Shenstone's estate, The Leasowes, the personal reproach of Gilpin's note that he 'laughed at his inscrip[tion] inviting the naiids to bath' has to be massaged in the published text into a more carefully worded discussion of why the inscription, by a muddy pool, might be deemed 'ludicrous'.[14] In turn, however, while Shenstone is on the receiving end of this kind of challenge within an apparently shared aesthetic, he could also inspire far more deferential responses. The anonymous Miss M— who appears in the selected letter of Shenstone's circle (1778) writes to him about her trip to Piercefield in 1760, and adopts the language of a self-professed 'giddy girl', a 'poor, prattling, insignificant Being'.[15] And yet, she continues:

I will venture to affirm, that my Merits . . . are equal to those of any other wild Female in the Circle of your Acquaintance. But is it come to this? And must I really take Pen in Hand, and describe our little Peregrinations? I must, for you have commanded me.

If Shenstone confers honour upon 'a poor, prattling, insignificant Being' by taking notice of her, Miss M— goes on to ask his 'humane Heart' to make allowance for whatever is 'unworthy your Judgment' as she sets about describing her trip to Piercefield with a gentleman and lady 'as wild and as whimsical as ourselves'. Gilpin was to find the shrubberies and flowers at Piercefield a disappointing contrast to the windings of the River Wye, the sublimity of cliffs, and the broad expanses of fields beyond (fig. 4.5). Miss M—'s account, however, subsumes such niceties within a language of excess. Doing 'justice' to the merit of these scenes, she asserts, is impossible, but 'though I am unequal to the Task, I must say something'. The description of landscape which follows is distinctly less 'wild' than she goes on to claim:

The Gardens are situated on the *Rocks*, I cannot call them the *Banks*, of the River *Wye*, and cut into Walks, in themselves excessively beautiful, but the superior Beauty of the Views they command, so entirely engrosses the Eye, that they can be very little heeded. Sometimes we look down upon the River, from an Eminence of near four hundred Feet, which winds itself round as in a Semi-circle. The opposite Side is bounded by Rocks of equal Height, some barren, and resembling the Ruins of old Fortifications; others covered with the most pleasing Variety of Greens the Eye can wish to behold, while at the Bottom, Cattle are feeding in the sweet Pastures by the River's Side: Cattle, we were told the Creatures were which we saw; but really our Faith had need be stronger to believe it, since they appeared to our View more like Hens and Chickens, and I do assure you, one of our Company took them for such.

Walks are 'excessively beautiful', the view 'engrosses the Eye'. But if this is the wild excess Miss M— claims, it is also an excess expressed in terms of conventional, of fashionable language. Indeed throughout the letter the language of aesthetic description becomes intertwined with the language of social action to

*Fig. 4.5   Piercefield, Gwent, view across the River Wye. Revd William Gilpin enjoyed the
sublimity of the cliffs and the broad expanses of the fields beyond. Photograph by Stephen Bending.*

the point where the experience of being carried on men's shoulders across a river
is as much a 'Piece of Variety' as that recognized in the formal organization of
landscape. In this sense Miss M—'s 'wild Description', is a recognition of the
garden as a space allowing the same social freedoms as polite discourse, but
recognizing also the threat to order inherent in that discourse. She adopts the
polite language of taste – beauty, delight, variety – even as she seeks to
marginalize herself from a perceived male domain of judgement and justice.
Equally, in using that language Miss M— both plays to and seeks to exploit a
gendered stereotype of female sensibility. In its stress on the excessive, the wild
and the whimsical, this is a language differentiating itself and offering deference
to the dominance of élite aesthetics, but one also looking for a mode of self-
representation, a means of registering individual experience.[16]

   While Miss M—'s account of Piercefield claims the limited view of a partial
traveller, others were more confidently expansive in their approach. Another
letter to Shenstone, this time from Robert Dodsley, who visited the garden a year
before Miss M—, also begins by adopting the language of the sublime but by
contrast has no need for the attempts at self-marginalization we find in that
other account.[17] Dodsley's visit is likewise made with 'a polite Party of
Gentlemen and Ladies' but is far from 'wild', instead it is 'altogether agreeable'.
Here, sublimity and excess can be safely assimilated as part of the recognized
language of taste, the language appropriate to the sophisticated male traveller.
Dodsley's account itself begins by categorizing Piercefield as 'of the great and
sublime Kind':

. . . most of the near Views are seen below you from the Top of high Precipices, consisting of steep Rocks, hanging Woods, the Rivers *Severn* and *Wye*, which last winds about the Feet of the Rocks below you, in a very romantic Manner, almost surrounding a very pretty Farm, where Cattle and Sheep are feeding in the Meadows, at such a Depth below your Eyes, that they seem very much diminished. The Rocks are bold and numerous, half covered with Woods, and rise almost perpendicular from the Edge of the Water to a surprising Height, forming, from the great Cliff, a kind of double Amphitheatre.

Like Miss M— 's account Dodsley speaks of 'bold and numerous' rocks, of surprising heights, of the romantic windings of the River Wye at the foot of the cliffs, of the 'Pride and Grandeur' of the scenes and of their extensive prospects (fig. 4.6). Unlike Miss M— 's account, no apologetic tone is apparent. What is introduced, however, by way of an extended footnote, is 'a more particular Description of the Scenes and Views I have attempted to describe', a description intended to give Shenstone a 'better understanding' of their situation. This takes the form of a list of objects from a Chinese Bridge (no. *X*) and a delightful shrubbery (no. *XIV*) to a Druid's Throne (no. *XIX*), cave above a precipice (no. *XXII*) and so on. Notably this latter account is unable to express the sublimity of Dodsley's letter; emphasis falls not on personal emotion but on a series of objects, not on social experience but on formal aesthetic organization.

Fig. 4.6 *Piercefield, Gwent, view across the River Wye. Robert Dodsley's account speaks of the 'Pride and Grandeur' of the scenes. Photograph by Stephen Bending.*

For Dodsley, the listing of objects produces a 'better understanding' and so demonstrates his own socio-aesthetic status, but the very particularity we find in such a list is rejected as aesthetic incompetence by other travellers. Accordingly, in the *Tour through Derbyshire to the Lakes*, by a 'Gentleman of the University of Oxford' (1797), Dodsley is abruptly taken to task.[18] The anonymous author writes, 'Particular descriptions, the more minute they become, are the farther from giving the reader a distinct idea of the place, whose beauties they enumerate; witness Mr Dodsley's tedious detail . . . I shall dwell only, therefore, on such beauties as may be relished, without passing through the medium of sight.' The attack on detail, on the mere tallying up of 'beauties', becomes a means of stressing a notion of the liberal arts repeatedly used by the apologists of patrician culture. Associating Dodsley with particularity associates him also with the mechanical arts, with a lack of liberal view, and with his earlier career as a mere footman. In moments like this the notion of a shared polite aesthetic starts to seem very fragile.

With that fragility in mind, I want finally to turn to Arthur Young, a figure all too aware of his own marginal status as a member of the impoverished gentry. Young once remarked that while his family had a coat of arms and his grandfather had kept a coach and four, the family had lately declined to the point where his estate was only able to maintain 'the establishment of a wheelbarrow'.[19] As an author championing practical agriculture as the source of national wealth we might expect him to reject the apparently non-productive landscape garden from which he was already excluded by lack of wealth. Instead he constantly finds himself caught between these two apparently opposing groups of concerns and seems strangely incapable of ignoring the aesthetic. Repeatedly, as he steps into a garden, economic discourse is dropped in favour of the language of taste (fig. 4.7). In this Young's writing plays out many of the tensions and contradictions of polite travel over the final third of the eighteenth century. Driven on the one hand by an apparently uncompromising concern for the means of agricultural production, Young exhibits on the other a desire to join that (polite) society not of the land but of the landed.[20] Thus, in his agricultural tours the garden becomes a valuable point of focus for our understanding of eighteenth-century culture in that it acts as a battleground for the conflicting but nevertheless intertwined interests of the propertied and the landed, the agricultural and the polite.

One way of understanding Young's apparently contradictory response is to return once again to Valentine Morris's gardens at Piercefield.[21] While describing the estate at Piercefield Young praises Morris for always having 'people ready to attend whoever comes, to conduct them every where, and not one of them is suffered to take a farthing; yet they shew every thing with great readiness and civility'. What Young draws to our attention is the idea of polite society itself, a culture in which he is keen to claim membership. However, it is also a culture in which he seeks to distinguish himself. And once again it is the unfortunate Dodsley who provides the foil for Young's necessary demonstration of socio-aesthetic competence. Summarizing Dodsley's style and differentiating it from his own Young writes, 'Mr *Dodsley*, with his dells and his dingles, *and such*

Fig. 4.7   Piercefield, Gwent, view across the River Wye towards the Lancaut Peninsula. Characteristically Arthur Young chose to describe the agricultural scene here almost wholly in terms of its aesthetic qualities. Photograph by Stephen Bending.

expressive terms, might make amends for the want of a *Claude Loraine*; however, such an idea as my plain language will give you, follows'. But inevitably Young's language is far from 'plain'. When he reaches a house he characteristically adopts the rhetoric of plain speaking – of calling a spade a spade, one might say – and claims not to be swayed by fashionable judgements but by his own feelings. Thus at Holkham, when considering the well-proportioned front of the house and especially its columns, he writes, 'It may be said the proportion of a pillar is stated, and always the same. . . . I know nothing of architecture, but view these at *Holkham* and others at *Blenheim*. . . . I never speak by rules, but by my eyes' (fig. 4.8). However, he then continued,

> Will you excuse these criticisms from one who knows nothing of architecture, but its power of pleasing the taste of individuals – As one among the many, I give you my opinion, but I wish you would pass over all these parts of my letters, till you see the objects yourself, for I cannot give you an idea of the building clear enough by description for you to see the propriety or absurdity of my remarks.[22]

Thus Young at once champions the response of the individual even as he drags himself away from such subjectivity with his concern for 'propriety and absurdity'. Similarly, at Earl Tilney's he remarks of the paintings, 'You will excuse me giving you my little criticisms; I am no connoisseur in painting, and may be so gothic as to praise a piece by a modern artist, when an antient one hangs by it.'[23] If the language and values of connoisseurship in art and architecture are dealt a rhetorical – albeit ambiguous – blow in favour of the 'Gothic' claim for a distinctly English (natural) taste, something rather different happens when Young steps into the garden. Notably, the problems in Young's claim not to be swayed by fashion become distinctly more apparent, and indeed the very emphasis on feeling places him firmly within a recognizably polite appreciation of landscape.[24]

It is at Piercefield once again that Young provides us with one of his fullest descriptions of a garden, and this takes the form of an exercise in the sublime and the beautiful, in the language of feeling employed by the polite traveller, and in the art of composing pictures. He writes:

> A little further we met with another bench inclosed with iron rails, on a point of the rock which here is pendent over the river, and may be truly called a situation of the terrible sublime: you look immediately down upon a vast hollow of wood, all surrounded by the woody precipices which have so fine an effect from all the points of view at *Persfield*; in the midst appears a small, but neat building, the bathing-house, which, though none of the best, appears from this enormous height, but as a spot of white, in the midst of the vast range of green: towards the right is seen the windings of the river.[25]

Thus, Young runs through the appropriate language of the sublime, setting vastness, precipices and enormous heights against a tiny 'spot of white'; and as the description continues this language is elaborated. If the united talents of 'a *Claud*, a *Poussin*, a *Vernet*, and a *Smith*, would scarcely be able to sketch' these scenes, Young nevertheless offers us a neatly composed verbal picture:

> The last point, and which perhaps is equal to most of the preceeding, is the alcove. From this you look down perpendicularly on the river, with a finely cultivated slope on the other side. *To the right* is a prodigious steep shore of wood, winding to the castle, which appears *in full view*, and a part of the town. *On the left* appears a fine view of the river for some distance, the opposite shore of wild wood, with the rock appearing at places in rising cliffs, and *further on to the termination of the view* that way, the vast wall of rocks so often mentioned, which are here seen in length, and have a stupendous effect. *On the whole*, this view is striking and romantic.[26]

Despite his claim that 'I do not write to make display of description', this is just what Young offers us. What we see here is Young's concern to demonstrate that he is a gentleman and can deal competently with the aesthetic as well as the agricultural: the aesthetic here becomes a demonstration of gentlemanly status,

Fig. 4.8   Holkham Hall, Norfolk. Arthur Young described the estate as it was during the life of Thomas Coke, 1st Earl of Leicester, known as 'Coke of Norfolk'. Photograph by Stephen Bending.

but a demonstration characteristically asserted at the expense of others. Thus it is that Young ostentatiously apologizes that he is not a liberal artist, but only in order to demonstrate a liberal understanding. At Hagley, he writes, 'A better assemblage of unconnected objects managed most skillfully to form one whole, can scarcely be imagined: Yet have I read a description of *Hagley*, in which it is *thus* mentioned: – "*You turn into a thicket*, and HAVE A LOOK *at the Doric Pavilion*, Thomson's *Seat, and the obelisk*."' [27] Young's phrase here, 'managed most skillfully to form one whole', is crucial for the management is of course that of Young himself; his description creates the whole, and it is this which he then underlines by quoting an author who is only able to 'HAVE A LOOK'. Young's concern, then, is to demonstrate gentlemanly status through a competence both aesthetic and agricultural. If anything, in a text apparently championing agriculture, the aesthetic becomes of central importance, for it is the aesthetic rather than the agricultural which allows a demonstration of his polite credentials.

In this respect, despite his claims for the greatest farmer being the greatest man, Young's tours represent no great challenge to the landowning aesthetic of patrician culture or to the cultural self-representation of the landscape garden. Gardens do not need to be productive, neither are they represented as a waste. They are at once set within the agricultural landscape of the tour and demonstrably apart from that landscape; in this they re-enact both the uniformity and the fundamental divisions within polite culture. With that in mind, Young's relationship with his aristocratic subjects is worth brief exploration. Of course elaborate descriptions of houses, gardens, and even farms act also as elaborate and extended compliments to their owners. And indeed Young's ability to avoid the political differences of landowners in favour of the landscapes they share – as for example at the nearby estates of Wentworth Woodhouse and Wentworth Castle in Yorkshire – is the very essence of polite travel. At Wentworth Castle, after describing the gardens and the house, Young turns not to the famous rivalries of the neighbouring families, or even to their highly politicized building programmes, but to politeness.[28] Thus we find him going out of his way to praise Lady Strafford for retiring from her apartment when he visits:

> I mention this as an instance of general and undistinguished politeness, a striking contrast to that unpopular and affected dignity in which some great people think proper to cloud their houses – such is the necessity of gaining *tickets* – of being *acquainted* with the family – of giving notice before hand of your intention; all which is terribly inconvenient to a traveller.[29]

At Piercefield, as we have already seen, he praises Morris for much the same reason. What Young repeatedly insists upon, then, is the idea of polite society itself, of a culture in which huge differences of wealth and rank, and indeed of politics, are smoothed over in the interests of social harmony among a propertied élite. Lady Strafford retiring from her apartments appears to treat Young with respect, though condescension may be a more appropriate term. Either way, Young can flatter himself that in this act of 'general and undistinguished politeness' he is being treated – almost – as an equal.

It is this concern with undistinguished politeness which also makes the apparently trivial issue of insolence from servants a matter of great seriousness, and for Young a repeated cause for anxiety. At Blenheim, he recounts an episode in which a gentleman meets with 'excessive insolence' from the porters at the park gate. They demand money of him despite his having already tipped the house porter, and when he refuses they abuse him 'in a very scurrilous manner'. Young concludes from the episode that, 'The vile custom of not being able to view a house, without paying for the sight, as if it was exhibited by a *showman*, is detestable; but when it extends to double and quadruple the common fees and impudence, the exorbitancy calls aloud for the public notice to be taken of it, which its meanness so well deserves.'[30] Paying money to visit a house or garden shatters the illusion of a polite 'public' which Young has been creating, and polite visiting is reduced to a further venture of the commercial world. Concomitantly, insolence is a threat precisely because it challenges the polite status of the traveller: the questioning of rank which it entails is an implicit questioning also of one's membership in a society of the genteel. The sheer number of Young's references to such episodes may well suggest his own insecurity on the edge of that polite world.

Finally, Young's views on gardens are expressed perhaps most clearly not in England but in the relative freedom of a foreign land. On arriving in Nice during his tour through France Young visits a number of noblemen's gardens where oranges are grown for profit. Of this he writes, 'the garden, which with us is an object of pleasure, is here one of œconomy, and income, circumstances that are incompatible. . . . that open apartment of a residence which we call a garden, should be free from the shackles of a contract, and the scene of pleasure, not profit'.[31] This, indeed, is how Young conceptualizes the landscape garden of England. His agricultural proselytizing claims productive landscape as crucial to national wealth and this would seem to leave no room for the ostentatious display of mere gardening. Instead, however, while articulating an agricultural discourse much of the time and aligning this with large-scale landownership and intensive farming, when Young reaches a garden he reaches – as we have seen – a recognizably different space. What we may also see, then, in the farms and gardens of Young's tours is the shift from economic to social aesthetic, and with it an attempt to place both himself and his concerns within the arena of polite culture. Young's insistent removal from farm to garden and back again demonstrates his acute awareness of the polite aesthetic of the liberal arts, and his recognition also therefore of the garden as a key site in which to rehearse that awareness. The problem this raises as a social venture can again be best explained with the help of the French tour. On visiting the King's Library in Paris, Young discovers a series of glass cases containing models of the instruments of various trades, preserved for the benefit of posterity. These include:

> . . . the potter, founder, brickmaker, chymist, &c. &c. and lately added a very large one of the English garden, most miserably imagined; but with all this not a plough, or an iota of agriculture; yet a farm might be much easier represented than the garden they have attempted, and with infinitely more use. I have no doubt but there may arise many uses, in which the preservation of instruments unaltered, may be of considerable utility; I think I see clearly, that such a use would result in agriculture, and if so, why not in other arts? These cases of models, however, have so much the air of children's playhouses, that I would not answer for my little girl, if I had her here, not crying for them.[32]

Young's annoyance at the lack of agricultural models is apparent, as is his clear evaluation of the usefulness of agriculture over that of the garden. This is something he studiously avoids mentioning in the English tours. What Young is confronting of course is not simply use, as he sees it, but polite culture's assimilation of the mechanical arts. And this act of assimilation itself throws further light on the reason for including gardens in his tours. The tours are constantly both playing off and combining gardens with his own agricultural concerns, using one form of landscape to convey the other into the polite world. This recognition of the garden as a crucial site for social advancement means that while Young's writing appears to represent an alternative culture of the land – one which is economic, practical, and unconcerned with conventional aesthetics – in fact he attempts the polite act of merging the garden's culture with the economic culture of the field.

Park landscapes of the later eighteenth century may well denote the physical exclusion of the poor as recent critics have noted, and they may also attempt the aesthetic exclusion of their visitors; but the responses made to them in the mass of polite writing mark more than this. In the writing of Young and Dodsley, of Miss M— and the 'Gentleman of Oxford', we see the attempts of polite culture to articulate itself, its own acts of exclusion, and the rivalries within a culture seeking to claim some kind of normative status. Notably, beyond simply the rejection of the poor and a broad consolidation of class interests is a series of socio-aesthetic discrimination within the propertied polite. While the designs of the landowner might be to seek the removal of any opportunity for engagement with the garden or with his personal presence, polite writing points to a range of possible responses to such acts of exclusion. In the picturesque traveller William Gilpin, or in the agricultural writer Arthur Young, we see the tensions within a society undergoing fundamental change but a society also searching for a means of maintaining its stability. While I have stressed the conflicts within polite responses to the garden we must recognize also the sense in which that garden offered a shared arena for discussion, for that socio-aesthetic interaction which cements the bonds of a shared culture. As a site in which to represent the cultural concerns of the nation, the English landscape garden was to remain contested social and aesthetic space throughout the eighteenth century, but a space also powerfully homogenizing in its creation of a shared identity within which those differences could be articulated.

5 Defining Femininity: Women and the Country House

Dana Arnold

This chapter explores how the country house represented and reinforced the role and status of women in the upper echelons of eighteenth- and early nineteenth-century society. This aspect of country house history has been written about only in fragments in studies which focus on marriage, domestic life or 'feminine' pursuits such as needlecraft.[1] Partly as a result of this, the role of women has been marginalized or associated with other sub-groups, such as servants or children, rather than presented as part of the mainstream history which remains a male preserve.[2] Yet, the very notions of house and family home – both central to the definition of the country house – have feminine associations. The aim of this chapter is to signal the importance of women to the evolution of the country house as a prompt for further research into this rich field. In doing so the intention is not merely to reconfigure established interpretations of the country house; rather, it is to add an additional layer of meaning which makes interpretation richer. Moreover, the country house is used as a means of exploring upper class femininity in the long eighteenth century. It is investigated in such as way as to reveal how aspects of the country house served to shape, determine or give physical expression to the role of women in Georgian culture and society.

Social definition

One of the areas in histories of the period relevant to the country house where the role and status of women has been underplayed is how they were defined in contemporary society. This can be demonstrated in several different ways. The most relevant starting point to consider this with reference to the country house is the way in which women could hold titles or be enobled. It is perhaps not widely appreciated that the number of title-bearing women outnumbered men in the eighteenth century.[3] Moreover, the conventions governing the conferment of titles were greatly in women's favour. If a woman married she took the female equivalent of her husband's title whether this was of higher or lower rank than her own. But women retained their own titles when they married commoners, although their

Fig. 5.1   William Hogarth, Marriage à la Mode: The Betrothal, *engraving, 1745. Hogarth is parodying the practice of using marriage settlements as a means of buying into the aristocracy.*

husbands' status remained unaltered. Also there was greater egality or anonymity of specific noble rank among women as the title 'lady' and 'ladyship' were generally used. A woman also had financial independence even if her husband predeceased her. Widows received a pension or jointure from their children. A survey of the Irish peerage in 1783 reveals that 72 of the 101 peers were making payments of this kind to dowagers.[4] Indeed, Lord Kildare whose octagenarian mother held parties every night complained 'I think it's very surprising that a single old woman should be distressed for the delay of paying £300 [for] a month or two when she has got £3,000 a year'. This sum was about a quarter of the Earl's own income.

The rules governing the place and treatment of women in society were different and distinctive, implying a recognition of some kind of independent status. Most notably women of noble birth were not redefined by men who were not of noble birth. And these noble women held important positions at Court. For instance, much has been made of Lord Burlington's official appointments under George I as Lord Treasurer of Ireland and Lord Lieutenant of the East and West Ridings of Yorkshire followed by his becoming a Privy Councillor and Knight of the Garter under George II. But Lady Burlington had an equally important role

Fig. 5.2 Sir John Soane, Design for a Pavilion and Garden Seat. *(SMAL Cupboard 22, folio 5 items 77 and 78). The inscription was added later. The exchange of copies of designs of this kind was indicative of women's developing interest in architecture. Courtesy of the Trustees of Sir John Soane's Museum.*

at Court as Lady of the Bedchamber to Queen Caroline and conducted her own successful career even after her husband retired from public life in 1733.[5]

Social status and rank underpinned the hegemony of the landed élite, so why has the role of women in the social and cultural history of the country house which gave physical expression to these norms been so underplayed and under-explored? This question becomes more puzzling when the economic importance of women to the country house and its estate in the eighteenth century is considered. There are two areas of particular interest here: inheritance and marriage.[6] Edmund Burke's observation that property is 'a partnership not only between those who are living, but between those who are living, those who are dead, and those who are to be born'[7] applies well to the concerns of those with landed interests in Britain and their attempts to protect their interests through property settlements. These, together with the law and custom of primogeniture, were important factors in preserving large estates and keeping family fortunes intact. Few entire estates were purchased in the eighteenth and early nineteenth centuries – although land was mortgaged, leased or even sold to cover debts or to finance expensive projects. For instance, Lord Burlington sold leases and land on his Irish estates in both 1729 and 1738. This raised over £30,000 alongside the £15,000 per annum he took in revenue from these lands.[8] But the opportunities to increase acreage and thereby augment one's social standing were limited. A

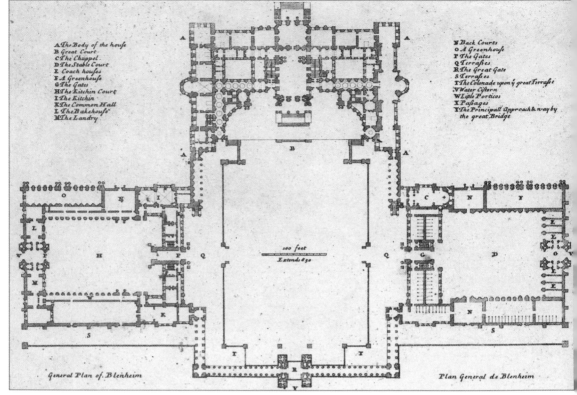

A The Body of the house
B Great Court
C The Chappel
D The Stable Court
E Coach houses
F A Greenhouse
G The Gates
H The Kitchin Court
I The Kitchin
K The Common Hall
L The Bakehouse
M The Landry

N Back Courts
O A Greenhouse
P The Gates
Q Terrasses
R The Great Gate
S Terrasses
T The Colonade upon ÿ great Terrasse
N Water Cistern
W Little Porticos
X Passages
Y The Principall Approach & way by
  the great Bridge

100 feet
Extends 650

General Plan of Blenheim   Plan General de Blenheim

Fig. 5.3   Plan of Blenheim, principal floor, Vitruvius Britannicus, *vol. I, plate 59.*

notable example of this was the purchase of the adjoining estates of Gawthorpe and Harewood (pl. 3) in 1739 by the Lascelles family. (Although the palatial Harewood House was constructed between 1759 and 1771, Edwin Lascelles was not enobled until 1790.)[9] But apart from isolated instances the position of men in landed society offered only limited scope for improvement. However, there was greater social fluidity for women through marriage. This had a fundamental impact on the country house and its estate. Established landowners could aggrandize their estates or wealth through opportune marriage. The conference of a title to a woman with a suitable dowry, even if she be from a lower social rank, oiled the wheels of matrimonial arrangements.[10] Indeed, generous dowry settlements were bestowed upon daughters of wealthy merchants and gentry as a means of buying into the aristocracy. And this wealth often supported the estate and enabled new investment in farming and property refurbishment or rebuilding. This practice was so well known in the first half of the eighteenth century that it is parodied in Hogarth's first scene from his *Marriage à la Mode* series (fig. 5.1).

On the other side of the coin, however, was the amount of debt run up by families to provide an adequate dowry for the female members of the family. One

Pl. 1   Holkham Hall, Norfolk, the marble hall, 1734–65.

Pl. 2   Goodwood House, West Sussex, enlarged and remodelled by James Wyatt, 1787 onwards. Courtesy of Lord March.

Pl. 3   Harewood House, Yorkshire, entrance front, 1765–71, designed by Robert Adam and John Carr of York. Courtesy of Harewood House Trust.

Pl. 4   Houghton, 1722–35, entrance front, Colen Campbell, 1722, domes added by James Gibbs 1729; the interiors were designed by William Kent 1725–35. Photograph by Dana Arnold.

Pl. 5 Kedleston, Derbyshire, 1760–8, the garden front, one of Robert Adam's finest houses. Photograph by Frank Salmon.

Pl. 6 Chatsworth: magnificent seat of the Dukes of Devonshire, but the 5th Duke (suc. 1764, d. 1811) preferred to live mostly in London, coming to Chatsworth only for recreation. Photograph by M.H. Port.

Pl. 7 Holkham Hall, Norfolk, 1734–65, the product of complex collaboration. Photograph by Dana Arnold.

Pl. 8 The Palladian Bridge at Stowe. Photograph by Dana Arnold.

Pl. 9 The Temple of British Worthies, Stowe, Buckinghamshire, by William Kent, 1735. Photograph by Dana Arnold.

Pl. 10   The Pantheon (Temple of Hercules), Stourhead, 1754–6 by Henry Flitcroft. Photograph by Dana Arnold.

Pl. 11   Shugborough, Staffordshire, Tower of the Winds by James Athenian Stuart, converted into a dairy in 1805 for Viscount Anson.

Pl. 12   Design for Offices, Brampton Bryan, Herefordshire, 1777, Robert Adam. Courtesy of the Trustees of Sir John Soane's Museum.

Pls 13, 14 and 15   A La Ronde, Devon, 1795, Jane and Mary Parminter. View of the grotto off the stairs leading to the shell gallery, (bottom left) a crown painted in honour of George III in 1800, watercolour birds and shells stuck on either side, (bottom right) shell-encrusted surround of shell gallery window. The National Trust Photographic Library / Geoffrey Frosh.

Pls 16 and 17   Lady Julia Calverley, needlework screen, 1727, wool and fine petit point, Wallington Hall, Northumberland, (left) detail of two panels, (right) detail of a panel showing a country house in a landscape. National Trust Photographic Library, left A.C. Cooper, right Derrick E. Witty.

Pl. 18   Sir John Soane, Hamels Dairy, Hertfordshire, 1781–3. Courtesy of the Trustees of Sir John Soane's Museum.

Pl. 19 Richard Westall, Orpheus.
Orpheus symbolized Greek civilization.
Here he is taming animals with music from
his lyre – a metaphor for him civilizing the
barbaric population. For Richard Payne
Knight this represented the connections
between the benefits of wild nature and
civilized society. Private Collection.

Pl. 20 Arthur Devis, The Crewe Conversation Piece, 1743–4, detail. The whole of the Crewe
family is assembled for the polite ritual of taking tea. The interior is probably fictitious as Crewe
Hall, Cheshire, was a Jacobean house. Here the classical architecture and garden ornaments
signify, like the tea drinking, the family's social status. Courtesy of the Spink-Leger Galleries.

way of gathering the necessary funds was to mortgage property but this sometimes led to large debts accruing for future generations. This estate capital was an important contribution to wealth and the marriage market in the period. But the most glamorous instances of augmentation of wealth and land were through marriage to heiresses with landed property. Once again these were particularly from the gentry classes. For instance, the aggrandizement of the great estates of such nobles as the Duke of Buckingham and the Duke of Leeds relied largely on the acquiring of more land through marriage.[11]

In all these areas women were the focus for a family's dynastic and economic ambitions. Moreover, as social conventions moved away from arranged marriages towards some kind of free will in the choice of partner the rules changed and women can be seen as having social mobility and economic significance within the upper echelons of society. Indeed, by the second decade of the eighteenth century the notion of the ideal husband and of male qualities potential brides should look for began to be discussed in publications aimed at women. Moreover, the *Female Spectator* (1744) spoke out against arranged marriages while the *Lady's Curiosity or Weekly Apollo* published an essay on 'The Unreasonableness in Confining Courtship to Men'.[12]

The corollary of this is that emphasis on feminine virtues and accomplishments came to the fore. As the passion grew for hot liquors – including tea, coffee and chocolate (which were then expensive, luxury goods) – so did the social

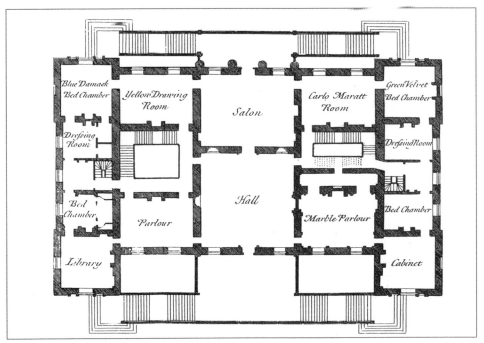

Fig. 5.4   Plan of Houghton, 1722–35, principal floor, from Horace Walpole, Aedes Walpolianae, *1767 edn. Houghton's design shows the interaction between communal and private areas of the house.*

Fig. 5.5   Luton Hoo, Bedfordshire, entrance front, by Robert Adam, 1767–74.

conventions surrounding the serving and imbibing of these drinks.[13] These focused on the female members of the family and made femininity separate and distinct. This is evident first of all in the growing importance of the equipage as a symbol of status and rank.[14] The pouring of these luxurious hot drinks from expensive and highly decorative services was seen as a bench-mark of feminine virtue and grace (pl. 20). This act was central to the definition of a family's status and was the linchpin of hospitality which was a fundamental part of polite society. It also made a connection between femininity, the decorative arts and good taste.

The emphasis on correct feminine behaviour can be seen in the growth of publications for women in the early years of the eighteenth century.[15] One of the earliest examples is the *Ladies Library* (1714) published by Richard Steele and 'written by a lady'; it was 'compiled from Writings of Eminent Divines for Guide to her conduct to be of some Service to Others of her Sex, who have not the same opportunities of searching into Various Authors themselves'. There were two volumes: the first contained essays on Chastity, Modesty, Meekness, Wit and Delicacy; and volume two gave instruction on how to be a daughter, wife, mother, widow and, perhaps surprisingly, mistress.

The intention here is not to paint an inaccurately rosy picture of the cultural practices concerning upper-class women in the long eighteenth century. Indeed, there is plenty of evidence that women were not always well treated, as witnessed in Lady Blayney's description of her marriage:

> I was married to my Lord Blayney against my own opinion; he had an agreeable outside but there was a terrible inside. I endured all sorts of indignity for several years, even frequent blows; after bearing this usage longer than perhaps most others would . . . I went back to my father.

More extreme was Lord Belvedere's imprisonment of his wife at the family mansion of Gaulston after she had committed incest and adultery; the incarceration did, however, receive some criticism.[16] Lady Luxborough suffered a similar fate. Her extensive correspondence with William Shenstone was partly the result of her exile in the country imposed by her husband after an extra marital affair which she denied.[17]

The definition of women within eighteenth-century society establishes their social and economic importance to the country house. Travel was arduous and time consuming; these factors together with family needs meant women spent more time in the country than men. As a consequence women often ran the estate in their husband's absence. Some, including Lady Orrery, did the job permanently and her actions and opinions are recorded in her regular letters to her husband.[18] If we then accept that the country house represents a distinct set of social and cultural values in which women played an important part there must be ways in which its form and function embody the feminine.

The definition of femininity within the country house

The most obvious starting point for a consideration of the relationship of women to the form of the country house is the role they took in its architectural design. Indeed, the tradition of the amateur architect is associated with the upper classes as it connotes the education, leisure and wealth that enabled the pursuit of this interest. And many country house owners had a keen interest in design. The education of women prepared them equally for involvement with architecture. They were taught drawing and mathematics and the art of surveying and so were equipped with the rudiments of design production.[19] The general growing interest in architecture is evident in the increasing popularity of subscription publications like *Britannia Illustrata* and *Vitruvius Britannicus*. Although the majority of subscribers were men, women also supported these volumes. It was Lord Burlington's mother, Lady Juliana, who subscribed to the first volume of *Vitruvius Britannicus* and Lady Marlborough paid for two volumes in addition to those bought by her husband. There is also evidence of women designing buildings or taking proactive roles as patrons. For instance Weston Park in Staffordshire was designed by Lady Wilbraham in 1671 using Palladio's first book of his *I Quattro Libri Dell'Architettura* as her chief guide.[20] And the Duchess of Rutland designed Belvoir Farm on their estate at Belvoir Castle for her husband the 5th Duke.[21] Women also commissioned designs and acted as patrons in their own right. For instance, Lady Elizabeth Craven commissioned Sir John Soane to produce several design for her garden in 1781 shortly after his return from Italy. Although none was realized, they included plans for several garden seats and Soane inscribed his design for a rustic dairy of the same year to Lady Craven.[22] The role women played in certain aspects of architectural design, most notably primitivism, is discussed more fully below. But here the gift by Lady Craven of some of Soane's garden designs to her friend Lady Penelope Pitt-Rivers gives an indication of the currency of architecture and design questions within female society (fig. 5.2).

Women were also actively involved in the building profession and its processes. At the top end of the scale Lady Margaret Tufton demonstrated her abilities as a patron and financial manager when she was left with debts of £90,000 after the

*Fig. 5.6   Harewood House, the music room, 1765–71,
by Robert Adam. Courtesy of the Harewood House
Trust.*

*Fig. 5.7   Harewood House, the music room, detail of
Terpsichore the muse of dancing, one of the nine muses
who accompanied Apollo, by Angelica Kauffman.
Courtesy of the Harewood House Trust.*

death of her husband Thomas Coke, Earl of Leicester. But she brought Holkham
to completion and spent a further £2,000 per annum until 1764 to ensure it was
finished in accordance with the original designs, although the style of the building
– deemed unfashionable on completion by some critics – was still associated with
her husband.[23] There is no doubt of the practical abilities and outstanding
technical contribution to the building trade made by Mrs Coade.[24] Her secret
recipe for a manufactured stone made a substantial contribution to the
architectural profession through the technical possibilities of the material.
Moreover, its cheapness in comparison to genuine stone made it highly attractive
and gave many buildings the illusion of grandeur and expense. The
embellishment of country house interiors was the concern of both the women of
landed families (see below) and professional practitioners like Angelica Kauffman
(figs 5.6 and 5.7). Her work with Robert Adam, where she painted, for instance,
some of the ceiling panels at Harewood, is equal to any other of his collaborators.

There is no doubt that further research and a re-evaluation of the way in which
designs for country houses and their interiors were developed might well reveal
that women played a much greater part in this area of country house history. But
that is beyond the scope of this brief survey. The purpose here is merely to
highlight this possibility and to bring together known areas to create a framework
for the more comprehensive understanding of the relationship of women and the
country house.

Planning

The planning of the country house might well be expected to reflect the social conventions regarding women. And during the eighteenth century a general trend away from formality in the country house plan to one which allowed a more private lifestyle can be identified.[25] The long enfilade suites of rooms were characteristic of this kind of planning; the use of long vistas through the house and a hierarchy of rooms reached through the enfilade emphasized the formality of the social conventions of the time. The importance of the reception of visitors of varying ranks in various parts of the house was expressed by how far they penetrated the private apartments. This protocol was observed by the occupants of the house and any guests using the state apartments – the most distinguished visitor being admitted to the inner most sanctuary, the bedchamber.[26] This kind of formal planning was adopted at Chatsworth – although only one suite of apartments was built because the south wing of the Elizabethan house was not long enough to accommodate the usual two. New-built houses provided the best examples of this kind of hierarchical formal planning, for example in Vanbrugh's Blenheim (fig. 5.3). A suite of apartments would comprise usually an ante-chamber, withdrawing chamber, bedchamber and closet with perhaps a dark room for servants. Husbands and wives sometimes shared bedchambers but all other rooms remained separate, allowing for privacy and the reception of different

Fig. 5.8   Osterley, Middlesex, 1761–80, eating-room by Robert Adam, paintings by Antonio Zucchi, Moorish dancers in a Ruin, and Offering to Ceres in the overmantel. Photograph by Dana Arnold.

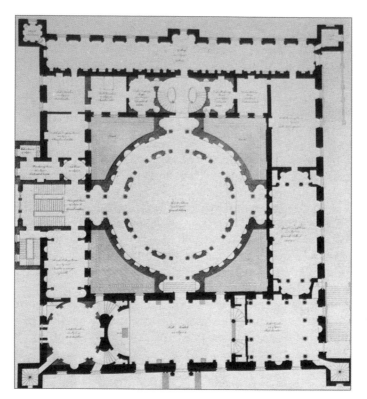

Fig. 5.9 Syon, plan of principal floor, Robert Adam, The Works in Architecture, *vol. I, part i, plate 5. Adam's design ensured women could retire to a room well away from the noise of men in the dining-room.*

groups of guests. The positioning of the saloon in the middle of the suites of apartments continued into the middle of the eighteenth century. Houghton (fig. 5.4) provides a useful example of this type of house in transition. The *piano nobile* comprised four suites of apartments two of which were occupied by Walpole and his wife. The remaining apartments and the double-height saloon and hall were used only on very special grand occasions. After this time the social rituals became more relaxed and the communal areas of the house became more widely used. The bedchamber moved to the upper floors of the house while the lady's dressing-room – a kind of private sitting-room open to select visitors – remained on the *piano nobile*, the principal floor of the house. This can be seen for instance in Robert Adam's designs for Kenwood and Luton Hoo (fig. 5.5). But apart from this rather obvious separation of the sexes in terms of suites of private apartments comprising dressing-rooms or bedrooms which endured throughout the eighteenth century there was little else in terms of planning that had feminine associations.

Turning the question on its head there was also little in planning and design that had masculine associations. And the classical language of architecture certainly provided enough vocabulary with which to articulate spaces according to gender – or purpose. The masculine associations of the Tuscan and Doric orders could connote 'men only' spaces, while references to Ceres or Bacchus might well be appropriate for a dining-room (fig. 5.8). Indeed, the different associations and uses of the dining-room and drawing-room are among the few aspects of country house design where male and female interests are expressed.

In the early part of the century dining had taken place in halls or saloons which usually occupied a central position on the main floor of the house. But during the course of the eighteenth century the fashion for a separate dining-room emerged. This became one of the biggest and most extravagantly furnished rooms of the house and dining became an elaborate array of courses brought in by liveried servants. Although men and women dined together, the dining-room was deemed to be male space being the site of sybaritic pleasures and excessive eating and drinking. As such it was separated from the drawing-room because once the women had 'withdrawn' to the drawing-room things could become raucous. While Sanderson Miller was still working on the plan for Hagley, Worcestershire, in 1752 Lord Lyttleton wrote to the architect to express the wishes of his wife that 'Lady Littleton wishes for a room of separation between the eating room and the drawing room, to hinder the ladies from the noise and talk of the men when left to their bottle, which must sometimes happen, even at Hagley'.[27] This attitude is endorsed by Robert Adam in his discussion of the Syon drawing-room (fig. 5.9) in the *Works in Architecture*, volume I. His explanation of plate i 5 reads thus:

[it is] an admirable room for the reception of the company before dinner, or for the ladies to retire to after it. For the withdrawing room lying between this and the eating room prevents the noise of the men from being troublesome.

Fig. 5.10   Castletown, Co. Kildare, Edward Lovett Pearce, c. 1722. It was the home of Lady Louisa Connolly who made significant alterations to the house. Courtesy of the Irish Architectural Archive.

Fig. 5.11   Lord and Lady Kildare, 1753. Emily was an accomplished designer. Courtesy of the Irish Architectural Archive.

Although these planning questions reveal interesting elements of the social history of country house life there is not enough evidence to gauge how women were defined in the house. But perhaps this is the wrong question to ask. It is clear women were in tune with design issues and sensitive to the social and cultural changes taking place in the period. Did this manifest itself in the country house in other ways? Did, for instance, the decoration of the interior betray traces of femininity?

Interiors

Women made a direct contribution to the country house interior in two ways. Firstly, their role in the general choice of materials and fabrics and the overall design. This is seen in Robert Adam's work for Fanny Boscawen at Hatchlands and the Duchess of Northumberland at her London town house and Syon. In both cases Adam worked with his female clients but attention has been focused on Adams' role. Furthermore, earlier in the century Lady Luxborough's lengthy correspondence with William Shenstone reveals her keen interest in matters of interior design.[28] The correspondence between Lady Louisa Connolly who lived at Castletown (fig. 5.10) and her sister Lady Kildare, later Duchess of Leinster (fig. 5.11), who lived at Carton (fig. 5.12) is filled with details about their choices of wallpaper, linen, embroidery and other furnishings. Both sisters also commissioned plasterwork from the Lanfranchini brothers and supervised architectural interventions in the built fabric of their houses – including an ambitious new staircase at Castletown (fig. 5.13).[29] Secondly, women made more specific contributions through activities like wall decoration and needlecraft. Needlecraft became a bench-mark of a leisured lifestyle and was seen as an appropriate feminine pursuit for the upper classes.[30] This was echoed later in the century in women's work in print-rooms and paper collage.

Debates about women's involvement with embroidery were current at the beginning of the eighteenth century. And it has been suggested that the decline in the art was partly due to an interest in other creative outlets such as poetry and shifting attitudes towards the role of women, particularly wives. This is seen in the debates around Addison's comment in the *Spectator* (1716).[31] When replying to a letter complaining of young women's declining interest in embroidery in favour of 'Gadding abroad', Addison remarked:

> What a delightful entertainment it must be to the fair sex . . . to pass their hours in imitating fruits and flowers. . . . This methinks, the proper way wherein a Lady can show a fine genius, and I cannot forbear wishing that writers of that sex had chosen to apply themselves to tapestry than rhyme.

Fig. 5.12 Carton, Co. Kildare, Richard Castle, 1745, wings added by Richard Morrison in 1815, the home of Lord and Lady Kildare. Courtesy of the Irish Architectural Archive.

Fig. 5.13   Castletown, the staircase and entrance hall, commissioned by Lady Louisa Connolly. Courtesy of the Irish Architectural Archive.

Needlework was an important feminine occupation and it was on display throughout the house in such forms as samplers, screens and chair covers. The iconography of some of the larger pieces shows that women were very much in tune with changes in society and attitudes towards the land. For instance, the two screens produced by Lady Julia Calverley in 1716 and 1727 (pls 16 and 17),[32] now in Wallington, Northumberland, had pride of place in the family possessions. The later screen comprised six leaves each representing scenes from Virgil's *Eclogues* and *Georgics* based on a series of illustrations published by Francis Cleyn in 1654. Later in the century embroidery moved away from the representation of pastoral scenes towards a more naturalistic representation of the landscape and those working in it. These representations of farm scenes are a comment on the changes in the management of farmland.

Paper hangings were another area of women's work in the country house interior. Women were involved with the embellishment of printed papers – especially those of Chinese design. Extra figures, commonly exotic birds cut from unused parts of the paper, were pasted on to give a very rich appearance. These papers were extremely expensive which gives some indication of the prestige this work had at the time. Indeed, at Temple Newsam Lady Hertford used Audubon's *Birds of America* to decorate the Chinese wallpaper given to her by the Prince Regent.[33] Lady Kildare created a Chinese room at Carton in 1759 (fig. 5.14) and

Fig. 5.14 Carton, the Chinese room, created by Lady Emily Kildare. Courtesy of the Irish Architectural Archive.

went to considerable pains to choose the correctly coloured chintz and matching paint to ensure the best possible effect.[34]

The print-room became another feature of the country house interior in the latter part of the eighteenth century.[35] This again was women's work. Individual prints were pasted onto walls, which were usually treated with a yellow or buff ground, and frames were made to surround them.[36] This was by no means a cheap solution to interior decoration because good quality prints were imported specially from the continent for the purpose. The decorative effect was stunning – perhaps no more so than at Louisa Connolly's print-room at Castletown (fig. 5.15). Indeed, as this fashion spread so papers which copied the look of print-rooms came into general manufacture.[37] The industry of women within the house and their contribution to its design and decoration is a fundamental part of its history. There is a flavour of this in Lord Aldoborough's remark on his return to Belan House where he found 'Louisa Wingfield at work, Martha painting a card table, Emily at other work . . . [and] the grotto going on . . . [with the arrival of] shells from Waterford'. The emphasis on feminine craft and the use or replication of natural elements in the decoration of interiors are important to the understanding of the relationship between women and the country house.

Women and nature – art versus craft

The link between women and nature goes some way towards providing a key to unlock at least some of the ways that women and femininity were embodied in the country house. This lies partly in a re-evaluation of what is now seen as craft as opposed to art as it is here that women were especially active. There are two main points. Firstly, decorative arts in the eighteenth century had an equal if not a higher perceived value than flat art. Chippendale settees took pride of place among the Rosas and Claudes. Horace Walpole's response to the interiors at Kedleston represents this attitude. He found the house 'magnificently finished and furnished. . . . In the Saloon, a fine room, door cases of Alabaster, Settees supported by gilt fishes & Sea gods.' Although, typically, Walpole snipes that the settees look 'absurdly like the King's coach'.[38] Secondly, present-day reaction to 'craft' is that it is a less cerebral and therefore less valuable art form and this colours our view of this aspect of the country house interior. If these attitudes are projected back into the eighteenth century and combined with a study of women who mainly carried out these pursuits it is clear that this kind of contribution to country house architecture or decoration could be marginalized.

Apart from needlework, women carried out other kinds of interior design, most notably paper collage and the decoration of print-rooms. But in all these forms the emphasis was to work from nature. These have received little attention from the historian in contrast to the work of Angelica Kauffman, but Kauffman was a painter and as such ties in with the notion of fine art being a gentlemanly and scholarly pursuit into which she was an anomalous visitor. Contemporary attitudes towards these crafts are exemplified by a comment in the *Female Spectator* (1746) by Eliza Heywood: 'Why do they call us silly women, and not endeavour to make us otherwise? . . . The Ladies themselves begin to seem sensible of the Injustice which has been done to them, and find a Vacuum in their Minds, which to fill up, they of their own accord invented ways of sticking little Pictures on Cabinets.'[39] Indeed, Mrs Delany's remark that 'The ornamental work of gentlewomen ought to be superior to bought work in design and taste' is indicative of how present-day attitudes obscure the definitions of upper-class femininity within the country house.[40]

Dairies and grottoes

The imprint of femininity spread beyond the confines of the house to the estate buildings. Just as embroidery demonstrated that women were in tune with changes in the landscape and in the social and economic status quo, so the emergence of the dairy as an independent feature in the country house landscape was associated not only with femininity but also with the increasing interest in primitivism and a return to nature expressed in the writings of theorists like J.J. Rousseau and the Abbé Laugier (fig. 5.16). Dairies emerged as buildings of interest to architects in the third quarter of the eighteenth century. By the closing years of the century dairies, like other farm buildings, were designed with the freedom of expression which was in tune with contemporary continental

Fig. 5.15   Castletown, the print-room, created by Lady Louisa Connolly. Courtesy of the Irish Architectural Archive.

Fig. 5.16   Frontispiece from Abbé Laugier's Essai sur L'Architecture, *Paris, 1753. One of a number of mid-eighteenth-century works showing an increasing interest in primitivism and a return to nature.*

architectural thinking about primitive and natural forms. The important point is that unlike other farm buildings dairies were designed for the lady of the house. Here, as in the use of embroidery, the association between women and nature was strong. The dairy acted as a return to the primitive and a variation on the simple rustic life; the milk fad, where cold milk was served to both rich and poor, endorsed this.

The feminine associations of the dairy go back to the musings of Marie Antoinette and her model farm and the *ferme ornée*. But more important is the link between women and nature, which throughout the eighteenth century was expressed in various ways through the medium of the country house. These 'feminine' buildings can be seen in the designs for dairies by Sir John Soane, Samuel Wyatt and Henry Holland. There is a conflict here between the female patron and user and the primitive and therefore 'masculine' associations of the architectural style. But the use of design elements like the baseless Doric or thatched roofs perhaps refer to the tradition of mother nature and the rustic life.

Sir John Soane's commission for a dairy from Lady Craven did lead to the production of one of his most inventive early designs. The Craven dairy showed Soane's understanding of the principles of primitivism and the return to nature.

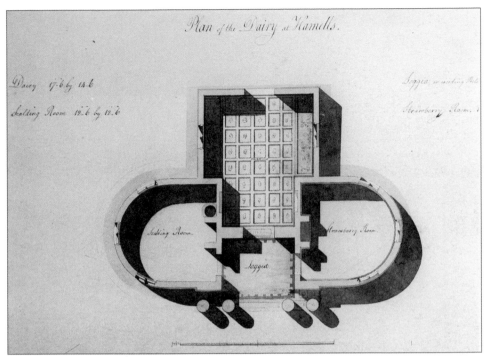

Fig. 5.17   Sir John Soane, Hamels Dairy, Hertfordshire, 1781–3, plan. Courtesy of the Trustees of Sir John Soane's Museum.

Indeed, it has been argued that Soane's design was greatly influenced by Lady Craven and that she was responsible for the architect's developing interest in primitive design.[41] Lady Craven had done much to promote the interest in the natural and the primitive in design. In 1776 she built a mock cottage called Craven Cottage on the banks of the Thames in Fulham, then just outside London. Soane's connection with Lady Craven influenced his design for Hamels Dairy (1789–94). The work at Hamels was commissioned by Philip Yorke but the designs went to his wife Lady Elizabeth (fig. 5.17 and pl. 18). The dairy was then the domain of women and there were other 'aristocratic' milkmaids than Soane's two clients. Samuel Wyatt designed one at Sandon, Staffordshire for Lady Hervey in 1784 and Henry Holland produced such a building for Lady Hillsborough at Hill Park in Kent. Lancelot 'Capability' Brown also joined the fray of designers encapsulating this rustic, natural feminine ideal with his dairy for Lady Digby at Sherbourne.

Like dairies, grottoes imitated and celebrated nature. Alexander Pope's grotto at his villa in Twickenham copied the rock formations of a Cornish tin mine. Pope even employed the services of a geologist to ensure accuracy. More usually grottoes were sites to show off rare and expensive shell collections. And shellwork was carried out by women.[42] For instance, Lady Walpole's grotto, which used shells from the Channel Islands, was praised in *The Gentleman's Magazine* of 1743:

*Fig. 5.18   Goodwood House, West Sussex, the grotto, by kind permission of Lord March.
Photograph by Rosemary Baird.*

> Each little isel with generous zeal
> Sends grateful very precious shell
> To make the Walpole grotto fine.

But praise was not universal. Mrs Delany, known for her needlework, paper collage
and shellwork, declared, 'Grotto I will not call it. The regularity is abominable;
besides all the coral is painted, mine shall not be made after that model.' Indeed
Mrs Delany went on to help the Duchess of Portland construct a grotto where over
1,000 snail shells were used. The cost of the materials was considerable and caused
many remarks. William Shenstone noted that Lady Fane's grotto, 'a very beautiful
disposition of the finest collection of shells I ever saw', cost three times as much as
her house. The Duchess of Richmond's grotto at Goodwood House, West Sussex,
was also extremely expensive (figs 5.18 and 5.19). It was begun in 1739 and the
Duchess and her daughters spent seven years making an exquisitely decorative
pattern of shellwork made the more dazzling by the inclusion of mirrored glass.
The skill and restraint of the design is stunning and in complete sympathy with the

Fig. 5.19 Goodwood House, West Sussex, the grotto, detail of the shellwork, by kind permission of Lord March. Photograph by Rosemary Baird.

coffered wall surface and vaulted ceiling of the architectural framework of the building. Grottoes were expensive and used valuable materials like shells that were indicative not only of wealth but of trading connections with the South Seas. As with the interior decoration of country houses, women were responsible for putting this wealth and taste on display. The work of the Parminter sisters and their cousin Mary at A La Ronde on the outskirts of Exmouth, Devon (1795 onwards), is perhaps one of the most outstanding examples of the expression of femininity through design. The sixteen-sided building was influenced by the octagonal basilic of St Vitale in Ravenna, which the women had seen on their Grand Tour. Designed by the Parminters, A La Ronde had a thatched roof and limewashed walls and was reminiscent of the 'feminine' dairy designs of the period. The women spent several years decorating the interior with shellwork, feathers and cut paper. The survival of the house was ensured by Mary who died in 1849; her will forbad any changes to the house and allowed only unmarried kinswomen to inherit it (pls 13, 14 and 15).

This chapter has presented only select sample of work carried out by women and the ways in which femininity was defined and represented in the country house. One of the functions of the country house was to represent the taste of aristocratic society and, through this to reinforce the social and cultural hegemony of the ruling élite. Women were an active part of this class and their interventions in the decoration and fabric of the country house and its estate are essential to this definition of the country house. If we realign our sights to appreciate the social and economic importance of women, the significance of their crafts, and the value and meaning of stylistic trends other than the classical, a new and vital field of investigation is revealed.

6 The Illusion of Grandeur? Antiquity, Grand Tourism and the Country House

Dana Arnold

The Grand Tour is one of the best known cultural activities of the long eighteenth century. Its appeal endured throughout the period. The dangers of the many wars which raged in Europe did little to dispel enthusiasm. Travellers either adjusted their route to suit the political climate of the time or waited until hostilities had ceased. Moreover, the frequent changes in stylistic taste and fashion across all the arts did not detract from the attraction of the offerings of mainland Europe, and in particular Rome. There has been considerable work done on the itineraries of the Grand Tour, the different kinds of tourist together and the social life they led. This is equalled by the detailed surveys of what was bought, whether original or copy, and shipped back to Britain for display, usually in the country house.[1]

This chapter considers why the Grand Tour remained such a popular activity in the Georgian period and why Rome remained its focal point. Of special interest is the role and function of the Grand Tour in the culture and society of the time. The lure of antiquity evoked feelings of nostalgia in those who had visited Italy, and later Greece and Asia Minor. Together with the influence of Renaissance Italy, this had a resounding impact on aesthetic attitudes and artistic production which manifested itself in the architecture and gardens of the country house as well as the collections which were frequently displayed within it. But ancient buildings were rarely copied *per se* and there were in any case few directly relevant precedents. The architecture of the country house was instead full of quotations and reinterpretations of the antique.[2] And, although more directly relevant, the palace and villa designs of sixteenth- and seventeeth-century Italy were only adopted on a piecemeal basis. Alongside this the practice of collecting artefacts, and copying them, also raises interesting questions about the role Grand Tourism played in defining social and cultural ideals in the long eighteenth century. And the lack of differentiation between the original and imitation raises important issues about the use of antique elements as a metaphor for a variety of sets of beliefs and values. In this way the

Grand Tour addresses the fundamental questions of taste, the reuse of antique forms and their appropriation for an important national language of the visual arts.

Georgian society was itinerant. Individuals and whole households moved between town house, country house and resort or spa town according to the dictates of the social or political season. As such, travel was an integral part of the activities of the social élite. It is necessary to consider the act of foreign tourism and what it meant for eighteenth- and early nineteenth-century culture and society. Chapter 2 has already discussed the importance of home tourism for the definition of different social groups and the maintenance of the political status quo. But travel in Britain was a kind of internal, reflexive, self-definition. Here the external or alien elements of Graeco-Roman art, architecture and aesthetic ideals were adopted as signifiers of a distinct set of social and cultural values. And the country house played a pivotal role in the expression of these values. Its role as a site of display extends from its function as a repository for artefacts, from quotations of *all'antica* elements in its architecture and decoration to a more metaphorical display of a unique and self-consciously defined intellectual culture.

The collections held in country houses are testament to the enthusiasm and purchasing power of eighteenth-century travellers. Among other collectables paintings and sculptures were brought back in substantial quantities. Some were copies, others originals – or in the case of the sculptures composite pieces made from antique fragments. These collections were housed in picture galleries like the one at Harewood House (fig. 6.1) specially designed for Edwin Lascelles by

Fig. 6.1 Harewood House, Yorkshire, 1765–71, the gallery by Robert Adam, designed to house Harewood's extensive collection of fine art. Courtesy of Harewood House Trust.

Robert Adam between about 1765 and 1770.[3] As the passion for collections grew, additions to existing buildings became necessary. Richard Colt Hoare added matching wings to house his pictures and his library nearly three-quarters of a century after Stourhead was originally completed. The sculpture gallery was a showcase for *all'antica* artefacts and architecture as seen in the examples at Newby and Woburn Abbey. But the collections inspired by the Grand Tour are too numerous and diverse for analysis in this short chapter. Furthermore, most practising architects took some kind of Grand Tour and many met their future clients while doing so. But this vast and fascinating area of designer/client interaction is also outside the scope of this study. Similarly the instances of quotations from antique architecture would, in this context, be reduced to a mere catalogue of stylistic elements. Instead attention is focused on how aspects of the Grand Tour inform the social and cultural meaning of the country house.

The Grand Tour

The Grand Tour first appeared as a recognized cultural activity in the seventeenth century. Richard Lassels codified this in his *The Voyage of Italy* (1670). Part guidebook, part treatise, the text formed the template for an itinerary and benefits of the Grand Tour which endured into the early nineteenth century.[4]

During the opening years of the eighteenth century the Grand Tour evolved into a kind of wandering academy. It was commonly the practice that young men or milords, aged around eighteen, would travel for up to three years through Europe, stopping at artistic centres like Paris, Venice and Florence (fig. 6.2).[5]

Fig. 6.2 Thomas Patch, A Gathering of Dilettantis around the Medici Venus. *Paul Mellon Centre for Studies in British Art, Brinsley Ford Collection.*

Their main purpose was to take in the sights and familiarize themselves with the art and architecture of ancient Rome (fig. 6.3).[6] Edward Gibbon remarked that 'according to the law of custom, and perhaps of reason, foreign travel completes the education of an English gentleman'.[7] But not all young men of rank were willing participants in the uncomfortable overland journey in unsprung coaches along dusty roads. There were also real dangers. Crossing the Alps was hazardous and the cocktail of sickness and disease – including plague – which was prevalent in mainland Europe at the time posed a constant threat. This less romantic view of the Grand Tour was identified by Laurence Sterne who commented that tourists were 'young gentlemen transported by the cruelty of parents and guardians'.[8] But they were accompanied by tutors, often academics knowledgeable in the classics, including scholars like Adam Smith, who ensured the quality of the journey's educational content. Their pupils' attention was, however, often more readily captured by raucous drinking parties.

These study trips were the subject of books published by tutors or 'bear-leaders' as they were known. Their travel accounts give an interesting insight into the activities of the tourists. The text was often in letter form as the correspondence between the tutor and the parent of his charge formed the basis of the book. Also it must not be forgotten that this kind of writing, alongside the emerging form of the novel, was new and the epistolary format was popular and effective. Edward Wright, a Cambridge graduate with good connections with the English virtuosi in Italy, wrote his *Observations Made In Travelling Through France, Italy &c in the Years 1720, 1721 and 1722* (1730) based on the letters he had written to Lord Macclesfield while travelling in Europe with his son between 1720 and 1722. Similarly Monsieur de Blanville had acted as tutor to the sons of William Blathwayt of Dyrham Park during their Grand Tour of 1705 to 1707. Some decades later his correspondence with his employer formed the basis of his three-volume account *The Travels through Holland, Germany, Switzerland and other parts of Europe but especially Italy* (London, 1743 and reprinted 1745).[9] The accounts of travels were not only published by tutors trying to earn a living as passive ciceroni from their good knowledge of Italy. The tourists' own letters also appeared in print as seen in the correspondence of the Earl of Cork and Orrery which was published as *Letters from Italy in the Years 1754 and 1755* (1773).[10]

This wealth of travel literature confirms the uniformity of the experience of the Grand Tour. A core number of cities were visited on standard itineraries which usually began in France and ended with a stay in Rome. Ancient texts such as the writings of Pliny were used by tutors to illuminate the sights and sites, and ensured a communality of experience for the young patrician élite. This was an important unifying factor in British society as the shared educational curriculum assured common ground between those of a certain class. Moreover, the volume of British tourists – in 1763 Winckelmann noted there were over 300 young men in Paris *en route* for Rome – meant the next generation of the ruling nobility met and fraternized on neutral ground. In this way the tour was a substitute for the élite melting-pot of a university education.[11] The nostalgia for this rite of passage is expressed in the architecture, landscape and collections of country houses to

Fig. 6.3   Attributed to James Russel, English Connoisseurs in Rome. *The Grand Tour gave travellers a set of shared experiences. Collection of Mr and Mrs Paul Mellon.*

which the milords returned. These elements of the country house became potent symbols of a shared cultural experience and signifiers of a distinctive set of social values.

Trips abroad were not solely the preserve of the single male. Newly-weds, families and even unaccompanied women undertook these extended journeys. Lady Mary Wortley Montagu, a recognized scholar and patron of the arts, travelled abroad extensively. Equally notable was the Grand Tour of the Parminter sisters: on the death of their father in 1784 Jane and her invalid sister Elizabeth together with Mary their orphaned cousin and a friend, Miss Colville, set off on a voyage that lasted ten years. The four women started by following a traditional route. They sailed from Dover and travelled to Paris via Chantilly, Abbeville and Versailles. The first two months of the journey, during which time they reached Dijon, are recorded in Jane's diaries which betray vivid and incisive responses to European art and architecture equal to her male counterparts. Like many of the milords, the sisters decided to make use of their experiences abroad and build a new house – A La Ronde in Exmouth, Devon (pls 13, 14 and 15).

Visits abroad were not always for the purposes of education. Georgiana, Duchess of Devonshire was one of many noblewomen who went to Europe to have her illegitimate child. And Lord Byron travelled the continent as a outcast from English society. But the majority of travellers undertook some kind of educative Grand Tour and the event itself was devoted to the positive benefits of travel – despite the physical discomforts from bed bugs to bad food. The acquaintance with other nations encouraged a kind of pan-European consciousness, or as Sterne observed: 'It is an age so full of light, that there is scarce a country or corner of Europe whose beams are not crossed and interchanged with others.'[12] This currency of intellectual and aesthetic ideals has perhaps been played down in deference to the role of cultural distinctiveness in the long eighteenth century. But these binary forces reveal some of the contradictions inherent in the Grand Tour.

The benefits of travel

Tourists of whatever era are sightseers in search of experience. But they remain outsiders and their experience of foreign cultures is both transitory and superficial (fig. 6.4). The Grand Tour offered two different strands of cultural edification: the exploration of the past (that is antiquity) and the present (that is contemporary Europe). These simultaneous but distinctive interactions with the foreign produced a variety of responses and reveal different facets of the cultural

Fig. 6.4 Thomas Patch, A Drinking Party – Grand Tourists at Play, *detail. The Grand Tour was about sybaritic as well as intellectual pleasures. The National Trust, Durham Massey, Cheshire.*

consciousness of eighteenth-century society. The Grand Tour offered the next generation of the ruling élite an intellectual experience essential for a gentleman. Their breeding was evident in their innate 'taste': travelling refined this quality and ensured the continuation of their cultural hegemony. The wisdom gained equipped them with the *sagesse* and right to rule. It was a rite of passage through which young nobles changed from adolescence into manhood.[13] This ritualistic element of the Grand Tour helped ensure its survival throughout the period. The knowledge of foreign languages and customs as well as the geography, history and material culture of mainland Europe helped to broaden the experience. On their return, the nobility could emphasize their status through this knowledge. But the Grand Tour and its participants did not go uncriticized. Laurence Sterne gives a voice to the notion that there was no need for improvement:

> Knowledge and improvements are to be got by sailing and posting for that purpose; but whether useful knowledge and real improvements, is all a lottery. . . . I am of the opinion that a man would act wisely, if he could prevail upon himself to live contented without foreign knowledge or foreign improvements, especially if he lives in a country that has no obvious want of either. . . . But there is no nation under heaven abounding with more variety of learning [in both the arts and sciences] . . . where there is more wit and variety of character to feed the mind with – Where then my dear countrymen, are you going?[14]

Nor were the Grand Tourists always proactive in trying to integrate into foreign society. In 1740 Lady Wortley Montagu remarked the milords had:

> an inviolable fidelity to the language their nurses taught them . . . [their principal concerns are] to buy new clothes, in which they shine in some obscure coffee house, where they are sure of meeting only one another.[15]

Whatever the shortcomings of the tourists, visiting and consuming sights and sites of cultural value was one way of subordinating these into an established set of values and ideologies belonging to the British tourist.[16] Grand Tourism is linked to the emergence of the self-consciousness of a class-structured society not only through the appropriation of alien forms but also, in almost complete contradiction, the definition of nationhood through the concept of otherness and the foreign. This is particularly relevant to Britain at the beginning of the eighteenth century.

The accession of the first Hanoverian King George I in 1714 established not only a stable constitutional monarchy but a Protestant dynasty. The political turmoil of the previous century emphasized the potential threat of Jacobitism to the new constitutional monarchy. The threat of invasion in 1717, 1719, 1720–21 and even as late as 1740, together with conspiracies and riots and the ongoing enmity with Catholic France, made a national identity a necessary part of a cohesive policy of resistance to threat.[17] The prodigious building projects of the period, of which the country house is the finest example, were part of this cultural reaction to political and social circumstances as they helped to establish a new national identity. There was also an attempt to construct a history of the recent past in volumes like Clarendon's *History of the Rebellion*. This gave validation to the series of events which had formed the present British state and the new social order. The interest in the history and formation of the new state also led to the celebration of Britain's own past. This is seen in monuments to King Alfred at Stourhead or the Temple of the British Worthies at Stowe which comprised portrait busts of intellectual and political figures such as Queen Elizabeth I, Francis Bacon and William III but these were housed in a setting derived from the architecture of antiquity. The literature of the period also reflected this trend. This is seen in Bishop Perry's *Reliques of Ancient English Poetry* (1765) and the widespread fabrication of the Ossianic legends across the British Isles.[18]

The fascination with antiquity was part of the rising interest in the past and the validating effect it could have on the present. But the general experience of travelling abroad did much to shed favourable light on the British social and political status quo. The constitutional monarchy stood out as a beacon of liberty in comparison with other European governmental systems. Allied to this was the moderation of the Anglican Church – a judicious marriage of religion and state. This stood in contrast to the perceived excesses of the papacy and the ritualistic practices of Catholicism. The combination of a national religion – notably the only one in Europe – and the ordnances of good government with sound economic policies defined the uniqueness and quality of Britain. The formative experience of the ruling élite did much to foster a cultural memory which was defined by its opposition to the foreign. In tandem with this was an invented memory of a connection with Roman antiquity, and, in the early part of the eighteenth century, with the Rome of Augustus.

In the opening years of the eighteenth century the move towards classical formulae in art, architecture and literature was indicative of a feeling in Britain that contemporary culture reflected and was akin to that of Augustan Rome. Inherent in this was a culture of collecting where the image of Augustan Rome was enriched through the assimilation of products from across the Roman Empire. Indeed, this attitude was outlined in Roman histories and epics and underlined the relationship between imperialism and commodification. In the period of colonization and economic expansion at the beginning of the eighteenth century Rome was the obvious model. The nation's belief in its cultural superiority over the rest of Europe meant it saw itself as the inheritor of the mantle of ancient Rome.[19] This self-conscious construction of culture made a classical past out of current beliefs and values. Classicism, in its broadest sense, was used according to its utility in a contemporary, i.e. Georgian, ideological system. In this way the reuse of antiquity was an invented memory with an ideological end. This helps define what the neo-classical movement (i.e. the use of antique forms throughout the whole period) means in a broader historical context. Neo-classicism, although rooted in antiquarianism, offers interpretations on the cultures which chose to cite it. The more we know about its use the more light this sheds on the system of beliefs and values which justified the status quo in Britain in the long eighteenth century.

Discovering and remembering Rome

In an era when history as a concept and intellectual discipline was nascent, the conceptualization of the past required imagination and the ability to map the unknown against the known. Baron d'Hancarville's assertion that 'Antiquity is a vast country separated from our own by a long period of time' is indicative of eighteenth-century attitudes towards the past. This statement is made in the baron's ambitious, if ultimately flawed, study *Antiquités Etrusques, Grecques et Romaines* (1767 but not published before 1776) which was based on the collection of Sir William Hamilton the British envoy in Naples.[20]

The idea that travel to foreign lands could lead to knowledge of the past was endorsed by the voyages of discovery of explorers like Captain Cook.[21] He found peoples untouched by Western civilization who appeared to be living history – remote geographically and culturally. The connection between travel and knowledge is essential to an understanding of the importance of the Grand Tour as an actual and metaphorical journey into the past.

The touristic appreciation and absorption of another culture, whether past or present, relied on the collection or memory of a set of displaced forms which were elements dislodged from their original natural and historical cultural contexts. This introduces the importance of the souvenir which validated the allusion to place. And the souvenirs brought back from the Grand Tour were plentiful.

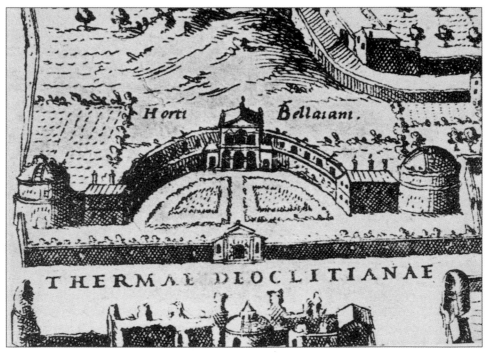

Fig. 6.5   Etienne Duperac, Map of Rome, 1577. Detail of the Baths of Diocletian, one of the guides to ancient Rome used by Grand Tourists.

Lord Burlington returned from his first trip to Europe in 1714/15 with 878 trunks and crates.[22] Other purchases were on a smaller scale but were for a specific project. In 1720 the 2nd Marquess of Annandale brought back over 300 paintings for his house at Hopetoun, while Edward Wright and his tutee, George Parker, bought works of art for the gallery at the latter's father Lord Macclesfield's newly acquired house, Shirburn Castle in Oxfordshire.[23] These kinds of bulk purchases were not uncommon and set the tone for the remainder of the century. The objects served in turn to construct a social identity.

This changing attitude towards commodities in the long eighteenth century reflected changes in the social order and the steady growth of a consumer society during the period. Remnants of antiquity, whether they were sculptures, coins or vases or architectural fragments, became part of a currency of material culture disembodied from their original context but with related sets of meanings. The importance of the emergent consumer society and with it the emphasis on material culture in the long eighteenth century is an essential element in understanding the relationship between antiquity and the country house.

Objects and commodities took on a system of meanings relating to religious, aesthetic and social values relevant to their time. In terms of the Grand Tour it is easy to see how the collectables brought back by tourists and displayed with such pride were seen as symbols of a distinctive social system and cultural beliefs. This fetishization of the object tells us even more about its meaning in the developing consumer society. Entrepreneurial Italian dealers fed the appetites of eighteenth-century travellers to whom export licences were sometimes an optional extra. The objects or souvenirs were cultural relics of antiquity or of Italy which appeared in a dislocated context. In response to their popularity British manufacturers produced goods based on designs from antiquity. D'Hancarville's volumes were an ideal visual reference for the mass-produced pottery of Josiah Wedgwood and his partner Thomas Bentley.[24] They also produced facsimile pieces which were used in the decorative schemes of country house interiors such as the library at Bowood, Wiltshire. Similarly the furniture designs of William Kent, Thomas Chippendale or Robert Adam show the appropriation of antique forms for prestige, modern manufactures.

There were other ways too in which Italy and antiquity became established parts of the eighteenth-century consumer society. Reproductions of well-known paintings were produced by a lively colony of British artists for the home market. Sculptures were also copied by professional cast makers; by the latter half of the century Matthew Brettingham the younger was one of the principal suppliers of these. Other dealers, including William Hamilton, sold originals or pieces composed out of fragments as well as antique vases.

The fact that an artefact might not be an original did not seem to concern eighteenth-century collectors. Copies of Renaissance paintings hung next to works by Claude in country house picture galleries. And casts of antique sculptures were as much a part of interior decorative schemes as originals as seen in the arrangement of the portrait busts in the entrance hall at Holkham where the two are used together (pl. 1). In contradiction to present-day attitudes the reproduction of the original seems only to have enhanced its aura and that of the copies themselves.[25]

The appeal of Rome

The growth of consumerism goes some way towards explaining the importance of souvenirs and quotations from antiquity. But what was the attraction of Italy and especially Rome and why did it endure? It might at first appear curious that Rome appealed to the cultural élite of a northern-European, Protestant country. Yet it was seen as the fountainhead of Western civilization and Rome stood for a set of timeless, rational values which were widely held. Its unique attraction and influence benefited from Italy's tradition of learning, as seen in its flourishing universities and urbanized societies. The intellectual response of thinkers like Edward Gibbon in his *The History of the Decline and Fall of the Roman Empire* (1776–88) demonstrates the rising importance of historical enquiry in the appreciation of the past. Britain was not the only nation to respond to Italianate and Roman culture. Secular classicism had been adopted by France as a means of self-definition. Conversely Germany asserted its identity through its opposition to classical taste by concentrating on indigenous literature, mythology and architecture.[26] Like Germany, religious forces had separated Britain from Italy. And the presence of the exiled Stuart court in the papal city from 1717 surely gave the message of a Catholic stronghold occupied by the Pretender to the British crown who opposed all the new constitutional monarchy represented. It was only with the defeat at Culloden in 1746 that the Stuarts finally became a spent force in European politics.

British attitudes towards ancient Rome are equally interesting and complex. Ancient Rome was a pagan place and the site of vigorous persecution of Christians. Knowledge and appreciation of this period was generally enhanced in the opening years of the eighteenth century through the study of textual descriptions of the writers of antiquity. For instance, Alexander Pope translated the works of Homer and used the literary styles of ancient poets in his own writings. And the 'Golden Latin' of Virgil and Horace represented the urbane refinement of Roman culture and society under Augustus. The linguistic and literary qualities of these powerful epics created a myth which modern European states found fascinating and compelling. This helped to engender a feeling of a connection and similarity between Augustan Rome and the new era in British history. But this connection was a feeling, an invented memory as in reality there were few connections between the two epochs. The absence of adequate alternatives to Roman *mythologies* and Rome might offer an explanation for the reverence for a society which had conquered and colonized Britain. Boadicea's valiant revolt did not fuel the nation's imagination. Instead, the urban and urbane culture of ancient Rome offered the polite society of the eighteenth century a more acceptable invented memory of itself.

The importance of invented memory – the exploration and ordering of ancient Rome in the conscious and the subconscious – is an important aspect of the appreciation of Rome and the larger significance of the Grand Tour. The problematic issue of the role of memory is addressed by Freud who explored the psychoanalytical consequences of memory trace and the connection between it, the human subconsciousness, and humankind receiving an intimation of a connection with the outside world.[27] In discussing the specific problem of

Fig. 6.6   Falda, Li Giardini di Roma, *c. 1683*. View of the gardens of the Villa Mattei, *detail*.

Fig. 6.7   A. Palladio, I Quattro Libri Dell'Architettura, *Section of the Pantheon, Rome, Book IV, ch XX. Palladio conjectured correctly that the portico was not part of the original Roman construction.*

memory Freud uses Rome, a key touchstone of Western civilization and thought, as a map of the human subconsciousness. Freud's discussion of the relationship between the subconscious, memory and experience sheds interesting light on the response to Rome by eighteenth-century travellers especially as he discusses it in spatial terms. He tries to reconstruct what a visitor equipped with a knowledge of ancient Rome would find and in so doing gives a flavour of what confronted the Grand Tourist:

> Of the buildings which once occupied this ancient area he will find nothing, or only the scanty remains, for they exist no longer. [S/he would only be able] at the most to point out the sites where the temples and public buildings stood. Their place is now taken by ruins, but not by ruins themselves but of later restorations . . . these remains of ancient Rome are found dovetailed into the jumble of the great metropolis. . . . This is the manner in which the past is preserved in historical sites like Rome.[28]

But it is Freud's use of Rome as a metaphor for a physical, living entity that reveals how the past and present resonated and informed each other in the mind of the eighteenth-century visitor. He emphasized the coexistence of past and present with the consequence that:

Rome and the palaces of the Caesars and the Septizonium of Septimus Severus would still be rising to their old height on the Palatine. . . . In the place occupied by the Palazzo Caffarelli would once more stand – without the Palazzo having to be removed – the Temple of Jupiter Capitolinus; where the Coliseum now stands we could at the same time admire Nero's vanished Golden House. . . . And the observer would perhaps only have to change the direction of his glance or his position in order to call up the one view or the other.[29]

The point Freud makes in this analogy is that historical sequences cannot be expressed in spatial terms. Space, or indeed a city, cannot have two different simultaneous contents; instead histories of the same geographical location must be juxtaposed. Yet this is precisely the experience of Grand Tourists. They were travelling through the past and the present. The way in which this experience was remembered is then surely indicative of fundamental processes of assimilation of different cultures.

Eighteenth-century guides and commentaries relied heavily on classical literary precedents. Joseph Addison's *Remarks on Several Parts of Italy etc.* (1705) is a narrative of his travels and relies heavily on ancient poetry. He uses classical verse as a means of commenting on key sites included in the Grand Tour. This made an important link between the past as a foreign country and the actuality of foreign soil. This connection was remarked upon by contemporaries and is perhaps best summed up by Horace Walpole who observed in 1740:

Mr Addison travelled through the poets, and not through Italy; for all his ideas are borrowed from the descriptions and not from reality. He saw places as they were, not as they are.[30]

The resonance between past and present is continued in the visual guides to Rome. Sixteenth- and seventeenth-century images, sometimes with text, were used by eighteenth-century travellers as guides to ancient sites. Seeing the ancient past through the eyes of the recent past in guides like Etienne Duperac's map of Old Rome (1577) (fig. 6.5) and Falda's *Li Giardini di Roma* (c. 1683) (fig. 6.6) gives an indication of how Rome was experienced by visitors like William Kent or Lord Burlington. Here the half-ruined forms of structures like the Baths of Diocletian were assumed to have always been surrounded by landscape.[31] The measured reconstructions of antique buildings by Palladio also revealed the duplicity of vision. The Pantheon was transformed from present-day Christian Church back into a Roman temple. Palladio even conjectured correctly that the portico was a later addition (figs 6.7 and 6.8).[32] These parallel experiences of ancient Rome find no better expression than in the garden designs of the country house. The Temple of Venus at Stowe or the Pantheon at Stourhead reflect these different experiences of antiquity and are indicative of the nostalgia for the memories of the Grand Tour.

The connection between Freud's ideas and the experience of the Grand Tourists is made more compelling by the fact that in the eighteenth century there was a growing interest in both the conscious and the subconscious mind. This is

Fig. 6.8   A. Palladio, I Quattro Libri Dell'Architettura, *an elevation of the Pantheon, Rome, Book IV, ch XX.*

evident particularly in the literature and philosophy of the period. The growth of the novel gave insight into human thought and the different emotional and aesthetic responses to things or events preoccupied contemporary philosophers. John Locke's *Essay Concerning Human Understanding* (1690) acknowledges the role of memory in the invention of fancy. Although Locke does not use the term imagination his views were the beginning of the evolution and recognition of two distinct languages: the metaphorical language of poetry and the literal language of science. The former developed into the philosophy of association which dominated eighteenth- and early nineteenth-century thinking.[33]

The philosophy of association played an important part in the appreciation of antiquity in the long eighteenth century. Key texts which developed and refined these ideas include Addison's *The Pleasures of the Imagination* (1712), Edmund Burke's *Philosophical Enquiry into the Origin of our Idea of the Sublime and the Beautiful* (1757), and Henry Home, Lord Kames's *Elements of Criticism* (1762).[34] These all developed the Lockian idea of the philosophy of association and throw interesting light on the question of imitation as posed with reference to the Georgian period. Sir Joshua Reynolds had addressed the question of copying in his *Discourses* – lectures given to the Royal Academy. He pronounced that imitation was the best way to invention and that this should not be concealed (*6th Discourse*). In the *13th Discourse* Reynolds addressed the question of architecture:

> Architecture certainly possesses many principles in common with poetry and painting. Among those, which may be reckoned as the first, is that affecting the imagination by means of the association of ideas. Thus for instance, we have naturally a veneration for antiquity whatever building brings to our remembrance ancient custom and manners is sure to give this delight.[35]

Kames continued this sentiment by suggesting that architecture could transmit the feeling of grandeur through association with antiquity. These elements come together to form a discussion around the nature of taste. This derives partly from the ability to relish beautiful objects and the pleasure associated with this. For Addison there were two kinds of pleasures that derived from actual buildings or artefacts – the pleasure itself and a secondary kind from remembered or fictitious objects.

These ideas about originality and the appreciation of beauty and imitation through intellect were crystallized into an embodiment of an élitist structure by David Hume.[36] Taste became a product of breeding; socially formed tastes should be recognized as absolute preferences and those who failed to accept them were to be considered inferior. Taste was equated with education – the intellectual ability to contextualize an object or building whether it be original or copy. Social pre-eminence was based on cultural superiority. The possession of taste indicated education and hence virtue and implied a fitness to rule. Antiquity was harnessed into the service of the propaganda machine of the social and cultural élite of Georgian Britain and exploited to its full potential to give the illusion of grandeur.

The originality of country house architecture, as opposed to the uniformity of Georgian town planning, allowed the reconfiguration of antique and Italianate architectural formulae. As such the country house, arguably the most important building type of the long eighteenth century, was an essential vehicle through which a patrician culture could express its values. This gave the ruling élite the freedom to express individual and national identity through the complex interaction of forms underpinned by a distinct set of intellectual systems and conventions. This was not merely trying to look like Rome. Instead, the aesthetic vocabulary of antiquity was appropriated and a new syntax formulated to create an effective national visual language of art and architecture with encoded meanings for the educated classes.

7 Town House and Country House: their Interaction

M.H. Port

The history of the country house has been exhaustively studied in many of its aspects; the aristocratic or gentry town house has also been examined in considerable detail, notably in the unsurpassable *Survey of London*. But the relationship between the two has failed to attract much notice. The purpose of this chapter is to attempt to sketch in some of the principal elements in that relationship and thereby encourage further in-depth studies.

That London during the Georgian period exercised an increasingly powerful influence in national life has been widely acknowledged by historians.[1] Wrigley has shown its dominant economic role;[2] the work of Namier, Sutherland, and succeeding historians of Georgian politics has underlined its political hegemony, extended to Scotland by the 1707 Act of Union and to Ireland by the similar Act of 1800; historians of fashion, the arts, theatre and music have demonstrated its social reign. It would have been surprising if the Georgian upper classes had resisted its lure in order to moulder in their traditional country residences. In his *New History of Gloucestershire* (1779) Samuel Rudder commented: 'Many gentlemen's seats in this county are totally deserted . . . and too many others, in compliance with the taste of the present age, are left by the owners for the greater part of the year, to partake more largely of the pleasures of the metropolis.'[3] Ten years later, the Honourable John Byng on a holiday tour in the Midlands, chiefly to visit country houses and old castles, commented on 'our not having met any family of any house we have stop'd at, except Sandbeck; marking the desertion of the country, or the extraordinary short time of quitting London: – old people shake their heads, and say "Aye, I remember rare doings, formerly, at the hall . . . but, lackaday, my Lord now only comes in September, for a fortnight's shooting!" . . . It should seem to me', Byng concluded, 'from my (trivial) observations, that noblemen and gentlemen have almost abandon'd the country . . . and that dowagers have gone away . . . and that as that encreasing Wen, the metropolis, must be fed the body will gradually decay.'[4] 'Many landowners, especially among the politically active magnates, spent only a modest amount of time on their estates, and in this respect were much more urban in character . . . than is commonly allowed (figs 7.1 and 7.2).'[5]

Fig. 7.1   Houghton House, Ampthill, Bedfordshire. A Jacobean house bought by the Duke of Bedford in 1738, repaired by his son, Lord Tavistock, who resided there from 1764 until his death in 1767, and demolished by his son, the 5th Duke, in 1793–4. Photograph by M.H. Port.

Fundamental, as Byng had observed, was the influence of Parliament. Georgian parliaments were essentially assemblies of landowners and merchants. By 1715, annual sessions of several months' duration had become essential. By the late 1720s, a regular pattern pertained of parliamentary session from mid-January to late May; from the late 1770s, the session not infrequently opened in November and ran regularly into mid-June; from the 1810s, it generally ran far into July – and by 1792 summer pleasures had extended the season to August.[6] Party passions apart, landowners often had personal or local business that demanded Parliament's attention;[7] or they might have ambitions which only parliamentary attendance could serve to realize;[8] or there might be wars or threats involving increased taxation (falling notably on land) to alarm them; nor must we omit sheer sense of duty. For a commoner, a seat in Parliament (even for a rotten borough) conferred prestige: and the more significant the constituency (a county seat or a great city) the greater the prestige and also the obligation.

Predominantly it was the country gentry who composed the House of Commons. As their stay in the capital lengthened into months, mere lodgings became inadequate,[9] especially when wives wanted to come too. Byng, indeed, blamed the wives of the gentry ('urging the old motives of *education* for the girls and of stirring interest for the boys') for driving the country gentry to Marylebone.[10] There was some truth in this: 'I miss a house in town very much. Living all the winter in the country [twenty miles from London] is not to my taste', wrote Mrs Calvert in 1815.

She complained that by her husband's costly rebuilding of their country house, Hunsdon, Hertfordshire, which had entailed giving up a town house, 'my pleasure and comfort were considerably diminished'.[11] A visitor to the Fludyers at Lee (seven miles from London) in 1764 found Lady Fludyer 'mighty busy about building her house in town [in Downing Street] . . . I do wish she had a better taste . . . 'tis entirely left to her, Sir Samuel only pays'.[12]

Thus the acquisition of a town house became a conventional gentry necessity. The western suburbs now being opened up by aristocratic or gentry landowners – notably the Portlands, Harleys, Scarboroughs, Grosvenors and Portmans – offered plenty of houses for hire; a gentry family might lease such a residence for a period of years from the builder or immediately from the ground landlord, or might hire one for the season from an existing leaseholder (figs 7.3 and 7.4). For the great aristocrats and leaders of political factions, a great town house was essential as a mark of status and a place of rendezvous for their followers.

The 3rd Duke of Portland, as the nominal leader of the Opposition Whigs, needed a house of rendezvous for his political friends, but the Portland family house in Whitehall was held by his mother until her death in 1785 and he was in

Fig. 7.2   Powis Castle. In 1784, John Byng found it 'sadly neglected . . . some great windows quite forc'd in.' The owner, the 5th Earl of Powis, was 'a mean, silly man, the bubble of his mistress . . . who rarely comes here, to sneak about, for a day or two', preferring to spend his rents 'in the prodigalities of London, and in driving high phaetons up St James's Street' (Torrington Diaries, I, 137; III, 295). Photograph by M.H. Port.

considerable financial difficulties. His residence at Bulstrode, Buckinghamshire, some nineteen miles from London, was too far off for a party meeting-house, but Portland was lucky to have been loaned Burlington House, Piccadilly, (fig. 7.5) inherited by his father-in-law, the Duke of Devonshire, to whom it was superfluous as he already enjoyed his neighbouring family mansion. Portland's other seat, Welbeck in Nottinghamshire, was altogether too distant for him, as a leading politician, to reside at and he made it over to his son, Lord Titchfield. When an increasing burden of debt led him in 1795 to consider the sale of either Bulstrode or his town properties in Soho, Titchfield urged him to sell the former as producing more immediate relief; as to the gardens and trees that Portland enjoyed there, he 'could find similar trees and gardens nearer to London and would be able to enjoy them much more frequently'.[13]

It was this desire to enjoy gardens and country delights that doubtless persuaded the great lawyer-politicians to purchase estates (*lex est magnum emolumentum*) on the edge of London rather than in the true country, so that they were constantly accessible for business even if out of town. Thus Lord Mansfield's town house (in Bloomsbury Square, sacked by the Gordon Rioters in 1780) (fig. 7.3), was complemented by Kenwood (fig. 7.6) on the Hampstead Heights, Lord Thurlow could be found in Dulwich just to the south of the City, and Lord Loughborough in Hampstead, all within four or five miles of Westminster. Similarly, Henry Fox could escape from Whitehall to the fresher air of Holland House, Kensington, before the end of the season, though official business followed him to make it 'quite a coffee house'.[14]

Of the politicians, perhaps the most obvious figure to consider is the 1st Duke of Newcastle (1693–1768), who held high office for more than forty years. 'Newcastle was in essence a London man, or perhaps more correctly, a court man', writes his biographer.[15] His town house in Lincoln's Inn Fields was 'the central office for conducting the business of [his] estates' in eleven counties. His principal country seat, Claremont, about sixteen miles south of the capital, where his wife spent most of her time, was near enough for him to conduct business there, though it was chiefly a place to relax in. Lists of servants at Newcastle House and Claremont in 1752 imply that, as was commonly done, a small resident staff in the country was supplemented by bringing others from London when requisite. Newcastle used his expensively maintained Sussex seats, Halland and Bishopstone, principally for political ends, nursing his family interest, though his not infrequent if brief visits enabled him to relax by riding and hunting.[16]

When in June 1789 Byng visited Worksop, a seat of the Duke of Norfolk, and Welbeck (the Duke of Portland's), he found them deserted. He could not

refrain [his] paltry wonder at the possessors of these charming domains, sacrificing health, and fortune, at the shrine of politics! . . . times are sadly changed; for one does see many noblemen, either dependent on ministry, or so linked to an ever-losing opposition, or so reduced in fortune, by gaming, or elections (the worst folly of all); that a country residence, at first tiresome, becomes at last impossible . . . whilst the fine air of Marybone parish is enjoyed to the highest perfection on two closets and a cupboard![17]

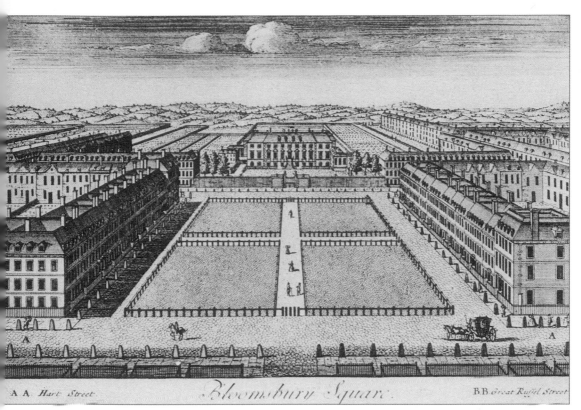

A A. *Hart Street* *Bloomsbury Square* B.B. *Great Russel Street*

Fig. 7.3 Bloomsbury Square looking north to Southampton (later Bedford) House, 1727, the first aristocratic speculative leasehold development in London, from 1661. Lord Mansfield, LCJ, was living here in 1780, when his house was burned down by the Gordon Rioters.

Some idea of the dimensions of this Parliament-linked influx of society shortly after the end of the Georgian era is provided by the *Morning Post*, which in 1841 reported over 4,000 movements in and out of London of members of the 'fashionable world' (a 'movement' might consist of an individual, a couple, or a whole family).[18] No doubt the true figure was considerably larger, many such movements having gone unreported. However, the *Survey of London*'s study of these movements shows that nearly 300 arrivals were reported in the last week of January for the opening of Parliament. By the third week in May the net number of arrivals (i.e. departures having been deducted)[19] was nearly 900, but the dissolution of Parliament near the end of June promoted a net outflow approaching 400. The assembling of a new Parliament at the end of August, following the general election, produced an exceptional insurge of some 200; there was then a steady drifting away until late November, by which time the net inflow, compared with the start of the year, was down to about sixty. Early December's meeting of the Royal Agricultural Society and the Smithfield Club's annual cattle show produced a temporary influx of about a hundred but nearly all had gone by the year's end.

*Fig. 7.4   Hanover Square, looking south, in 1761. First of the great Mayfair squares,
developed principally by Lord Scarborough from about1717, and immediately favoured by his
military colleagues. For much of the later eighteenth century, the very rich Earls of
Hillsborough (later Marquesses of Downshire) lived at no. 15.*

These figures, although incomplete, indicate the powerful magnetic effect of
parliamentary sessions in drawing the fashionable world from the country to the
capital at the end of the Georgian period. Similarly, in 1759 the end of the session
had emptied the metropolis: 'Nothing can be more solitary than the environs of
London after midsummer.'[20] That Parliament was not the only influence is shown
by the pull of the December agricultural meetings in 1841 but these were too
brief to require the special setting up of a town establishment.

The magnetism of the parliamentary session also produced significant spin-
off. The presence in London for nearly half the year of the majority of the
leaders of society created a critical mass that demanded transportation, housing,
furnishing, foddering, embellishing, entertaining, medicating, nourishing
spiritually, providing with legal and financial services – and all of high quality
and in many respects of the latest fashion. Thus London's professions and
trades came to offer services generally superior to those normally available
elsewhere, and thereby attracted that fashionable world that extended beyond
Parliament and led parliamentarians' wives and daughters to demand a town
house in the capital for the season.[21] And that meant that London became the
great marriage mart of the empire: 'my Lady Dss' remarked the Honourable
John Byng of the Duchess of Ancaster in 1789 '(like other Ladies), fancys that
London is the only Place for a Girl to get a Husband in, and her daughter is of
the same opinion'.[22]

Fig. 7.5   Burlington House and Gate, as remodelled by Colen Campbell for the 3rd Earl of Burlington, c. 1717–20. It was subsequently inherited by the 4th Duke of Devonshire, who loaned it to his son-in-law, the 3rd Duke of Portland, a political party leader.

*Fig. 7.6   Kenwood, or Caen Wood. A small suburban retreat, remodelled and enlarged by
Robert Adam for Lord Chief Justice Mansfield, 1767–9.*

In order to determine the relationships between town house and country house
we need to make some analysis of this mass of itinerants. Possession of the two
types of house clearly implies some degree of movement between country and
town: it is only that sector of society whose movements were recorded that is our
concern. We may classify them by the distance of their properties from London,
by their degree of political activity, by their marital/familial status, by their
wealth, and by the character of their London house (insulated/square/terrace;
freehold/leasehold/short-hire), which is not always identical with their wealth-
ranking.

We may say at once that, although wives were frequently blamed for the
flocking to London, lifelong bachelors (e.g. 4th Duke of Queensbury, Horace
Walpole) maintained both town and country houses, as did widowers as well as
widows (e.g. Lady Mary Coke, Mrs Montagu, Duchess of Portland) (fig. 7.7). A
tendency for dowagers who would previously have lived on in the country seat to
desert it for permanent residence in London has also been noticed.[23] An heir may
have needed his own London establishment upon marriage; or a young nobleman
might acquire a town mansion in compliance with the agreement on his marriage
to an heiress;[24] but in examining the relationship between country house and
town house marital status otherwise made little difference.

The increasing number of dowagers occupying town houses has been
established by the *Survey of London*; one-third of the ratepaying occupants of

aristocratic Upper Brook Street in 1749 were female, and of the 343 persons listed under 'No occupation' in a survey of Mayfair in 1790, nearly 200 were women.[25] Though a number of these were certainly spinsters, a considerable proportion were dowagers. The widow of Sir Everard Fawkener was said in 1759 to have taken a house in town: 'she has £1,200 a year . . . she must live upon it, and educate her three children, two of which being boys, whose educations are now very expensive; . . . she has let her place in the country . . . as she could not live in town and there too she thought it better for her children to live in the world, and in the way of making friends'.[26] In Grosvenor Square itself, five aristocratic widows (not including the late king's mistress) were among the fifty-one first occupants listed by the *Survey of London*.[27]

Is there perhaps any significance in the type of town house or the tenure on which it was held? I have explored this problem elsewhere.[28] Given the strong tradition in the aristocracy of renting a metropolitan mansion, there was no derogation in doing so, the possession of vast wealth did not oblige one to set about acquiring an insulated freehold mansion, and the decision seems to have depended on personal factors and family custom (fig. 7.8). Some noble families traditionally had possessed great London 'inns' or town residences – Northumberland, Devonshire, Bedford. Although they might move west with the fashion, as did the latter two dukes, such magnates usually still owned very large town houses surrounded by gardens, pleasure grounds and outbuildings hidden behind high brick walls. Others, however, no less rich or politically engaged – the Rockinghams and the Derbys for instance – might be satisfied with a leasehold in the most fashionable square, though that by no means implied a shoebox. Rockingham's house was one of the largest in Grosvenor Square (fig 7.9), with twenty-three male servants in house and stables in 1782, and was held, like the Derbys' nearby, for several generations. The 12th Earl of Derby had the interior of his house reconstructed in the richest vein by Robert Adam in 1773–4 with 'a sequence of ceremonial rooms "well suited to every occasion of public parade" with a distinct private part of the house', a very costly business (figs 7.10 and 7.11).[29]

What then of the effects of distance from London? It might seem reasonable to conclude that those with a house within two or three hours' ride would be less concerned to establish a town house. Nevertheless, the inconvenience of such travelling to men of affairs at a time of indifferent roads was clearly a powerful incentive to acquire a town house. The 1st Duke of Chandos (1673–1744), despite having a palatial villa at Cannons only ten miles from London, planned to build himself a town palace in Cavendish Square – though he was prevented by the failure of his financial speculations. In the 1760s, the Lambs required both Brocket (Hertfordshire, about twenty-eight miles from London) and Melbourne House, Piccadilly. Two decades later, the 3rd Duke of Portland, as we have seen, could not function as even a figurehead of the Opposition Whigs from his seat at Bulstrode. In the 1800s, Nicolson Calvert, of Hunsdon, near Ware, twenty-one miles from London, found a town house necessary for effectively executing his parliamentary duties; when hard times hit, in 1810, he and his wife gave up their large establishment in Albemarle Street, but substituted a smaller house in Hanover Square.[30] Although Holland House, at Kensington, was only two miles

Fig. 7.7   Berkeley Square, no. 44. Built 1742–4 by William Kent for Lady Isabella Finch, spinster First Lady of the Bedchamber to Princess Amelia, daughter of King George II. Photograph by M.H. Port.

Fig. 7.8   Brook Street, Mayfair, nos 68 and 66. The former house was occupied by the 10th Earl of Rothes (a Scottish representative peer), 1741–56, and Sir William Mildmay Bt, and his widow, 1757–96; and the latter by Nathaniel Curzon MP and his second son, Assheton Curzon, MP, later Lord Curzon of Penn, 1729–1820. Photograph by M.H. Port.

west of London, Henry Fox as a minister found it much more convenient to live at the Pay Office, Whitehall; his wife wrote (8 May [1759]) that she had been chiefly alone since she came to Holland House, 'for when we settle here so early Mr Fox has always business that calls him a great deal to Town, and there have been some long days in the House [of Commons]'.[31] Thus even a suburban house within easy reach of Westminster did not rule out the need for a town house – if one played an active political role. Clearly then, for those whose country seat lay further from the capital, a town house was regarded as a necessity, for the bulk of the session at least. The debt-encumbered Marquess of Powis in 1726 'could not bring himself to sell his London house' in Great Ormond Street (that he had himself built in 1708), though holding on to it entailed the failure of his debt-reduction scheme.[32]

None the less, Professor Mingay has suggested that 'the preference for one's own countryside increased with the distance from the capital', commenting, 'Perhaps necessity was converted into a fashionable virtue', although he produces little evidence in support.[33] On the contrary, Dr Roebuck's study of Yorkshire

Fig. 7.9   Grosvenor Square, east side, c. 1750. The house on the extreme right, no. 46 (later 50), was then occupied by the 1st Earl of Guildford, and later by his son, Lord North, the prime minister. Nos 1–7 (reading from right to left), a symmetrical block built 1727–31, were in 1750 occupied respectively by the Duke of Buccleuch, Sir Edward Turner, Earl of Coventry, Marquess of Rockingham, Dowager Lady King, Bishop of Durham, and Dowager Countess of Essex.

baronets in their distant fastnesses shows that 'permanent residence in the countryside became less common, and, indeed, was eventually regarded as desirable only when retrenchment was a high priority'.[34]

When the owner was not in seasonal residence, the great town house could be used as an hotel, whether as a stopover for the owner out of season[35] or for visiting relations. Lady Caroline Fox, 'vastly crowded' at the Pay Office (her husband as Paymaster-General lived above the shop), sent her Fitzgerald nephews just down the road to stay in Richmond House in October 1758, remarking 'my brother [the Duke of Richmond] and the Duchess are never in London till February to stay, so that they will be no trouble to them' (fig. 7.15).[36] The following April she reported that the newly widowed Lady Carlisle 'has got Sir Thomas Robinson's house in Whitehall' for that winter, Robinson being her late husband's brother-in-law.[37]

One might have to desert the country and return to London unseasonably to seek urgent medical attention: 'I left Goodwood sooner than I intended,' wrote Lady Caroline Fox, 'the Duchess coming to town in a great hurry to have a tooth out, which had kept her awake two nights.'[38] Similarly, Lord Pery was in such poor health that 'he suddenly determined on leaving Hertford Castle' for his daughter's house in London.[39] Lady Caroline Fox recommended lying-in in town, 'when I think one wants company more than at any time'.[40] Lady Sarah Lennox in October 1776 took herself to London because she felt unwell, waking with a sore throat, suffering toothache, and having a weakness of the eyes; she also wanted to consult a surgeon about her small daughter's physique.[41]

When Henry Fox lost the Paymaster-generalship and had to leave the Pay Office, he bought a house in Piccadilly; his wife's description notes key desiderata: 'with a court before it and a fine long garden behind, so conveniently situated for everything, such a healthy part of the town, and so little pavement to drive over when I go to Holland House'. Yet even without these attractions, a well-situated house could command a high price: Lord Granville's house, without 'a foot of ground to it, and . . . a most melancholy gloomy place', sold for almost as much as Fox paid for his new house.[42]

London was also the great source for fashionable goods of every description. When Lord Kildare came from Ireland to London in 1759, he was entrusted with his wife's commissions for 150 yards of Indian taffeta, bottles of Ward's scurvy drops, and patterns of India paper; he asked Lady Hillsborough to choose for her a birthday gown, and posted her a new play, *The Orphan of China*, and 'a new book of Voltaire's call'd *Candide*' (fig. 7.12).[43] On a later visit, in 1762, he was commissioned to buy stockings with coloured clocks (which had to be made to order), table-cloths 'of that pretty kind', with napkins, and 'a very handsome French frame' for the portrait of himself by Ramsay; and bought 'Fielding's *Works* that is just come out in quarto', as well as bracelets for Lady Kildare, and tuberoses and narcissus roots, seeds and young trees.[44] Again, in 1759, Lady Sarah Lennox and Lady Louisa Conolly were sending to their sister in Ireland details of the latest fashions, including how to arrange one's diamonds, and executing commissions for her, including ordering carpets.[45] In 1789 Byng complained that the late Duchess of Kingston's seat, Thoresby in Nottinghamshire, 'seems like one in St James's Square, fitted up with French furniture'.[46]

The advantages of residence in London were summed up by the Duchess of Northumberland's list of metropolitan entertainments: three theatres, four opera houses, two sets of strollers, five wells, two puppet shows, five Gardens, three riding exhibitions, seven assemblies, four displays of geographical models, three series of lectures (including Thomas Sheridan on Oratory); numerous exhibitions ranging from the Westminster Abbey wax effigies, through Breslaw's 'Deceptions . . . illuminated with wax', to Behiron's anatomical figures; the Tower, the Royal Academy, Christie's, the St James's clubs, the Royal and Antiquarian Societies, debating societies, Bach's and Giardini's concerts; besides '20 inferior Assemblies, 100 Lectures on Anatomy, Law, Astronomy, &c, &c; Disputation Clubs . . . Concerts, Billiard Tables, and Cockpits'(figs 7.13 and 7.14).[47]

So evident were the pleasures of metropolitan life by the end of the eighteenth century that it was taken for granted that gentry families even in reduced circumstances would pass part of the winter there.[48] Nor was staying in the country necessarily a recipe for economy, as is indicated in the correspondence of Lady Caroline Fox. In 1762 when discussing the marriage of her poorly dowered

Fig. 7.10   Derby House (no. 23 Grosvenor Square): the third drawing room, designed by Robert Adam in 1773–5 for Lord Stanley, later 12th Earl of Derby; Lady Derby's dressing room lies beyond.

sister with Charles Bunbury she wrote: 'The father will give up an estate of £2,000 a year, a house in town and one in the country at present . . . The house in the country I should hope they would not yet take, as 'tis in the county he is chose for [as MP], and where he must keep up an interest, which is very expensive'.[49] A month later, she returned to the subject, again stressing the advantages of the newly-weds living in town: 'My brother [the Duke of] Richmond wanted them to live only in the country and have no town house; that I objected to of all things. I have no idea of young people burying themselves . . . Indeed I believe Mr B. would not have come into it, for as he is not very fond of sports, few men love the country that have not that amusement; besides his necessary attendance on Parliament must bring them often to town. The house in London is ready furnish'd and very well; Sir William gives them his plate, so they want but little to set out with.'[50]

Given the two establishments, and the increasing amount of time spent by the upper classes in London, how did living in two (or even three) houses work out? Although the 4th Duke of Devonshire is said to have spent over £40,000 in constructing a new entrance, office wing and stables to amend the deficiencies of Chatsworth during his short reign (1755–64),[51] inventories taken after the death of the 5th Duke in 1811 suggest that in his time Devonshire House was the real

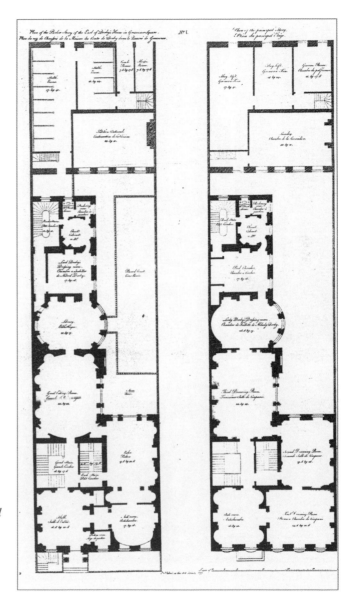

Fig. 7.11   Plans of ground and first floors of Derby House, showing the extent of accommodation that could be obtained in the grander terraced houses.

focus of family activity, Chatsworth serving as a holiday home (pl. 6). Although the value of 'household goods and furniture' in the enormous 'Palace of the Peak' was 1.7 times that of those in Devonshire House, the best paintings, plate and horses, and twice as many books were kept in London, where the total valuation for 'Books, Prints and Pictures' was £13,312, against a mere £3,428 at Chatsworth. The corresponding valuations for 'Plate, Linen and China' were £6,820 against £1,721; 'Horses and Carriages', £976 against £271; and 'Wine and other Liquors' £1,610 against £980.[52] Only a four-wheeled landaulet was

Fig. 7.12   Shops in Exeter 'Change, off the Strand, 1772. London's supply of luxury items and the latest fashions proved magnetic.

kept at Chatsworth: but Piccadilly called for a 'Yellow-Bodied Barouch', a similar landau and chariot, a brown landau, a curricle and a phaeton; and all twenty-one horses seem to have been in prime condition – whereas Chatsworth stables resembled a hospital, with a blind stallion, an old stallion, a broken-winded gelding, and two brood mares among its dozen horses.[53] This picture gives substance to the Honourable John Byng's account of his visit to Chatsworth in June 1789: 'All is asleep! More money may be lavish'd in follies, or lost at cards, in

Fig. 7.13   A coffee house: a convenient watering-hole for Georgian men before the rise of the social clubs. Often, an inner room was provided for approved customers.

one year than wou'd render this park a wonder of beauty', though certainly inside the house he found the Duchess had made a fine display of 'frippery French furniture'. Apart from 'some portraits', he thought such 'other paintings' as there were displayed 'much indecency'.[54] The correspondence of Duchess Georgiana (between 1774 and 1796) suggests a rough pattern of a withdrawal from Piccadilly to Chatsworth from the end of the London season towards the end of July and throughout much of August and September, and sometimes October, though that was often the time for militia camps; the New Year usually saw a return to Devonshire House.[55]

The close connection between Devonshire House in Piccadilly and the family's out-of-town villa at Chiswick is shown in the 1811 Chiswick inventory and in the common 'Abstract of Household Accounts for Chiswick and Devonshire House' from 3 October 1764 to the end of 1771, and a similar abstract for 1774, embracing 'Kitchen', 'Servants' wages', and 'Stables'; while another for 1784 to 1788 analyses the costs under seventeen headings, which are then all totalled under 'Devonshire House', a small sum only (averaging nearly 7 per cent) being

Fig. 7.14   Brooks's (built 1778), in St James's Street, a notable Society club, established a reputation for heavy gambling. Charles James Fox ran a faro bank here. Photograph by M.H. Port.

appended for 'Chiswick'.[56] Chiswick, the 1811 inventories suggest, was for relaxation (as the architect-earl, Burlington, had originally intended): although the household furniture and fixtures totalled £7,290, linen and china were valued only at £576, 'Books prints &c.' at £373, and wine and other liquors at £346, plate being included in that valued at Devonshire House. Accounts for 1829 and 1830 show no charge for liveries at Chiswick, while 'Laundry' is charged only under Chiswick. And although the 6th Duke of Devonshire was more Chatsworth-oriented than his father, the annual average for servants' wages and board wages at the two houses in 1825–31 was Chatsworth £1,012, London, £2,215.[57]

But Chiswick's role also as a source of food supplies is suggested by the valuation of its farming stock and instruments of husbandry at £1,415.[58] In 1776 filling the ice-house in London was charged in the Chiswick farm account.[59] The game department at Chatsworth, the cost of which in 1825 to 1828 averaged £881 annually, doubtless contributed its quota to supplying Devonshire House.[60]

The relation of Syon (about nine miles from town, fig. 7.16) to Northumberland House was similar to that of Chiswick to Devonshire House. The Syon estate diary of 1808 records the carter 'driving cart to town 3 times a Week with Garden Stuff

Fig. 7.15 The Pay Office, Whitehall, sandwiched between the Horse Guards and Admiralty House. Office and House of the Paymaster General, a lucrative post often held by important politicians, including Henry Fox, 1757–65. Photograph by M.H. Port.

and Farm produce during the Season'; in November, it was faggots that were brought to London. But unlike the Foxes running the Pay Office (fig. 7.15) in tandem with Holland House in the early summer, when the Percies moved to Syon it was a full-scale migration. In the early eighteenth century, when the Duke of Somerset held the Percy estates in right of his wife, the family used to spend the summer at Syon, the servants then travelling upriver by barge with the household goods.[61] The pattern subsisted: a century or so later, utensils and plate as well as wine were brought from Northumberland House for the summer removal.[62] Syon was not, however, merely a place of relaxation; a house of surpassing grandeur, like Northumberland House it was used for top-level dinners (fig. 7.17). Having given a 'magnificent dinner' to the Ministers of State and foreign noblemen at Northumberland House on 29 March 1787, the Duke used the gilt service for a 'magnificent dinner to Foreigners of distinction' at Syon on 28 July 1787, followed three weeks later by HRH the Duke of York and a 'great number of nobility'.[63] The 1st Duke of Northumberland also restored the ancient Percy seat of Alnwick Castle in distant Northumberland, and his family frequently spent the later part of the year there, plate and other required equipment being taken by sea and the servants by land. But the household accounts list no resident housekeeper at Alnwick, such as is found at both Northumberland House and Syon.[64]

Writing to her grandson John Spencer in 1738 about the benefits of the rangership of Windsor Park, Sarah, Duchess of Marlborough remarked, 'As for

Hay, there is so great a quantity this Year, which I have paid for the making of, that if the keepers don't cheat you, you will have not only enough to serve you at the Lodge, but to bring to London if you like it. And for the Wood, you may carry from the Park what you have present Occasion for. I remember my Lord Godolphin had so much wood from Wind-falls with one thing, or another, that he sent some to his house at London, till he found it manag'd so ill, that the Charge was more than it was worth.'[65] Clearly, one of the problems about supplying the town house from the country seat was the management of the transportation; there was not only the actual cost, which might make it an uneconomic exercise, there was also the possible 'leakage' on the way.

It was not only in London that the town house was furnished with provisions from the country estate; similar practices were to be found in Ireland between the country house and the Dublin house. The 1758 household book of the premier Irish nobleman, the Marquess of Kildare, laid down that a cart was to go from Carton, some fifty miles from Dublin, to Kildare House every Tuesday and Saturday to take meat and 'garden stuff' for the family, and a mule was to go every Monday, Wednesday and Friday, to carry rolls, butter, eggs, fowl, game and salad.[66] In 1769, the Duke of Leinster (as Kildare had become) ordered that the Tuesday and Saturday carts should each send one 'good, fat sheep', twelve or eighteen good chickens, a goose or two, a turkey or two, and a pair or two of duck; churned butter was to be sent three times a week.[67] There can be little doubt that this supply of produce was a normal practice where a country estate was no more than a half-day's journey from the town house.[68]

Fig. 7.16   Syon House, Twickenham. Exterior view. The Syon farm supplied produce to Northumberland House, Charing Cross. Photograph by M.H. Port.

Fig. 7.17 Syon, the anteroom. The out-of-town seat of the Duke of Northumberland was most richly transformed by Robert Adam in 1762–9 as a setting for grandiose entertainments. Photograph by M.H. Port.

Sometimes a country house was acquired specifically as a holiday retreat. Thus Henry Fox, with the Pay Office as his town house and Holland House as his seat only two miles out of town, took Kingsgate, near Margate, seventy-two miles from London, 'by the sea . . . not a place to be at above three summer months in the year, but very pretty for that purpose'; 'a little quiet retreat within a day's journey of Holland House at any time, the situation the most healthy imaginable and as beautiful as an open country can be, with the sea as near the house as Mr Fox could wish it. . . . We purpose being here in August', as Lady Caroline Fox reported to her sister.[69] It was convenient also for the holiday over Easter week, or for a week in May; for the exhausted party manager, it was a bolt-hole: 'No people of business coming to Mr Fox; no dressing to go to Court, or any other stupid engagement; no loo, no great dinners, in short none of the things *qui sont faits . . . pour me faire enrager*'.[70]

That, of course, was quite distinct from the country seat at which the owner expressed his dominance in the locality, with 'great dinners', balls, and hordes of aristocratic visitors engaging in amateur dramatics. Further study needs to be made of holiday houses. Those who were less keen on escaping society could hire a house in one of the fashionable resorts, notably first Bath and then Brighton, where one could enjoy many of the dissipations of metropolitan society in a less soot-ridden and more relaxed atmosphere: in his 'marine villa', George, Prince of Wales, showed himself much more affable than in the stuffy atmosphere of Carlton House, shooting 'with an air-gun at a target placed at the end of the room', or sitting between a famous violinist and Lord Lauderdale's daughter, 'for hours beating his thighs the proper time for the band, and singing out aloud, and looking about for accompaniment'.[71]

The relationship between country house and town house thus appears to be wide in range, varied and complex. At one end of the spectrum we have the country house that is the real home of the family, the owner (in all likelihood of the squirearchical class) – and probably his wife and daughters – moving to a hired house in London for a comparatively brief sojourn. At the other end stands the great magnate, deeply immersed in the political game, essentially an urban figure retreating to one or other of his country seats for occasional relaxation or to keep up his political interest in the locality. In the former instance, there would be little meaningful relationship between the country and town houses; in the latter, probably a constant flow of goods and services from one to the other. Somewhere between them lies the unexplored territory of the gentry or aristocratic house in the county town or provincial capital.[72] Tangentially situated lies the country house deliberately acquired purely for recreational purposes, be it hunting box or marine villa, which again for goods and services may have a direct relationship with one or more of the regular family residences. And further to complicate these interweaving connections is the chronological factor: the increasing importance of London in the life of the upper classes over the course of the Georgian era, the increasing enthusiasm for fox hunting,[73] and the growing popularity of holidays by the sea.[74]

8 Jane Austen and the Changing Face of England

Philippa Tristram

In the summer and autumn of 1814, Anna Austen sent her aunt instalments of the novel she was writing. In December she married. The novel was never completed and the manuscript, in a fit of despondency, was later burnt, but the letters from Jane Austen still survive,[1] and it is not difficult to deduce from them that at the age of twenty-one Anna was inspired as much by literature as life. Like her aunt, Anna was the daughter of a country vicar[2] but, in common with many novelists and readers at the time, she had a voracious appetite for high life and her pages apparently teemed with aristocrats. Jane Austen's sparing and constructive criticisms are nearly all directed at accuracy, particularly in matters of idiom and manners: Lord Orville is too formal to be natural; Lady Clanmurray would be too well bred to be so pressing; Lady Helena would not be introduced to her inferior, but vice versa; a country surgeon would not be introduced to 'men of rank' at all, and, if he were, Lord Portman's younger brother would not be called 'the *Hon*[ble]' for '*That* distinction is never mentioned at such times; at least I beleive not'. Although distantly connected with the aristocracy on both sides, Jane Austen always kept to the society she knew best, and never aimed higher than a baronet (a commoner) in fiction.[3] By September she was relieved to find that Anna's characters had been collected 'into such a spot as is the delight of my life; – 3 or 4 Families in a Country Village is the very thing to work on'. But what this starry cast can have been doing there is another matter.

Jane Austen's own creative periods coincided with settled residence in two such villages, Steventon and Chawton, both in Hampshire. Between 1795 and 1799 the early drafts of *Sense and Sensibility*, *Pride and Prejudice* and *Northanger Abbey* were written, probably in that order, and the first recast, in her father's rectory at Steventon where she was born.[4] When the family moved to Bath in 1801 and subsequently to Southampton following her father's death in 1805, an unproductive period intervened. It was only in 1809 when she settled with her mother and sister at Chawton that Jane Austen's inspiration really returned. *Sense and Sensibility* was revised; *Pride and Prejudice* was recast; *Mansfield Park*, *Emma*, and *Persuasion* followed at intervals of almost two years, and *Sanditon* was begun in

1818, the year in which she died.[5] All her novels are set in whole or part in the country villages of southern England[6] where she preferred to live and from which she drew her inspiration despite the very restricted social opportunities they offered. Together, the parishes of Steventon and Deane, where her father also held the living, numbered no more than 300 souls and visiting beyond a reasonable walking distance was a problem. Even when a family did possess a carriage, horses were not always available at times of harvest and although the unconventional Elizabeth walks three miles to Netherfield in *Pride and Prejudice*, the same distance for the delicate Anne Elliot in *Persuasion* puts Kellynch and Uppercross in different worlds. Nevertheless, it was through minute attention to this restricted circle of visitable houses that Jane Austen came progressively to generalize England as a whole. Although the description of living space which became so popular in Victorian novels is generally held to have been introduced by Dickens, her sparing detail had come to serve a similar purpose, indicating larger social changes, more than twenty years before *Boz* and *Pickwick* first appeared.

Houses in fiction are always fictional houses and the same is true of their locations. It is an attractive but ultimately idle occupation to suggest what particular house any novelist, but particularly Jane Austen, had in mind. Attribution can distract from the significance of such buildings in their fictional context and in the case of her most distinguished houses, Pemberley and Sotherton, she prevents identification by introducing some unusually specific details. Conversely in the case of houses that are not unusual, she achieves the same result by remaining unspecific. Mansfield Park has, for example, been compared with Godmersham, her brother Edward's mansion (and with Goodnestone, also in Kent),[7] but by describing Mansfield merely as a 'spacious modern-built house' (*MP* 48), she categorizes rather than identifies it, for she uses an identical phrase for Cleveland in *Sense and Sensibility* (*SS* 302), and a very similar one for Rosings – 'a handsome modern building' – in *Pride and Prejudice* (*PP* 56).[8] Godmersham Park was actually built in 1732, and Wellington dates Mansfield *c.* 1740;[9] but 'modern' to her means simply 'Georgian' and she leaves the reader to supply the rest. Her sparing detail serves a different purpose; for her houses are always human spaces, defined by and in turn defining their fictional inhabitants. Fanny's refuge, the former schoolroom, is the only interior specifically described at Mansfield because its wealth of personal associations is in marked contrast to the generalized dignity of the other rooms. Similarly, the lavish glazing and expensive fireplace at Rosings (possibly Chevening Park) are not mentioned to define the house but to contrast with Pemberley's natural adornments and pass judgement on Lady Catherine's very public face.

Yet although fiction can never be regarded as documentation by those interested in the history of country houses, it can tell attentive readers a great deal about the significance of such buildings at the time. Lord Chesterfield was undoubtedly right in claiming that when Richardson 'goes . . . into high life, he grossly mistakes the modes',[10] but his idealization of Grandison Hall where 'the very servants live in Paradise' at least suggests what a working printer considered a great country house should be.[11] Jane Austen, with her care for accuracy in modes of all sorts, and her fidelity to her own immediate experience, can be a far more revealing guide to the social topography of country houses, small as well as great, for she traces in them not only the features of her characters, but, through her power to generalize, the changing face of England in her time.

Like Anna Austen, historians of country houses tend to focus on the great. If the houses in Jane Austen's novels had actually existed, only two, Pemberley and Sotherton, would receive a mention in the work of writers like Mark Girouard today. When a visit to Pemberley is proposed by Mrs Gardiner, it is the last in a succession of tourist attractions for Elizabeth protests 'that she was tired of great houses; after going over so many, she really had no pleasure in fine carpets or satin curtains' (*PP* 240). Sotherton, 'one of the largest estates and finest places in the country', appears to be in the same category, for the author caustically remarks that the heir's mother, Mrs Rushworth, 'had been at great pains to learn all the housekeeper could teach, and was now almost equally well qualified to shew the house' (*MP* 38, 85). Mansfield itself, like all Jane Austen's other grander houses, is not in the tourist class, although, like Godmersham, it deserves 'to be in any collection of engravings of gentlemen's seats' (*MP* 48).[12] Its modernity may also tell against it for Jane Austen for, although she welcomes the comforts of modernization, and pokes fun at Catherine Morland who thinks she would prefer Northanger Abbey in a romantic state of semi-ruin, a historic house has for her a value of its own. She had actually stayed at Stoneleigh Abbey in Warwickshire (but at too late a date for it to feature as Northanger) and in her letters mentions it quite respectfully despite its somewhat pompous grandeurs. Both Sotherton and Pemberley are older houses, the first specifically said to be Elizabethan, and the second, to judge from its gallery, either Elizabethan or Jacobean. To Miss Bingley, Pemberley is the model of a country seat, but like its library it is 'the work of many generations', and cannot be imitated, only purchased, as her brother points out (*PP* 38). Jane Austen's own ideal is the humbler and still older Donwell Abbey; though 'rambling and irregular' in structure with only 'one or two handsome rooms', it is 'sweet to the eye and the mind, English verdure, English culture, English comfort', when seen in the setting of its prosperous state (*E* 358, 360). Houses built from abbeys were to have a special aura for Victorian novelists as diverse as Disraeli, Trollope and George Eliot, for in an age which romanticized the Middle Ages, the spiritual values connected with the abbey were expressive of an idealized vision of what a great country house should be.[13] But Jane Austen was never a romantic.

Although, to her, its age may give a country seat a title to respect, the same is never true of lineage *per se*. Pemberley, yielding an income of £10,000, is nevertheless a greater house than Sotherton, which produces £12,000, because Mr Darcy is a much better man than the congenitally stupid Mr Rushworth. However, Jane Austen's morality in such matters is pragmatic. She does not exclaim with Fanny Price, whose ideals seem formed by Richardson: '"There is something in a chapel and a chaplain so much in character with a great house, with one's ideas of what such a household should be!"' (*MP* 86). The landlord's cure is not of souls, but bodies: his crops and woods, his tenants and his buildings.

Mr Darcy, like his father before him, is involved in the life of his estate, and the testimony of his housekeeper – '"the best landlord and the best master . . . that ever lived"' – leads Elizabeth to reflect, 'How many people's happiness were in his guardianship!' (*PP* 249, 250). Sotherton has not been the childhood home of Mr Rushworth who has only just succeeded to it, and the outlook for his tenants is a bleak one. The approach to the house itself has been repaired, and he has large ideas for improving his grounds, possibly with the assistance of Repton; but the prosperity of his estate does not feature in his thinking, much less the happiness of his dependants. According to his betrothed, Maria Bertram, the cottages in the village are 'really a disgrace', but this only leads her to celebrate the mile which separates the great house from the village and its church bells, a distance unusual 'in old places' (*MP* 82). Jane Austen's brother Edward owned a secondary estate at Chawton where the Jacobean great house is adjacent to the church and village. When he was staying there in 1813, she remarked, 'We like to have him proving & strengthening his attachment to the place by making it better.'[14] Unlike General Tilney at Northanger Abbey who never mentions farming activity or tenants, Mr Knightley's preoccupation with his estate, his concern for dependants like the farmer, Robert Martin, and his pleasure in discussing the affairs of Donwell Abbey with his brother, a London lawyer with an equal interest in his ancestral home, all confirm that Donwell is 'the residence of a family of . . . true gentility, untainted in blood and understanding' (*E* 358). In contrast, the absorption of Sir Walter Elliot in the *Baronetage* is made even more ridiculous by his indifference to 'the duties and dignity of the resident land-holder' (*P* 138). When Kellynch Hall has to be let and he departs for Bath, Jane Austen comments acidly that he has only 'condescending bows' to offer 'all the afflicted tenantry and cottagers who might have had a hint to shew themselves' (*P* 36).

Baronets do not, however, feature very often in the novels, and gentlemen with incomes in five figures are still more uncommon; even Sir Thomas Bertram, with additional revenue from his West Indian estate, has a smaller income than Mr Rushworth, as his daughter, the future Mrs Rushworth, observes with satisfaction. The mainstay of rural society is the landed gentry with estates like Donwell Abbey, husbanded through several generations, prosperous but not conspicuously rich: Mr Knightley, though affluent in Highbury terms, is no wealthier than Emma's landless father. In all Jane Austen's novels, but particularly the first three, women are assessed by the capital they bring to an estate, men by the income they derive from it. Lady Bertram 'with only seven thousand pounds' is held to have made a great match when she captivates Sir Thomas of Mansfield Park: 'her uncle, the lawyer, himself, allowed her to be at least three thousand pounds short of any equitable claim to it' (*MP* 3). Conversely, the importance of a country estate tends to be defined by revenue, not its capital value or its acres, perhaps because it is regarded as a living organism, rather than a passive asset. John Dashwood's Norland Park in Sussex and Henry Crawford's Everingham in Norfolk both yield an income of £4,000; Colonel Brandon and Mr Bennet draw half that sum from Delaford and Longbourne; Willoughby's estate, Combe Magna, produces an annual return of £700. Of those five owners, only John

Dashwood, who has inherited money from his mother and married a wealthy wife, is said to have an additional source of income, and part of this is reinvested when he inherits Norland. The enclosure of Norland Common has 'been a most serious drain', and the purchase of an adjacent farm at a time when stocks were low, would have been an embarrassment had he not already had the 'necessary sum' at his banker's (*SS* 225). John Dashwood is a mean man and his wife still meaner, but his investment in Norland is not censured; it is his parsimony towards his father's second wife and her three daughters that attracts an adverse judgement, for an estate is not merely farms and land, but human lives. Improvements to a property and moral improvement are interrelated, provided they are directed to communal benefit, not 'envious show'. Henry Crawford shows himself to be no better than Mr Rushworth when he declares that he landscaped Everingham as soon as he acquired it; but when, in deference to Fanny's finer moral sense, he determines to spend more time on his estate and investigate the conditions of his tenants, his life is pointing in the right direction – until he dawdles in London on the way to Norfolk. The proper care of an estate gives meaning to the lives of those who inherit country houses, and the possession of land of almost any kind confers significance on a family. Charles Hayter, the heir to 'Winthrop, without beauty and without dignity . . . an indifferent house, standing low, and hemmed in by the barns and buildings of the farm-yard', is nevertheless regarded by the Musgroves as a suitable match for Henrietta, for, as her brother seeks to persuade his wife, the possession of '"good freehold property"' is not to be despised, and Charles Hayter '"will never be a contemptible man"' (*P* 85, 76).

Jane Austen invariably describes such landed gentry as 'country families': the Musgroves at Uppercross are 'an old country family of respectability and large fortune' (*P* 6); an acquaintance with 'a proper unobjectionable country family' helps to establish the self-made Coles in Highbury society (*E* 214). In relation to families, the word 'country' is equivalent to 'county' in modern usage, but when Mr Musgrove is described as 'a man, whose landed property and general importance, were second, in that country, only to Sir Walter's' (*P* 28), the word appears to mean 'locality' or 'neighbourhood', as it does when it is used of Sotherton. Jane Austen's counties are never fictional like Trollope's Barsetshire or Hardy's Wessex, and Kellynch, though probably built at the time of the Restoration, is not grand enough to dominate Gloucestershire. Her England is invariably small-scale, and a locality is defined by the circle of houses with which visits are exchanged. Whether a house does, or does not, belong within that circle is not a problem in the early novels; it contains a 'country' family when it has a name, and that family will often be referred by their house name rather than their patronymic. The same is true of relatives, however humble. In *Sense and Sensibility*, when Mrs Dashwood and her daughters are reduced to living in a cottage on an annual income of £500, they remain a country family, and visits are exchanged between Barton Park and Barton Cottage almost daily. But in the last two novels the question of which families rate as country and which do not becomes an issue indicative of larger social change, for in the twenty years between the first draft of *Sense and Sensibility* in 1795 and the completion of

Emma in 1815 that distinction has come to be less definitely marked. Emma herself is not in doubt about it – "'The yeomanry are precisely the order of people with whom I feel I can have nothing to do'" (*E* 29)[15] – and she makes a point of waiting in the carriage when Harriet calls on the Martins, although Abbey Mill Farm has not only acquired a name but can claim that title to gentility, two 'very good' parlours, which are probably larger than those 'about sixteen feet square' at Barton Cottage (*E* 27, *SS* 28). However, the Martins are not beyond the pale to Mr Knightley or to his brother who invites the tenant farmer to see a play and dine with his family in London, and Emma, whose social perceptions frequently mislead her, is eventually forced to concede that 'it would be a great pleasure to know Robert Martin' (*E* 475). Sir Walter Elliot's youngest daughter, Mary Musgrove, is equally reluctant to call on the Hayters at Winthrop, for although they are connected to the Musgroves, are freeholders and have a son in orders; the family is otherwise under-educated and 'hardly in any [social] class at all' (*P* 74). But at Uppercross Mary is in a minority of one, for the Musgrove family is easygoing, and the parents, who themselves are 'not much educated', move – or are moved by their children – with the times.

The visiting circle was not of course confined to those who owned the land but embraced the few professions considered suitable for younger sons. When Edmund Bertram disappoints Mary Crawford by revealing that he is shortly to take orders, he sets out the other options: "'You must suppose me designed for some profession, and might perceive that I am neither a lawyer, nor a soldier, nor a sailor.'" (*MP* 91) The church had many advantages. When presented to a family living, a younger son was assured of a competence for life and did not have to depend upon his talents. In isolated villages attached to large estates, he had immediate entry to the best society available, since the parsonage provided the only unfailing source of sociability for the great house. When Lady Catherine has no resident visitors at Rosings in Kent, Mr Collins is almost as welcome to her as she always is to him, and Mansfield Park in Northamptonshire springs to life when the company of the phlegmatic Dr Grant is leavened by Mrs Grant's step-siblings, Henry and Mary Crawford. The profession had also become much more prosperous and its members were more educated than they had once been. At the beginning of the eighteenth century, country clergymen lived in cottages and augmented their pittance with weekday farming like Fielding's Parson Trulliber, 'stript into his waistcoat, with an apron on, and a pail in his hand, just come from serving his hogs'.[16] At its end, when the revenue from glebe land had been greatly increased by enclosures and agricultural developments, the care of pigs was left to others and many parsonages became substantial buildings; the rambling house at Steventon had seven bedrooms and the two daughters had a small sitting-room of their own. Parsonages do not rank as country houses but some of them could certainly have served as such. Mrs Norris is scandalized to discover that Dr Grant's new dinner table is even wider than the one at Mansfield Park, which suggests that the room is a very large one, even if diners are aware of servants passing behind their chairs. Henry Crawford is even more impressed by Edmund's future parsonage at Thornton Lacey, which he describes as '"a solid walled, roomy, mansion-like looking house such as one might suppose a respectable old country family had lived in from generation to generation, through two centuries at least, and were now spending from two to three thousand a year in"', a figure at least equal to, and even substantially above, the revenue from Delaford and Longbourne (*MP* 243). Though Edmund's income does not exceed three figures, the appearance of the house suggests to Henry that with '"judicious improvement"', it could '"receive such an air as to make its owner be set down as the great land-holder of the parish, by every creature travelling the road; especially as there is no real squire's house to dispute the point"' (*MP* 244). Edmund concedes that he will have to move the farmyard but when he resists Henry's more ambitious plans, protesting that he aims no higher than comfort and 'the air of a gentleman's residence', his objections are not only financial but moral. Like Donwell, which 'was just as it ought to be, and . . . looked what it was' (*E* 358), Thornton Lacey must not assume a false identity, but appear to be what it is, a parsonage and not a country house.

Lawyers appear less frequently in the novels, and their houses, unlike parsonages, do not acquire a presence. The legal profession has many levels, ranging from the distinguished judge who is mentioned in the same breath as his relative, Mr Darcy, to the country attorneys, Mr Philips at Meryton and Mr Shepherd at Kellynch, who are on the margins of the social circle and would, for preference, be outside it, if Elizabeth Bennet and Anne Elliot had their way. Rising men in the profession live in London, like Mr John Knightley who cultivates domestic virtues in all the respectability of Brunswick Square. The military men among Jane Austen's characters do not have houses at all, unless they inherit them like General Tilney, for in the course of their profession they are always on the move; the militia is only stationed at Meryton for the winter and then migrates to Brighton. Jane Austen's regard for them does not seem high; both Wickham and Frederick Tilney are profligate philanderers and General Tilney is an egocentric martinet. Of her six brothers, only the mercurial, optimistic Henry tried the Army, before moving on to banking and the Church, and that early disappointment in the brother who in early life seemed to have most promise may have affected her perceptions. Conversely, her enthusiasm for the Navy was undoubtedly fuelled by her sailor brothers, Francis and Charles, both of whom had flourishing careers,[17] and the impact of sailors on two of her most important country houses became exceedingly significant. In the histories of Mansfield Park and Kellynch Hall, Jane Austen anticipates the very different attitudes to domesticity, morality and social conscience which the Victorian middle classes were to introduce.

Francis and Charles went to sea at an early age, but it was not until Jane Austen wrote *Mansfield Park* (1811–13), when both were well into their thirties, that naval officers came to represent to her what can fairly be described as the development of a new and invigorating meritocracy in England. Although influence in the profession was needed to secure promotion, talent was essential; the 'troublesome, hopeless' Dick Musgrove, whom his family 'had the good fortune to lose' at sea, could never have succeeded (*P* 50). But even Henry Crawford with his prosperous estate in Norfolk envies the bright ambitions of William, Fanny's brother, a midshipman of humble origins, who has 'seen and done and suffered [so] much' before the age of twenty: 'He wished he had been a William Price, distinguishing himself and working his way to fortune and consequence with so much self-respect and happy ardour, instead of what he was!' (*MP* 236). It was possible in time of war for naval officers to make a fortune at sea, for proceeds from the capture of an enemy vessel were divided among the victorious officers (the crew sometimes included) in proportion to their rank. From this point of view, the Napoleonic Wars were a prosperous time and when a temporary peace returned the Navy to land in 1814, following the First Treaty of Paris, many officers were relatively wealthy.[18] As Charles Musgrove remarks when considering Captain Wentworth's merits as a husband for Louisa, '"he had not made less than twenty thousand pounds by the war"', and would improve on it if war returned, for he was '"as likely a man to distinguish himself as any officer in the navy"' (*P* 75). When on land, sailors were unemployed and had to find their own accommodation, and another interesting aspect of Jane Austen's novels is the number of houses, some with estates, which are available to rent. In *Pride and Prejudice*, Netherfield, the major seat near Meryton, is let to Mr Bingley and Mrs Bennet lists four other substantial possibilities in the neighbourhood.[19] In *Persuasion*, Admiral Croft and Captain Harville have both rented houses, each accommodating a brother officer with the open-heartedness typical of the Navy. Both, moreover, are among the tiny number of happily married couples in the novel, for sailors seem particularly gifted with domestic virtues. At a practical level, they have the handiness and eye for detail typified by Francis Austen, and are expert in fitting up their temporary homes; Captain Harville, though no reader, has 'a mind of usefulness and ingenuity', and 'contrives excellent accommodations . . . he drew, he varnished, he carpentered, he glued' (*P* 99). As in Victorian novels, where this nautical gift is often celebrated,[20] one is led to feel that those who can fit up a cabin and run a tight ship, can also manage an estate and even govern a country as well as or better than those who are born to it. The true heirs of Mansfield Park are not Sir Thomas Bertram's unsatisfactory daughters and wayward elder son but the children he assists in the nautical Price family, who have only 'the advantages of early hardship and discipline, and the consciousness of being born to struggle and endure' (*MP* 473). Sir Walter Elliot objects to the Navy '"as being the means of bringing persons of obscure birth into undue distinction"', but when Admiral Croft becomes his tenant, Kellynch at last has found a fitting master; Anne 'felt the parish to be so sure of a good example, and the poor of the best attention and relief, that . . . she could not but in conscience feel that they were gone who deserved not to stay, and that Kellynch-hall had passed into better hands than its owners' (*P* 19, 125).

Unusually for her, Jane Austen tended to romanticize the Navy. The changes in the social face of England are explored with more detachment in the case of those who do not belong to the acceptable professions but have acquired their houses with fortunes made in trade. For generations, those in trade were social outcasts. When John Dashwood refers to Mrs Jennings as '"the widow of a man who had got all his money in a low way"', he does not mean that the late Mr Jennings had gone in for shady dealings but only that he had made, and not inherited, his wealth (*SS* 228). The marriage of his two daughters to landed gentry, Mr Palmer of Cleveland and Sir John Middleton of Barton Park, does much, however, to remove the stain. The Dashwood sisters can suitably stay with Mrs Jennings in London since 'excepting a few old city friends, whom, to Lady Middleton's regret, she had never dropped, she visited no one, to whom an introduction could at all discompose the feelings of her young companions (*SS* 168). The fidelity to old friends shows that the good-hearted Mrs Jennings is a better woman than her daughter in the author's view, but the tension between social valuations of 'low money' and the claims of individual merit remains a marginal theme in *Sense and Sensibility* and is barely mentioned in *Northanger Abbey*. However, in *Pride and Prejudice*, which was totally recast at a later date *c*. 1812, it features prominently.

Because Netherfield Park is the most important house in the neighbourhood, Meryton society rejoices when Mr Bingley moves in with his two sisters. He is a wealthy man with capital of nearly £100,000 from his father but he has yet to purchase an estate and although his tenancy of Netherfield transforms him into the foremost local figure, the Bingleys are not exactly landed gentry. They come from 'a respectable family in the north of England' but this is a 'circumstance more deeply impressed on [the sisters'] memories than that their brother's fortune and their own had been acquired by trade' (*PP* 15). Bingley himself is not pretentious and 'low money' does him no damage with Jane Austen but the same cannot be said of Sir William Lucas, 'formerly in trade in Meryton', who has been knighted, following a royal visit to the town when he was Mayor. Although he has no more than 'a tolerable fortune', he promptly quits his useful business and retires to a house about a mile from Meryton, 'where he could think with pleasure of his own importance' and allude repeatedly in conversation to his presentation at St James (*PP* 18). Lucas Lodge is very like the house erected by a banker, Mr Thompson, in the fragment of a novel subsequently named *The Watsons* which Jane Austen began to write but then abandoned in 1804; both pretend to be country houses but are barely in the country and their grounds extend no further than a carriage sweep and shrubbery. Jane Austen does not object to the increasing fashion for such houses in itself but to the dissimulation of those who buy or build them to disguise their origin in trade. Moreover, in the intelligent and honest who do not conceal the sources of their income, trade is not regarded as a blemish. Mr Gardiner, Mrs Bennet's brother, is also in trade and lives in London 'within view of his warehouses', but the Gardiners (another happy couple) are the only relatives, Jane apart, for whom Elizabeth feels 'no need to blush' when she introduces them to Mr Darcy (*PP* 139, 255). Mr Gardiner is 'greatly superior to his sister as well by nature and education', his wife is 'an amiable, intelligent, elegant woman', and neither of them pretend to be other than they are. We know only that their house is in an unfashionable area of London and full of children, but if they were to retire to a property in the country, it would certainly not be titled Gardiner Lodge.

In more populated areas like Emma's Highbury, sixteen miles from London and nine from Richmond, landless country houses were proliferating. Mr Weston, of respectable family which has 'been rising into gentility and property' for two or three generations, is perhaps rather out of date when he realizes an old ambition and purchases Randalls, 'a little estate' which is not designed to support him since he is 'constantly occupied . . . with his business in town', with a house so modest that even its two parlours in combination cannot accommodate five dancing couples (*E* 16, 12, 247–9). The 'landed property' of Mr Woodhouse is even more restricted, for the grounds of Hartfield are contained within 'a sort of notch in the Donwell Abbey estate', but Mr Woodhouse does not need to demonstrate gentility; he is descended from 'the younger branch of a very ancient family' who have been settled at Hartfield for several generations (*E* 136). When Mrs Elton insists (as she constantly does) that Hartfield is 'astonishingly like' Maple Grove, a house near Bristol belonging to her brother-in-law Mr Suckling, the comparison appears to be quite accurate but the implication – that the two families are social equals – certainly is not. Both the Eltons have no connections that are *not* in trade and Maple Grove is scarcely an ancestral residence; Mr Suckling has lived there for only eleven years, though Mrs Elton insists, somewhat insecurely, that his '"father had it before him – I believe, at least – I am almost sure that old Mr Suckling had completed the purchase before his death"' (*E* 310). Again, it is not the association with 'low money' but the effort to misrepresent it that incurs Jane Austen's irony. The Coles, who have been settled for some years in Highbury, are also 'of low origin, in trade, and only moderately genteel' but they are 'friendly, liberal and unpretending' (*E* 207). However, an increase in their city profits leads to an extension of their house with a comparable expansion in their views and 'their love of society, and their new dining room, prepared every body for their keeping dinner-company'. Emma hopes they will not presume to invite 'the regular and best families . . . neither Donwell, nor Hartfield, nor Randalls', and is determined to teach them a lesson by refusing the invitation if they do. But in the event it is she who learns the lesson, for Donwell and Randalls are invited, and have accepted before an invitation reaches Hartfield. By this time, the prospect 'of being left in solitary grandeur' for the evening has begun to prey on Emma's spirits, and although she feigns reluctance, Hartfield quickly follows where Donwell and Randalls have led the way (*E* 208).

There can be no doubt that in those extraordinarily creative years at Chawton, Jane Austen had learnt to generalize the detail of lives in country villages to larger themes. One cannot read the fragment of her final novel, *Sanditon*, and fail to see that her interest in the changing face of England, particularly as it was registered in buildings, which she first began to explore when recasting *Pride and Prejudice* in about 1812, had gathered pace by 1817. The pre-eminence of Bath, the aristocratic brainchild of her distant connection, the Duke of Chandos, where visitors could be confidently placed by the location of their lodgings, had passed to less exclusive resorts like Brighton and Weymouth where everyone who could afford it indulged in the new fashion for sea-bathing. Sanditon is 'a quiet Village of no pretensions' on the coast, much as Weymouth used to be before it was developed, with the customary social circle (*Minor Works, MW,* 371). There is a baronet, the impoverished Sir Edward Denham of Denham Park, and a landed country family, the Parkers, with 'a moderate-sized house' surrounded by gardens, orchard and meadows, where the family has lived for generations (*MW* 379–80). The 'great Lady' of the neighbourhood is the twice-widowed Lady Denham of Sanditon House, 'born to

Wealth but not to Education', who first improved her status by marrying 'a man of considerable Property in the Country' and then acquired her title from Sir Edward's father (*MW* 375). However, this small society is very different from other country villages in one respect: it is downwardly, not upwardly, mobile. The enthusiastic Mr Parker has decided to develop Sanditon into a resort and has transformed his neighbours into ardent speculators. Lady Denham has become his partner in the enterprise and Sir Edward has invested such money as he can 'in running up a tasteful little Cottage Ornée, on a strip of Waste Ground' allowed to him by Lady Denham (*MW* 377). In order to set the right example, Mr Parker has even abandoned his 'honest old Place' in favour of 'a light elegant Building' named Trafalgar House, newly erected on a bare and windy hilltop, 'an hundred yards from the brow of a steep, but not very lofty Cliff' (*MW* 380, 384). The new resort is springing up about him and already includes a 'short row of smart-looking Houses called the Terrace', 'a Prospect House, a Bellevue Cottage, & a Denham Place', while the name and form of a Waterloo Crescent, still at the planning stage, is expected to yield a choice of future lodgers (*MW* 384, 380). Mr Parker intends the resort to be exclusive but the criterion is money; a West Indian heiress, half mulatto, will be the catch of the season if only he can land her. Even cottage windows display new curtains and are advertising rooms to let, for the fishermen too are now angling for lodgers, infected by 'the Spirit of the day' (*MW* 383).

Cobbett knew exactly what he felt about such places, 'to which East India plunderers, West India floggers, English tax-gorgers, together with gluttons, drunkards, and debauchees of all descriptions, *female* as well as male, resort, at the suggestion of silently laughing quacks'.[71] Jane Austen was always less doctrinaire, more speculative. After her aunt's death, Anna attempted to complete *Sanditon*, but again, she gave up. She probably knew how the plot was to develop but Sanditon, although another country village, is a new world in the process of formation. Although in retrospect one can see just how predictive Jane Austen's observations were, Anna herself could only guess at the impression that this new mercantilism was about to make upon the changing face of England.

The many redraftings of the first three novels, which register in the ambiguities of their internal dating, make it difficult to include them confidently in a historical sequence where buildings serve as indices of social change. However, there can be no doubt that in those last eight years at Chawton Jane Austen looked back to the last years of the eighteenth century, the period when she had embarked upon her first three novels, and recognized that the topography of country villages had undergone a radical change. *Persuasion*, completed in 1816, is a retrospective work in many senses, from the emotional history of its heroine, Anne Elliot, to the neighbourhood in which that history has developed. After many generations, Kellynch has not only lost its baronet and gained an admiral, but Uppercross, where the Musgroves still preside, is changing too:

Uppercross was a moderate-sized village, which a few years back had been completely in the old English style; containing only two houses in appearance to those of the yeomen and labourers, – the mansion of the squire, with its high walls, great gates, and old trees, substantial and unmodernized – and the compact, tight parsonage, enclosed in its own neat garden, with a vine and a pear-tree trained round its casements; but upon the marriage of the young squire, it had received the improvement of a farm-house elevated into a cottage for his residence; and Uppercross Cottage, with its viranda, French windows, and other prettinesses, was quite as likely to catch the traveller's eye, as the more consistent and considerable aspect and premises of the Great House, about a quarter of a mile further on. (*P* 36)

The ironies in this passage point in both directions. The country village, as it was, is expressive of an order acceptable to every previous generation but one which is dependent on exclusion, the high walls, great gates, and enclosing gardens which separate those who rank from those who do not. Uppercross Cottage contests that order by vying with the Great House for the traveller's attention, but in a manner that Jane Austen always ridiculed.[22] One cannot 'elevate' a farmhouse into a cottage, and to her 'the Pride that apes Humility'[23] in the cottage *ornée* is quite as meretricious as the parsonage that apes the pride of a squire's mansion. Her objection is not to change as such, however, but to its vanity in this particular form.

A similar overthrow of traditional style is rather differently regarded in the Great House, where readers are introduced to

the old-fashioned square parlour, with a small carpet and shining floor, to which the present daughters of the house were gradually giving the proper air of confusion by a grand piano forte and a harp, flower-stands and little tables placed in every direction. (*P* 40)

This of course is the 'lived-in look' which Disraeli was to celebrate in great houses because it humanized them and proved that even idle hands had work to do.[24] To many Victorians, devoted to family values and the work ethic, it continued to appeal and in fictional drawing-rooms at any social level good women are invariably occupied. Jane Austen's pleasure in this spectacle is less sedate for she exclaims:

Oh! could the originals of the portraits against the wainscot, could the gentlemen in brown velvet and the ladies in blue satin have seen what was going on, have been conscious of such an overthrow of all order and neatness. The portraits themselves seemed to be staring in astonishment.

The Musgroves, like their houses, were in a state of alteration, perhaps of improvement. The father and mother were in the old English style, and the young people in the new. (*P* 40)

The modern manners of the younger Musgroves, and the freedom of their domestic arrangements, have their negative aspect; their interiors are invariably noisy, and the French windows at the Cottage may admit unwelcome visitors, unannounced, at any time. But on balance the emphasis falls upon improvement.

Anne Elliot on entering the cheerlessness of Bath looks back 'with fond regret to the bustles of Uppercross' where even the roaring Christmas fire insists on being heard above the clamour of 'chattering girls' and 'riotous boys' (*P* 134–5). Fires are uncommon in Jane Austen's novels but once more she is anticipating Victorian fiction where the hearth, particularly at Christmas, becomes the heart which animates the home.[25]

Jane Austen is often described as conservative, even Augustan, in her attitudes and values but she was certainly no reactionary. On balance, she seems to have welcomed the 'state of alteration' which had overtaken the society of country villages but whether it did, or did not, amount to an 'improvement' was a matter for each specific case. Unlike Dickens, who often burns great houses down,[26] she had no wish to disrupt the established order for its own sake and her approval of a meritocracy of endeavour, whether in the professions or in trade, was never automatic. If Admiral Croft has a better moral claim to a great house like Kellynch than Sir Walter, the same cannot be said for Admiral Crawford, whose unprincipled domestic conduct has an unfortunate influence on his niece and nephew in *Mansfield Park*. In every area of life, including architecture, morality remained Jane Austen's touchstone and to that extent she *was* Augustan. When Wellington alleged that she was indifferent to the visual arts he was perhaps forgetting that to eighteenth-century writers like Lord Shaftesbury taste and morality were intimately related. Although Jane Austen's emphasis on education prevented her from believing sentimentally with Dickens that good people invariably produced good houses, moral values, particularly humanity and candour, when combined with education did produce an architectural aesthetic. Whether the changing face of England was to grimace or smile at Sanditon would ultimately depend on those unchanging touchstones.

9 Living off the Land: Innovations in Farming Practices and Farm Design

Dana Arnold

Land ownership was an essential part of the definition of social class in the Georgian period. Central to this was the country house, surrounded by its garden or parkland and set within the working farmland of the estate. These different kinds of landscapes functioned as signifiers of the social and cultural pre-eminence of the ruling élite through their layout, function and size. This was achieved partly through the design and symbolism of the landscape garden, and the feelings of admiration and nostalgia evoked by the use of classical architecture, antique remains and imitation ruins in the decoration of these landscapes. The importance of antiquity and the sensitivity and appreciation of landscapes and the picturesque by viewers and visitors are given full consideration in other chapters of this book.

The working estate was equally important to this definition of the ruling élite principally through the number of acres owned. Moreover, the income yielded from the land enabled the social conventions and cultural practices which made the country house the fulcrum of English society. The relationship of this farmland to the picturesque principles used in designing gardens has already been considered to some extent with specific reference to the activities of landowners in the Wye Valley. Uvedale Price's estate at Foxley has been the focus of convincing arguments for the adoption of picturesque principles of design in the laying out of the working landscape.[1] And similar observations have been made about Richard Payne Knight's nearby estate at Downton. Here the woodlands could provide a sustainable source of fuel for the factories owned by Payne Knight as well as a suitable setting for his intellectual interests. This work gives a coherent and well-argued picture of a very specific set of circumstances bound together through the three main protagonists of the picturesque movement in the later eighteenth century. The close proximity of Price and Payne Knight's estates and the template supplied for viewing the whole area by the Revd William Gilpin make a powerful and persuasive combination.[2]

The concerns of this chapter are rather different. Two distinctive but complementary aspects of the country house landscape are brought together to show how economic imperatives and revised social relationships affected the countryside. Firstly, the effect changes in farming practices had on the relationships between different classes and the consequences of these developments for the landscape are considered. Secondly, the influence these social and economic changes had on the architecture and planning of the estate is explored.

The country house estate could provide a substantial amount of wealth for the landowner, but established methods of farming and systems of land management restricted growth and change. Income from farming remained static if there could be no improvement in productivity. It would only increase or decrease according to the vicissitudes of market forces, disease or bad weather. Furthermore, the total acreage of the estate might be broken up into different kinds of productive land, for instance woodland, arable, and cattle/sheep according to factors like the region and soil type. Also many estates were subdivided into smaller farms and tenancies. These kinds of farming arrangements reduced the possibility for economies of scale and the widespread adoption of new techniques. This fragmentation of the agrarian economy put a premium on the small tenant farmer. Indeed, the relationship between landlord and tenant was a vital part of farming practices and the social fabric of the countryside. The changing relationship of the country house and its estate to local communities is an essential element in the history of the country house in the long eighteenth century. The process of enclosure is usually identified as the most dominant economic factor to influence the country house landscape and the structure of rural society. But this was not itself the prompt for such far reaching and fundamental changes which completely transformed the character and complexion of the English countryside. These physical changes to the landscape and developments in farming practices were the manifestations of shifts in society and the attitudes towards wealth and wealth creation. Moreover, the broader questions of attitudes towards science, technology and progress and land ownership also come to the fore.

Social structures

The social structure of England was bound up in the patterns of land ownership. The Glorious Revolution of 1688 had established a distinctive political status quo and system of rule. The constitutional monarchy restricted by law meant that the king served as head of state but had only limited powers. There was a small standing army but the enforcement of law and order, if necessary, was largely the duty of the aristocracy This land-owning class formed a kind of paternalistic oligarchy which had a slightly ambiguous relationship with the lower orders.[3] Up until the eighteenth century the presence of a land-owning élite had, by definition, an antithesis in the body of rural dwellers who owned no land or property. These people had few rights and no political say; this governmental system endured in the long eighteenth century and enfranchisement of the middle classes did not come until 1832. The system created a paternalistic framework for society, the emphasis being on loss (without choice) of freedom and rights in exchange for a sense of responsibility and benevolence on the part of the landowner. The country house and its estate is a focal point of these social contracts.

The economic rationalization of the long eighteenth century in all areas of production gradually eroded the bounds of paternalism as a means of social control and as an economic system. This is particularly the case with the country house as here the economic and social relations were intrinsically bound together and expressed as bonds between different classes rather than payment for services rendered or received. This is seen, for instance, in the tradition which waned in the eighteenth century of servants dining at the great table. Servants – here used in the broadest sense to include a variety of members of household from coachmen, to gardeners and gamekeepers – continued to be supplied with food and lodging by their employers. The level of ecomonic dependence on the country house owner by this class was enormous whether payment remained in kind or became cash. An indication of the level of indebtedness and the enduring nature of these paternalistic ties can be seen in the gratitude expressed by these ranks if their children were taken into service, so perpetuating the relationship. The tenants of small farms on estates also had some measure of protection because landowners were required to maintain their buildings. Although their position was more precarious than that of servants it does imply some kind of connection or responsibility across the estate for its inhabitants. These set roles of the landowners and their tenants underpinned the cultural hegemony in England.

There was a second layer of economic dependency on the great estate. This social group made money from the landowning classes in return for the supply of goods or services and included purveyors of luxury items, vintners, dressmakers and innkeepers. These were cash transactions which led to a loosening of the paternalistic bonds and the development of a 'free labouring class' operating small units of production in both towns and the country.

But the relationship of ruler to ruled was distanced by the growth of the gentry farmer who usually worked upwards of 300 acres.[4] This was not always their own land. Indeed, the distribution of landed property in the eighteenth century shows that there were different kinds of land owners but the proportion of land owned by each class did not change dramatically.[5] What did change was the kind of farmer. The nobility – or more accurately landed aristocracy since patterns of elevation to the peerage fluctuated throughout the long eighteenth century,[6] held between 15 and 20 per cent of workable land in 1688. This had increased to between 20 and 25 per cent by 1790. The gentry, comprising wealthy country notables and the less wealthy and influential squirearchy, held between 15 and 20 per cent throughout the period.[7] Despite the relatively stable pattern of land ownership, the number of gentleman farmers working leasehold land did increase. An indication of this can be seen in the building of new model farms by the owners of great estates. This proved to be a particularly popular activity in the latter half of the long eighteenth century.[8] For instance, Coke of Norfolk, who became a peer only in later life, consecutively built seven farms on his estate at

Fig. 9.1   Raby Castle, County Durham, south front, by James Miller The Earl of Darlington considerably extended his farmland Paul Mellon Centre for Studies in British Art.

Holkham between 1784 and 1807 at an average cost of £2,000 per farm. All of these were designed by Samuel Wyatt.[9] Perhaps even more impressive is the Marquess of Stafford's construction of over twenty farms on his estates at Lilleshall and Trentham between 1811 and 1819 at an average cost of £1,500–1,600 per farm.[10] But here, instead of using an architect, the farms were mostly designed by Stafford's estate steward William Lewis. These new farms expanded the class of leasehold gentlemen farmers who were then responsible for the landless labourers who had traditionally worked the farmland. But the profit-led agricultural reforms of these 'professional' gentlemen farmers ruptured the social framework and created a feeling of disharmony and anger between land-owners and the poorest members of the rural community.

Perhaps the most brutal social consequence of these new farming practices was the demolition of cottages of the rural poor to force them to move on; the trend resulted in a huge displaced population. In this way parish poor law rates could be kept low which was of direct benefit to the farmers because the rates were payable by the tenant rather than the landowner. Ultimately, however, the responsibility for these impoverished social groups must be attributed to the landowners while any remnants of a patriarchal system of government remained. It was their negligence and absenteeism that allowed this middle-ranking group of tenant farmers to continue their activities.[11] The aristocracy was increasingly becoming an urban species; its physical and social distance from the rural communities left the poor vulnerable to the solely profit-oriented activities of the gentleman farmer.

These changes in the physical layout and social structure of the landscape as a result of developments in farming practices were cause for great concern among writers and social commentators by the mid–eighteenth century. This underscores the relationship between landowners and the well-being of their tenants and confirms that this kind of paternalistic status quo was accepted, if not endorsed and admired, by many. But the strength of the reaction against improvements is perhaps stronger than the force of the improvements themselves.

The comments of John Mordant in his *The Complete Steward* (1760)[12] are a candid example of these attitudes:

> Nothing is now to be seen but a few wretched cottages, and as wretched inhabitants, without furniture, and almost without clothes, who are slaves to these all grasping farmers, who can now lay in their port wine by the pipe, and send their daughters to boarding schools, to make as genteel an appearance as those of their landlords.

These are indeed harsh words but the available statistics for the size of farms and patterns of land ownership seem to show that in reality small farms continued to exist in substantial numbers and even dominated the agricultural scene in certain counties. For instance, even in the later part of the eighteenth century the Board of Agriculture noted that small farms of 100 acres or less dominated the counties of Cumberland, Westmorland, Lancashire, Cheshire, Worcestershire, Derbyshire, Nottinghamshire, Rutland, Oxfordshire, Herefordshire, Middlesex and Cornwall and were still common in the North Riding of Yorkshire, Kent, Sussex, Hampshire, Devon and Shropshire.[13]

Moreover, as Mordant suggests, the harshness of the new improvements were not the result of the few 'spirited landlords' like Thomas Coke, 1st Earl of Leicester, at Holkham. Coke of Norfolk, as he was known, who had been identified with running estates on new lines. He points the finger of blame at the rather more anonymous group of wealthy freeholders and substantial tenant farmers for whom profit was everything and the paternalistic 'social contract' of the rural community was meaningless. The rise of this class of gentleman farmer, and his success, is confirmed by Henry Colman; the American traveller and writer remarked that:

> Lord Yarborough has more than sixty thousand acres of land in his plantation . . . 600 tenants in all, 150 tenant farmers . . . many of these farmers pay 1,400 guineas per annum in rent and live like nobles.[14]

Looking back on the developments of the final decades of the eighteenth century, Arthur Young saw these changes as inevitable remarking that 'these little arable occupiers . . . must give way to the progressive improvement of the kingdom'.[15] This is a comment which, in the light of the continuing Napoleonic Wars, betrays

Fig. 9.2a   Tower of the Winds by James Athenian Stuart, plate from The Antiquities of Athens, *1762, the source for Stuart's design for his garden ornament at Shugborough.*

Fig. 9.2b   Shugborough, Tower of the Winds by James Athenian Stuart, 1764–5, engraving attributed to Moses Griffith.

the imperative to maintain the nation's self-sufficiency in food production. This became more critical as the population nearly doubled over the course of the eighteenth century. Although small farms provided a subsistence living and catered for the specific taste of the city dwellers, the new efficient large farms fed the population at large. The economic and political imperatives together with technical advances were important factors in the inevitable but slow decline of the small farm during the Georgian period.

Physical changes in the landscape

The implementation of the physical changes to the landscape are the result of a mixture of improvements in technology, agricultural theory and economic imperatives. Perhaps surprisingly, enclosure – frequently cited as the root cause of the social and economic upheaval of the agrarian community – was only another factor that had intermittent influence on the course of agricultural improvements. Between 1730 and 1754 only fourteen acts of enclosure were passed whereas the startlingly high number of 1,124 were passed in the next twenty-five-year period.[16] This pace gradually slackened only to gain momentum again during the Napoleonic Wars. Enclosure was a cumbersome procedure. It required an Act of Parliament followed by legal processes and not least usually some form of compensation for those displaced and made homeless by its introduction. As such enclosure is an easily traceable act of deliberate intervention in the rural environment. There were other equally unsubtle ways of changing the landscape. As the fashion for landscaped parks continued to grow, farms, kennels and workers' housing began to appear to be incongruous elements. Many were disguised as gothic ruins or classical temples or moved out of the way so as to allow the landscape designer a free hand to achieve the optimum effect. Whole villages were moved as part of the improvement of the estate or grounds.[17] This could be done for purely aesthetic reasons or as the result of rationalizing farming practices which led to a logical regrouping of residential properties. Sometimes this kind of housing had philanthropic undertones and these new model villages were forerunners of the garden city.[18] One of the earliest schemes was implemented at Castle Howard in 1699. Others were New Houghton in Norfolk (1729) and Milton Abbas, Dorset (1774–80) for the 1st Lord Milton. The motivation for Milton Abbas was purely aesthetic. The house was rebuilt by William Chambers (1771–6) in the Gothic style. At the same time Lancelot 'Capability' Brown improved the park. Part of this redesign included the workers' housing being moved away from view of the house. The new village was designed by Brown and Chambers[19] and comprised rows of semi–detached cottages, built using sham techniques to emulate local cob construction, lining gently curving streets.

But there were more subtle means though which patterns of rural life and the physical appearance of the countryside were changed. Engrossing was another way in which traditional rural life was eroded. This involved the consolidation of farms and land on an estate whether the land was enclosed or not. It required no Act of Parliament and no legal process. It is therefore much harder to quantify as a social and economic phenomenon but it was as effective as enclosure in disrupting the character of the village and rural life that had preceded it. In the late eighteenth century there was much rearrangement of estates and farms. As leases fell in, tenant farms could be amalgamated either to form larger farms for re-leasing to wealthier, more competent tenants or, as in the case of Coke at Holkham, several tenant farms were amalgamated to form the landowner's own park farm of around 3,000 acres. This was one of the largest in England and it attracted both visitors and admiration on account of the progressive farming techniques employed there. Other great landowners followed suit. For example, the Earl of Darlington expanded his farm at Raby Castle in Durham (fig. 9.1) to 1,080 acres; and at Shugborough in Staffordshire the 1st Viscount Anson increased his park farm to a vast 2,000 acres.[20] This interest in more effective farming and the creation of larger farms gave rise to the construction of new farm buildings often relocated to a more central position on the farm. For instance, the 1st Viscount Anson employed Samuel Wyatt to build two groups of workers' cottages and carry out substantial developments to his house, stables and farm at Shugborough between 1803 and 1805. Even James Athenian Stuart's earlier Tower of the Winds (1764–5) (figs 9.2a and b and pl. 11), which was part of an earlier landscaping scheme at Shugborough, was not safe from this tide of agricultural improvements. This most prestigious of garden ornaments was turned into a dairy.[21] Perhaps there is a no more appropriate metaphor for the shift in attitudes towards the landscape and ways of living off the land.

Fig. 9.3   Wentworth Woodhouse, Yorkshire, c. 1735–70, east front by Henry Flitcroft. The owner of the estate, Lord Rockingham, was a successful farmer praised by Arthur Young for mixing waste to create a substance 'in so complete a state of corruption that it cut like butter'.

The aristocracy certainly led the way in changes and were no doubt encouraged by George III. He gave the agricultural improvements the stamp of royal approval and seal of social respectability not only through his own farming endeavours but also through his contributions, under the name Ralph Robinson, to Arthur Young's *Annals of Agriculture* first published in 1784. Furthermore, the Board of Agriculture, established in 1793, had the king as its patron and 500 honorary members drawn from the nobility. But the more trained eye of agricultural writers, like Arthur Young, identified the freehold 'gentry' farmers and substantial tenant farmers as those primarily responsible for changes in farming methods and consequent changes to the physical landscape. Larger farms meant economies of scale in terms of labour costs and machinery as well as greater bargaining power for maintaining prices at market because there were fewer suppliers. Indeed, the kind of tenant farmer who had the financial capital to take on leases of larger farms was rare and lower rents and better buildings could be exacted from landlords in return for taking up leases. By the same token landlords vetted farmers carefully[22] to ensure they had the correct knowledge and credit worthiness and leases often contained clauses enforcing levels of production and the use of certain kinds of progressive farm practices such as marling[23] and folding.[24]

Alongside the changes to the physical layout of estates there were also technical and scientific improvements. The reclamation of land, improved drainage and irrigation techniques as well as the introduction of more effective methods of cultivation dominated the opening decades of the eighteenth century. These developments were essential for the successful implementation of new scientifc farming techniques and land management which came at the latter end of the eighteenth century. The improver landlords were at the forefront of these changes, although the gentry farmers were the mainstay of the implementation of agricultural improvements. But of the aristocracy those most noted for their farming techniques and successes were the 1st Earl of Leicester, the 1st Marquess of Rockingham, the 5th and 6th Dukes of Bedford, the 3rd Earl of Egremont and the 2nd Marquess of Stafford. The list also includes the Duke of Portland of whom Henry Colman remarked that on his estate at Welbeck '[he] has drained . . . and now irrigates three and four hundred acres of land . . . yielding three crops a year'. Colman also remarked that the Duke had built 'several hundred miles of drains'.[25] Colman, a qualified and experienced commentator on agricultural matters, was clearly impressed by the improvements carried out by the Duke of Portland and had no less admiration for the work of the Duke of Bedford at Woburn. In his opinion:

> The Duke of Bedford next to the Duke of Portland is the largest improver in England; his estate at Woburn Abbey being no less than 20,000 acres . . . and his reclaimed land exceeds 18,000 [acres]. . . . His farm cstablishment at Woburn Abbey is deemed the most extensive and complete of any in the kingdom.[26]

Colman offers a very different, but equally relevant appraisal, of Woburn's significance compared to, for example, Dr Waagen's admiration of its architecture, collections and sculpture gallery.[27]

The combined efforts of the improver landlords saw the introduction of selective stock breeding, model farm building and the more efficient arrangement and management of the estates. Farming became a highly fashionable occupation for the aristocracy and the new methods were widely disseminated through publications, societies and events like the Holkham and Woburn sheep shearings. The combination of all these elements led to fundamental changes in farming practices and a prodigious increase in productivity. The country house and its estate was central to these developments. But behind all this was the need for venture capital to implement changes and invest in new equipment, livestock and buildings. This change in attitude to the economic possibilities of land precipitated a change in attitudes of the aristocracy towards commerce. The social impact of this was far reaching and a powerful force behind the changes in the landscape. Early in the eighteenth century Daniel Defoe recognized the relationship between land and Wealth in his remark 'Multitudes of People make Trade, Trade makes wealth, Wealth builds Cities, Cities enrich the Land around them, Land Enrich'd rises in Value, the Value of Lands Enriches the Government.'

But this correlation between land and trade touched a fundamental cord in the make-up of English society. The interests of the landed élite and their consequent social standing was seen as different and distinctive to those who practised commerce. But as Paul Langford has remarked:

> Agricultural improvement . . . could complicate the old simple assumptions about the line of demarcation between land and commerce. The intermingling of the supposedly distinct worlds of finance, trade, and agriculture did much to promote the sense of a broad commercial consensus in the age of Walpole and Pelham. . . . The readiness of landowners to invest in paper securities, the anxiety of merchants to acquire a share in the land market, the rapid growth of credit and assurance facilities for all sections of propertied society, made the traditional notions of the specialised nature of commercial enterprize manifestly untenable.[28]

Indeed, by the mid-nineteenth century Henry Colman remarked 'farming here is a profession, and one of the highest that can be pursued'.[29]

The alteration of this attitude towards the fundamental relationship between land and landed wealth, and commerce ruptured the structure and fabric of English society. When the South Sea Bubble burst in 1721 so did the conviction that the interests of commerce and land should remain separate.[30] Not only were many of the high-ranking culprits shown to be as money oriented as their 'lower rank counterparts' but also Walpole's scandalous protection of those of high rank from prosecution turned public opinion and certainly by the mid-eighteenth century there was a general acceptance that the best political system acknowledged the interdependence of land, trade and finance.

The impact of farming

The influence of picturesque principles of design on the layout and planning of estates has been widely considered. But the impact agricultural improvements had on the landscape has received less attention. The most obvious general effect was the creation of large fields necessary for the new farming practices. This produced landscapes of uninterrupted spaces which vividly contrasted with the patchwork of tiny plots that had been there before. These changes to the physical geography of Britain represented the new social order.

Arthur Young perhaps gives the most accurate general overview of the changes in the landscape. Here he is discussing the changes in Norfolk which give a flavour of the evident modernity in the landscape:

> All the county from Holkham to Houghton was a wild sheep-walk before the spirit of improvements seized the inhabitants . . . and this spirit has wrought amazing effects; for instead of boundless wilds, and uncultivated wastes, inhabited by scarcely anything but sheep, the county is all cut into enclosures, cultivated in a most husband-like manner, richly manured, well peopled, and yielding an hundred times the produce it did in its former state.[31]

But travellers also remarked on other evidence of the interventions of progressive farmers. Benjamin Silliman, an American visitor to Britain at the beginning of the nineteenth century, commented on the high yield of English farms and remarked on the farmers' understanding of the importance of manuring. Moreover, his

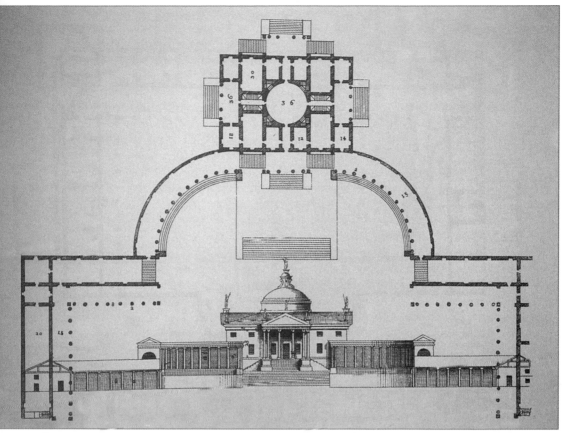

Fig. 9.4   A. Palladio, Villa Trissino at Meledo for Count Ludovico de Trissini, I Quattro Libri dell'Architettura, *Book II, plate 43, showing the house and the working farm elements enclosing a central courtyard.*

description of the countryside presents an interesting and vivid counterpoint to the usual eulogies of the picturesque views. The majority of the country estate was working land providing substantial revenue:

> Nothing is more common, when one is travelling in England, than to see in the roads adjacent to the fields heaps of compost, consisting of turf, tops of vegetables . . . dead animals, the offals of the yards and stables . . . everything . . . which is capable of being converted by putrification into vegetable mould.[32]

Indeed the national preoccupation with manure is also mentioned by Arthur Young. He heaps enviable praise on the Earl of Darlington at Raby Castle whose 'management of manure is much more masterly than that of his northern neighbour'.[33] But Young is even more impressed by Lord Rockingham at Wentworth Woodhouse (fig. 9.3). He was an enthusiastic and successful farmer whose technique of mixing manure with other waste produced a substance which Young observed 'was in so complete a state of corruption, that it cut like butter; and must undoubtedly be the richest manure in the world'.[34]

Model farms were an important part of the changing nature of the landscape. The increase in the size of farms led to new buildings and layouts. Well-designed buildings were essential for the improver landlords and new style farmers and this was recognized by agricultural theorists like Young. This aspect of country house design was perhaps closest in terms of function to Palladio's designs for his villas and their working farms in the Veneto.[35] Palladio established a hierarchy of parts in his designs. The villa was the central feature with the working farm elements flanking on either side often creating an enclosed courtyard space (fig. 9.4). In Britain, however, new farms were frequently moved away from the house to another part of the estate. The new rationalized farm comprised many parts and the layout of these was given careful attention to ensure maximum efficiency. It might be expedient, for example, to situate farm units requiring water power near to a stream. For those buildings grouped together the quadrangular layout was favoured. This had echoes of Palladio's planning ideals with the principal buildings ranged around a central court ideally in the following configuration. The house of the farmer or steward occupied the south run; this was usually a substantial dwelling of up to six bedrooms to represent the social status and wealth of the occupant. The

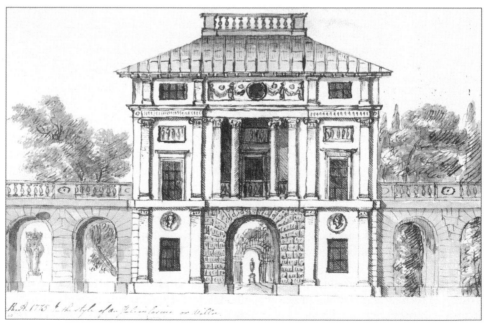

Fig. 9.5 Design for a Gardener's House, *Cullen, Grampian, 1775, Robert Adam, influenced by sixteenth-century Italian architecture. Courtesy of the Trustees of Sir John Soane's Museum.*

barn made up the north side of the farm with the stables and cattle sheds to the east and west. The remaining buildings were usually separated from this central unit. Pigsties were at a discrete distance owing largely to the smell. But these together with the poultry yard, often combined with a pheasantry or aviary, and dairies were often free-standing decorative buildings that attracted much attention and praise.[36]

In the first half of the eighteenth century farm designs were disseminated through architectural pattern books. Among these were Daniel Garret's *Designs and Estimates for Farm Houses* (1747) and William Halfpenny's *Twelve Beautiful Designs for Farm Houses* (1749). But it was only in the latter part of the century that farm buildings became a serious concern for the great landowners. As a result rational and utilitarian design principles were employed to ensure maximum efficiency. The new challenges presented by and the prestige of these projects attracted well-known architects. The likes of Robert Adam, James and Samuel Wyatt, Henry Holland and Sir John Soane all produced designs for model farms and estate buildings. Styles ranged from the Gothic and the Chinese, for instance Holland's Chinese Dairy at Woburn (1792) and James Wyatt's Gothic Dairy at Belvoir (1810), to the more predictable Italianate and neo-classical styles. Robert Adam's designs for a gardener's house at Cullen House, Grampian (1775) (fig. 9.5) borrows heavily from sixteenth-century Italian architecture.[37] Indeed, the influence of the Grand Tour and ideal landscape painting can be seen on Adam's designs for offices at Brampton Bryan, Herefordshire (1777) (pl. 12). These were intended to be set in the parkland across a public road. The design is based on Adam's studies of Roman antiquity and published survey of *Ruins of the Palace of Emperor Diocletian at Spoletro* (1764).[38] Adam was not the only architect to use antique sources for the designs of subsidiary estate buildings. The distinctive thermal windows of the ancient Roman bath complexes proved particularly popular in barn design. Lancelot 'Capability' Brown and Henry Holland's Cadland home farm, Hampshire (1777) for the Honourable Robert Drummond is a good example of how this form was adapted (fig. 9.6). The austere façades of Cadland were studied by Sir John Soane and may have influenced his own approach to farm design. Indeed, the use of primitivism in the design of model farms is best explored through the work of Soane.[39] His geometric approach to primitivism, based among other things on Abbé Laugier's *Essai sur l'architecture* (1753) and William Chambers's *Treatise* (1759), appears in the Burn Hall cow barn (1783).[40] Moreover, Soane's brick barn at Malvern Hall, Solihull (1798) is one of the most splendid examples of the baseless Doric revival.[41] These innovative designs are equal to any being produced in Europe at this time.[42]

The country house and its estate was an important representation of national identity throughout the long eighteenth century. The ways in which this identity was created developed and changed. The pictorial iconography of the landscaped garden gave way to a more general way of seeing and appreciating the landscape. Both these traditions established the symbolic nature of land and provided a cloak of respectability with which to dress the new farming practices. The importance of farming to Britain's social structures cannot be underestimated. And the

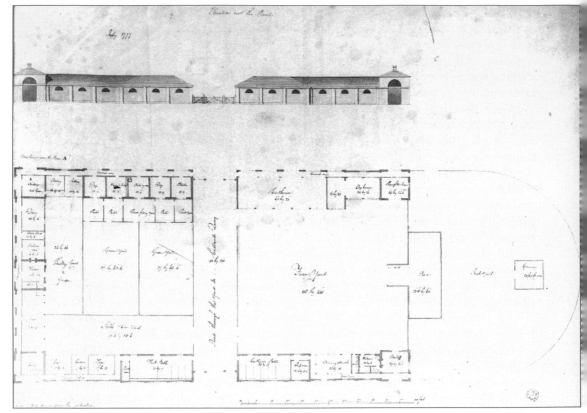

Fig. 9.6   Sir John Soane, Drawing of Cadland home farm, *1777, by Lancelot 'Capability' Brown and Henry Holland. Courtesy of the Trustees of Sir John Soane's Museum.*

identification of social and political systems with farming is widely manifested. Arthur Young affectionately describes the population as 'turnips' and George III was known as 'farmer George'. These factors together with a productive landscape and efficient model farms made the country house estate a potent symbol of a progressive nation.

10 Richard Payne Knight and the Picturesque Landscape

Andrew Ballantyne

The English landscape garden had its origins in the Garden of Eden, or so Horace Walpole claimed. He had written his account of the development of landscape design by 1770, soon after the publication of the works of his exact contemporary Winckelmann which are generally credited with having begun art history as we know it today.[1] However, whereas Winckelmann was writing about the art of the ancient world, which had, he said, reached its perfection in Periclean Athens in the fifth century BC, Walpole was writing about an art which had found its highest achievements in Walpole's own day. The hero of his story was William Kent who, by considering the imperfect efforts of others and by studying landscape paintings, managed to work out a method for the composition of gardens which achieved grandeur of effect by apparently effortless means. Kent, said Walpole, leaped the fence and saw that all of nature was a garden. The technical means which meant that he could achieve a blurring of the boundary between cultivated garden and natural countryside, was the ha-ha, an arrangement of ditch and sunken wall which prevented animals from wandering into the gardens, but which was practically invisible when seen from the garden side.

The idea that natural countryside might be seen as a garden, which this technical device made into a practical possibility, could be traced back, in Walpole's view, to the description of Eden in Milton's *Paradise Lost*.[2] He believed that this description owed nothing to the Italianate gardens which were fashionable in Milton's day, but represented a wholly original conception of the garden. This reading of Milton is now challenged, but the fact that it still can be challenged says much for the longevity and pervasive influence of Walpole's view:[3] we do not find long-dead views under attack – for example no one today would take the trouble to argue that the idea of phlogiston is wrong; more illumination is to be had from considering what the idea had to recommend it; we all know already that it is wrong, so completely that we have in general quite forgotten what it is, whereas the rival idea of oxygen is used all the time. The system of gardening which William Kent (a generation older than Walpole) devised was exploited most extensively in Walpole's day by Lancelot Brown whom we know as the great

Fig. 10.1   Thomas Hearne, A Landscape in the Manner of Capability Brown, *plate from Richard Payne Knight,* The Landscape a didactic poem *(1794).*

'Capability' Brown who remodelled most of the country's grandest parks and who is so universally admired that it might come as a surprise to find that he was ever criticized at all. Criticized he was, however, in the 1790s, when Richard Payne Knight (1751–1824 – a generation younger) published his didactic poem *The Landscape* (1794), a work which certainly annoyed Walpole, though Knight's subsequent poem *The Progress of Civil Society* (1796) annoyed him still more. It is not clear whether Walpole actually liked Knight when he first met him but certainly there was no instant hostility. When Knight wrote his book about phallic worship he wanted to include an illustration of an antique object in Walpole's collection and Walpole allowed it. He was given a copy of the book when it was published, in response to his hint that he would like one.[4] He excessively admired Knight's collection of antique bronzes and so he must have looked them over at some point, most likely in Knight's company. Knight regularly showed visitors round his collection, and in later life is to be found in a guidebook for visitors to London, particularly recommended for his abilities with foreigners.[5] For a time Walpole forbore to criticize Knight, because it would have disobliged a near

Fig. 10.2   Thomas Hearne, A Picturesque Landscape, *plate from Richard Payne Knight,*
The Landscape a didactic poem *(1794).*

relative who admired him, but then later he criticized him in print and felt that by
doing so he had debarred himself from seeing the admirable bronzes ever again.[6]

Knight made his particular criticisms of 'the modern taste in landscape
gardening' in tandem with Uvedale Price (1747–1829) who, like Knight, had an
estate in Herefordshire. Their ideas were evidently developed in conversation
and Price had for years been meaning to write and publish an essay on landscape
design but he did not get round to it until Knight, with an application and industry
which Price envied, worked his ideas into a poem. Knight suggested that his poem
and Price's essay might have been bound together in one volume but Price did not
want to recast his writing and in the event the poem was ready for publication
before the essay, and the two works were published independently.[7] It is possible
that this is how Price would have wished it, because his manner was much milder
than Knight's – his *Essay on the Picturesque* seems to make suggestions for the
refinement of a modern taste in landscape design, whereas Knight's poem was not
only more robust in its treatment of professional landscape designers but linked the
landscape itself with subject matter drawn from politics and religion which made
his notions seem at the time to be absolutely inflammatory.

It is worth pointing out that so far as practical gardening was concerned,
Walpole and Knight were hardly at odds with one another (and Knight

professed his agreement with Price to be complete).[8] They believed that apparently natural scenery was the best and that landscape designers should develop their taste by learning from landscape paintings. Walpole said that Kent had done this and thereby devised his system. Knight said that Brown was ignorant of paintings and just applied the system unthinkingly.[9] All were opposed to the sweeping away of older formal gardens simply for the sake of making the grounds conform to the modern taste. Uvedale Price wrote particularly evocatively about having himself done just such a thing at his own house, and how he had come to regret it – had his formal terrace survived then he would later have reformed it more gently, by allowing it to become overgrown.[10] Whereas in the late 1760s Walpole said that Kent had taught the stream to serpentize in an apparently natural way, by the 1790s Price and Knight saw the serpentine line as a shorthand means of signifying the idea of the natural, and they saw this sign as being as artificial and geometric as the straight edges and swirling parterres to be found in French gardens of the *ancien régime*. Knight's poem was illustrated with two plates to designs by Thomas Hearne, which are well known because they aptly summarize the whole debate of the 'picturesque controversy' of the 1790s. Both views show the same scene but in one case it has been tended with a view to picturesque principles and in the other it has been made to conform to the stereotypical landscape which Knight attributed to the followers of Brown (figs 10.1 and 10.2). In the first illustration we see a symmetrical Palladian house sitting in rolling countryside planted with small clumps of trees. The path to the house follows a serpentine line as does the stream in the foreground. By contrast the picturesque scene gives an image of a richly fertile ancient forest, similar to the forest on Knight's estate at Downton (of which Hearne made a series of a dozen highly finished watercolour views, see figs 10.3, 10.4 and 10.5). The relationship between paintings and landscapes was reciprocal: landscapes could inspire artists to paint, then designs for landscape could be inspired by paintings, and scenery could be inspiring on account of the ideas which it brought to mind (figs 10.5 and 10.6). It was undoubtedly the love of such scenery which gave Knight his conviction that there was an alternative to the prevailing tendency for parks to be made to conform to the ideal of open land sprinkled with trees – a tendency which he attributed not to Brown himself, who had died some years earlier, but to people who revered Brown and implemented what they took to have been his principles, but sometimes did so ineptly. There is no doubt that criticism of this kind was justified, as even Knight's opponents had to concede.[11]

However, the outraged response to what Knight had to say went beyond these matters of gardening, to include alarm at the political and religious views which were associated with them. These views were not chance associations of ideas which Knight's opponents introduced as a spurious means to attack him but were securely planted by Knight in his poem, which is about politics and religion every bit as much as it is about landscape design. Indeed, the content of the poem shifted between its first and second edition as Knight introduced some new verse and many pages of footnotes in order to answer his critics, especially Humphry Repton (1752–1818) who, as the leading landscape

Fig. 10.3   Thomas Hearne, View of Alpine Bridge, in the Teme Gorge at Downton. *Private Collection.*

gardener of the time, had assumed Brown's mantle and whose livelihood was threatened by the attacks. Therefore, in the second edition the gardening content of the poem increased. If we read the poem (especially in the first edition) all the way through then we find that Knight's subject matter shifts during the course of each of the poem's three books. Each book began with material which would have seemed innocuous and decorous but ended with forthright views on highly contentious topics. Each book began with conventional subject matter, modelled on Dryden's translation of Virgil's *Georgics,* but the conclusions of Books I and II of *The Landscape* both attacked superstitious aspects of Christianity, which show the influence of Lucretius, whom Knight (unlike most of his educated contemporaries) thought a better poet than Virgil.[12] Book I's ending described a monk:

The monk, secluded by his early vow,
The blessings of retreat can never know . . . (I, 391–2)
Dark rankling passions on his temper prey,
And drive each finer sentiment away;
Breed foul desires; and in his heart foment
The secret germs of lurking discontent. (I, 395–8)
In vain to distant Hope, Religion calls,
When dark vacuity his mind appalls:–
Without, a dismal sameness reigns around;
Within, a dreary void is only found.
 From mere privation nothing can proceed,
Nor can the mind digest unless it feed;
For understanding, like the body, grows
From food, from exercise, and due repose. (I, 403–10)

  The conclusion to Book II of *The Landscape* drew on similar material.
Knight inveighed against superstition, comparing Christians with Vandals, and
finding the Vandals to have been relatively harmless:

[Roman culture sleeps . . .]
But short its slumbers: – see fierce bigots rise!
Faith in their mouths, and fury in their eyes;
With mystic spells and charms encompass'd round,
And creeds obscure, to puzzle and confound;
While boding prophets in hoarse note foretell
The ripen'd vengeance of wide–gaping hell;
And pledging round the chalice of their ire,
Scatter the terrors of eternal fire.
 Touch'd by their breath, meek Science melts away;
Art drooping sinks, and moulders to decay;
Books blaze in piles, and statues shiver'd fall,
And one dark cloud of ruin covers all.
 Much injured Vandals, and long slander'd Huns!
How are you wrong'd by your too thankless sons;
Of others actions you sustain the blame,
And suffer for your darling goddess Fame:
For her, or plunder, your bold myriads fought,
Nor deign'd on art to cast one transient thought;
But with cold smiles of cold contempt pass'd by
Whate'er was fashion'd but to please the eye;
The works of Glycon and Apelles view'd
Merely as blocks of stone, or planks of wood.
 But gloomy Bigotry, with prying eye,
Saw lurking fiends in every figure lie,
And damned heresy's prolific root
Grow strong in learning, and from science shoot;

> Whence fired with vengeance and fierce zeal, it rose
> To quench all lights that dared its own oppose. (II, 406–33)

And the third book, which as the last has the general conclusion to the whole work, ends not by making a point about landscape design but with a lengthy passage on the French Revolution, written with strong sympathy for the revolutionaries – and written by an MP at a time when Britain was at war with France. These passages are quoted at some length in order to demonstrate that their presence in the poem is by no means slight – they go on for pages at a time, and being placed at the conclusion of each of the books they seem to be not so much asides from the real subject matter as the major point of the writing. It is as if, by selecting his symbols and metaphors from the gentlemanly realm of garden design, Knight was trying to introduce his ideas about politics and religion to a genteel audience. Of course the poem is about gardening as well as politics and religion, and when the poem is read today it is usually for the sake of the views about gardening. However, in Knight's mind they were all linked, so that for example the free growth of trees and the free flowing of water became in his imagination enmeshed with the idea of political liberty.[13] The idea that a well-regulated landscape might be taken as indicative of a benign political order was far from new – we find it very explicitly in Alexander Pope's verses on Windsor Forest, for example – but Knight's views were not (like Pope's) a flattering reflection on the current order, but were controversial to the point of being dangerous. They were close to being taken for seditious and had his poem had a more popular audience he might well have been imprisoned, though his views were actually very carefully expressed and were punctiliously defensible.[14]

The religious views expressed in the poem were equally contentious, and fed part of the hostile reaction, particularly enraging the Revd William Mason, Lancelot 'Capability' Brown's executor and one of Horace Walpole's correspondents. Mason was a poet and he had composed the epitaph on Brown's tombstone, that praised him not only as a genius but also as a virtuous 'Christian, Husband, Father, Friend!'[15] None of these epithets applied quite comfortably to Knight. He was certainly not Mason's friend, he was neither a husband nor a father, and he was only a Christian in so far as the law of the land required it of him – his father had been a vicar and as an MP he had to be a member of the Church of England, but his theory of religion made him a pagan by conviction. There are passages in *The Landscape* which are in many ways like passages in Mason's poem *The English Garden*, and Knight was suspected of having plagiarized them, which he denied by saying that he had never read Mason's poem.[16] Although the similarities are undoubtedly there, the verse in these passages is so pedestrian as to be inconclusive as evidence of plagiarism – both authors drawing from a shared reservoir of clichés – but clearly this, coupled with Knight's abuse of the followers of Mason's hero Brown, meant that there was no sympathetic rapport between the two men. After the publication of *The Progress of Civil Society*, when Mason knew *The Landscape* but had seen only the first few lines of the new poem, he wrote to Walpole to say that 'The extract,

Fig. 10.4   Thomas Hearne, Oak Tree, possibly at Downton. *British Museum, Payne Knight Bequest.*

Fig. 10.5   Thomas Hearne, The West End of the Teme Gorge. *Private Collection.*

which I have before me, contains only six lines of his last production, taken from the very first page, which contains so much rash scepticism, if not worse, plainly contending that, in his opinion, none but *learned fools* would *decide* that there was a *God*, that it moved my indignation';[17] and Walpole sympathetically replied that he was 'offended and disgusted by Mr Knight's insolent and self-conceited poem; considering the height he dares to carry his impious attack, it might be sufficient to lump all the rest of his impertinent sallies in one mass of censure as trifling peccadillos'.[18] These responses show that the religious content of Knight's verse did not pass unnoticed and it raised the temperature of the reaction to his work.

The view of Christianity which Knight presented in *The Landscape* was wholly negative. The only explicitly Christian figures in it were medieval bigots – the unhealthy monk and the iconoclastic zealots who were worse than Vandals. If we turn to Knight's positive views about religion they turn out all to be pagan. It is possible for this to go unnoticed in the poem because the imagery of gods and nymphs was so very commonplace in verse of the time and it need not signal any lack of Christian orthodoxy on the part of the writer. However, in Knight's case

Fig. 10.6   Claude Gellée, called le Lorrain, Study of Rocks and Trees. *British Museum, Payne Knight Bequest.*

we know from other works that he took the paganism of ancient Greece and Rome to be an unsuperstitious religion which was pleasing and poetical, and simply involved giving human character to the principles which were at work in nature.[19] Knight thought that the ancients had made the act of sexual intercourse the ultimate basis of their religion through such figures as Venus and Priapus. That fertility should be paramount among these principles might have seemed plausible enough at any time to someone who had a farmer's as well as a gardener's interest in the land, and in the wake of Freud the claims no longer seem outrageous, even to city folk.

Most eighteenth-century poetry, on any subject, now sounds outmoded and contrived, partly because of the classical symbolism which was commonly used. The career of William Wordsworth really began with the publication of *Lyrical Ballads* in 1798. He avoided classicizing motifs in his work and it has endured, though at first his poetry was received as coolly as was Knight's. Wordsworth's poems can still convey his profound and rapturous involvement with the landscape and nature:

> Therefore am I still
> A lover of the meadows and the woods,
> And mountains; and of all that we behold
> From this green earth; of all the mighty world
> Of eye and ear, both what they half-create,
> And what perceive; well pleased to recognize
> In nature and the language of the sense,
> The anchor of my purest thoughts, the nurse,
> The guide, the guardian of my heart, and soul
> Of all my moral being.[20]

Knight worshipped nature as devotedly as Wordsworth but did so through a range of symbols which now seem too lightweight to be convincing: nymphs and

Fig. 10.7   Claude Gellée, called le Lorrain, Landscape with Narcissus and Echo. *National Gallery, London.*

dryads sound too whimsical to do serious duties, but they haunted the dark places in *The Landscape*; and Knight's practical project in gardening seems to have been to restore their presence in the natural landscape. 'The Nymphs,' he said, were the 'emanations of the female productive power of the universe'; and 'Upon the monuments of ancient art, they are usually represented with Fauns and Satyrs, frequently in attitudes very lascivious and indecent; but in the Homeric times, they seem to have been considered as guardian spirits or local deities of the springs, the valleys, and the mountains.'[21] Nymphs are to be found, for example, in Claude's evocative *Landscape with Narcissus and Echo* (fig 10.7) a painting which Knight greatly admired.[22] One nymph (who may be a late introduction into the painting by another hand) is apparently asleep by a pool, failing to attract Narcissus' attention, the others, Echo herself – appropriately doubled – lurks in the bushes, hardly visible, merging harmoniously into the scene. There is no possible haunt for nymphs in the tidy Brownian landscape (fig. 10.1) but abundant hiding in the proposed alternative (fig. 10.2). Knight favoured gardens which were rampant and unchecked, preferring even old formal gardens to those designed by Brown, because although the old gardens had worked against nature, Knight argued that so did Brown's and his unnatural designs were far more extensive.

> kings of yew, and goddesses of lead,
> Could never far their baneful influence spread;
> Coop'd in the garden's safe and narrow bounds,
> They never dared invade the open grounds;
> Where still the roving ox, or browsing deer,
> From such prim despots kept the country clear;
> While uncorrupted still, on every side,
> The ancient forest rose in savage pride;
> And in its native dignity display'd
> Each hanging wood and ever verdant glade;
> Where every shaggy shrub and spreading tree
> Proclaim'd the seat of native liberty . . . (II, 29–40)
>   But ah! how different is the formal lump
> Which the improver plants, and calls a clump!
> Break, break, ye nymphs, the fence that guards it round!
> With browsing cattle, all its forms confound! (II, 51–4)

This is nature-worship in the guise of politics. The old order of kings and goddesses was despotic but not very powerful and the ancient forest retained its sacred mystery. By contrast Brown's gardens threatened the forest and therefore natural forces (personified as nymphs) were justified in rising up to overthrow the despotic oppression, just as the people of America and France had overthrown despotic rule. Knight seditiously roused trees and nymphs to break down fences and to 'spread promiscuous o'er the plains' (III, 2). The voluptuous fertile landscape was to be settled by ancient gods, and Knight's imagery was both religious and erotic.

Fig. 10.8   Cave in the Teme Gorge, Downton. Photograph by Andrew Ballantyne.

> —Ye woodland nymphs, arise,
> And ope your secret haunts to mortal eyes!
> Let my unhallow'd steps your seats invade,
> And penetrate your undiscover'd shade. (III, 9–12)

Knight's landscape was imbued with religious feeling, albeit of a pagan turn. A good Christian who gave full weight to Knight's religious symbolism would have thought it demonic, as William Mason evidently did. In the garden at Downton Knight hollowed out a series of caves in the gorge through which the River Teme ran and arranged a circuit of walks around them. The best of the caves was entered by way of a tunnel cut through the rock – the chamber opens up on one side, very dark indeed, but illuminated from high up by a fissure in the rock, a device which means that the full height of the cavern can be appreciated (fig. 10.8). It is like the type of Greek temple in which Pan was worshipped: caves were set up with shrines to him in ancient Greece, as Knight knew, and moreover, he identified Pan with Priapus, the subject of his early treatise and the root of all religion.[23] There is a painting by Knight's protégé Richard Westall (1765–1836) which shows *The Bower of Pan*, one of the forest's secret haunts, which confirms the potentially erotic character of such places (fig. 10.9). We also find Greek gods at Downton, or in an ancient forest which looks very like it, in paintings which Knight bought from Westall. Knight thought that Richard Westall was among the

Fig. 10.9   Richard Westall, The Bower of Pan. *Manchester City Art Gallery.*

greatest artists of his day, and had him to stay at Downton.[24] This high estimate
of Westall's merit was generally shared by his contemporaries (though there were
dissenting voices) even though it now seems mistaken. Knight owned more
paintings by him than by any other artist, and they included rustic and classical
scenes, including some pictures of Greek gods in rural scenery: a sleeping
Bacchante, Flora, Pomona and Orpheus. They are shown against the background
of ancient forest. While Flora's flowers and Pomona's fruit link them
straightforwardly with their rural settings, Orpheus invites further interpretation
(pl. 19). He is portrayed as a melancholy youth with a soulful expression, playing
a lyre and charming an implausible array of animals with his music: an eagle, a
lion, a tiger, a leopard, a stork, a stag, some squirrels, snakes and brightly coloured
birds are gathered around him harmoniously, anticipating one of Westall's most

widely circulated images, *The Peaceable Kingdom of the Branch* (1813) which became well known in America in Edward Hicks's many versions of it (fig. 10.10).[25] Explaining the origin of the mystical rites of ancient Greece, Knight said that 'General tradition has attributed the introduction of the mystic religion into Greece, to Orpheus, a Thracian; who, if he ever lived at all, lived probably about the same time with Melampus, or a little earlier.'[26] Orpheus therefore was, at least symbolically, the founder of Greek religion and thereby of Greek civilization – a point which can be clarified by turning, as Knight might have done, to Giambattista Vico, who said that 'Orpheus, the founder of Greece, with his lyre or cord or force . . . met his death at the hands of the Bacchantes (the infuriated plebs), who broke his lyre to pieces (the lyre being the law)'.[27] Orpheus taming the animals is seen symbolically as a representation of him civilizing the barbarian population, by binding them in a social contract with the cord of the law, which is stretched and turned into a musical instrument whose harmonies have a similar civilizing effect.[28] Here we find music becoming political, the harmonious relations between sounds finding a counterpart in the unexpectedly sociable relation between the wild beasts: both music and politics are arts of relationships.[29] This is a recurrence of a familiar refrain in Knight's thought, making connections between the benefits of wild nature and the benefits of civil society: Orpheus plays his lyre and conjures an ideal society into being; Westall's paintings show the forest as the haunt of pagan gods, embodying natural principles; Flora shows the sensual beauty of nature, in her body and in the show of richly coloured flowers; Pomona, surrounded by fruit, is emblematic of fertility and is shown in an amorous dalliance with Vertumnus, while Orpheus brings harmony and civilization to the scene.

At the point in his life when he bought these paintings Knight divided his time between his house in Soho Square in London (where he built a gallery and hung Westalls next to paintings which he believed to be by Rembrandt and Raphael to show that modern artists could produce work of a quality to equal the Old Masters) and Stonebrook Cottage, a modest dwelling set among trees on the Downton estate where he worked on his edition of Homer and took long daily walks in the forest feeling himself to be close to nature. An early commission from Thomas Lawrence shows how he imagined Homer's poetry to have been delivered – orally, to a group of listeners who are arranged in various states of undress, at ease in countryside which we should of course take to be Greek but which in fact does not look characteristically Greek (neither the artist nor the patron had been there) and has more of the appearance of the countryside of the west Midlands, from where both the artist and patron came (fig. 10.11). These images have the effect of associating the ancient forest at Downton with Greek culture, just as Knight's poem did by having nymphs and dryads haunt the woods and gods wander among the trees. There is a portrait by Westall of Knight's friend Lady Oxford in forest scenery in the attitude and costume of Psyche from Claude's painting which in Knight's day was known as *The Enchanted Castle* (now in the National Gallery).[30] Another Westall seems to be related to the Lawrence picture of Homer: it shows a bard in natural scenery but the image is unspecific about the location, which looks thoroughly British,

Fig. 10.10   Richard Westall, Peaceable Kingdom of the Branch. *Courtauld Institute of Art, Witt Library.*

despite the Grecian costumes of the bard and his audience (fig. 10.12). William Blake had a vision of Jerusalem in England's green and pleasant land but Knight and the artists he commissioned seem to have been trying to locate Hellas or Attica there.

Knight was enthralled by Homer and ancient Greece and does not seem to have succumbed to the romantic longing to find an indigenous equivalent, as did those who fell for McPherson's *faux-antique* verses written under the name of Ossian. The only indigenous British people known about from ancient sources occur in Roman accounts of Gaul and were the priestly caste of Druids but hardly anything was known of them then, and all that we now know of them as tree-worshipping white-robed figures was invented or inferred from the eighteenth century onwards. Knight's cousin Thomas Johnes (1748–1816) was of an age with Knight and the two were relatively close neighbours when Johnes lived at his family seat, Croft Castle, which, however, he sold. He set up an extraordinarily romantic, if remote, estate at Hafod in Wales where there were raging torrents and mountainous scenery along with calmer pastures and gentler streams. He planted about 3 million trees, making Hafod into a forest set in bleaker surroundings. On a plan of the estate a 'Druid Temple' is shown on one of his hills, which demonstrates a susceptibility to this kind of reverie, and indeed George Cumberland (whose reverie it was) can be found evoking Ossian in his response to the place.[31] But in Knight's work there is only one recognizably Druidic figure – he makes an appearance in Knight's last and least serious book, *Alfred; a romance in rhyme*, a narrative poem set in Anglo–Saxon England. A sage is encountered who has a flowing white beard and is in command of arcane knowledge and he explains a system of reincarnations which is taken from Plato's *Timaeus*.[32] The autochthonous sage turns out to have Greek wisdom. Similarly Knight recounted how the ideal Greek figure of the Apollo Belvedere had reminded Benjamin West, the American-born painter (who became president of the Royal Academy in London), of Mohawk warriors.[33] There is an idea here, related to Rousseau's idea of the noble savage, that the natural uncorrupted man may turn out to be not only the noblest of men but may turn out to be classically Greek.

The ancient forest of Knight's imagination, then, was a sacred space; but Knight's idea of the sacred was not Christian and so his forest was populated with spirits which were (to his mind) authentic spirits of the place, and, as always with Knight, the completely natural state of affairs had a pagan Greek character. Nevertheless, Knight's 'ancient forest' has much in common with Milton's version of the Garden of Eden – the starting point for the development of English landscape design, as we have seen. Knight was not ignorant of Milton, who was, and remains, one of the most admired, revered and conspicuously pious Christian poets. Knight acknowledged his greatness but found his language confused, obscure and inverted.[34] Where Milton advanced a case for non-rhyming poetry, following classical models, Knight (who generally adopted classical models whenever he could) found rhyming couplets more idiomatic in English verse.[35] In Knight's scheme of things Milton fared badly when compared with Homer, and in print he defended Milton in one point only: his characterization of Satan. 'Milton has been censured for making the devil too amiable and interesting a character,' he said, 'but Milton could not have done otherwise, without destroying all the interest of his poem. . . . Throughout the poem, the infernal excite more interest than the celestial personages, because their passions and affections are more violent and energetic.'[36] Knight was acting, as he so often did, as the devil's advocate, saying that even if Satan in fact were not attractive it would be necessary for Milton, on technical literary grounds, so to present him: the attractiveness of Satan would be required because of the effects of rhetoric, not because evil itself were attractive.

In fact we can go further than this and show that Knight was very clearly on the same side as Milton's Satan if we take Milton's Comus as one of Satan's avatars. In Milton's *Maske Presented at Ludlow Castle* in 1634 (Ludlow being the town nearest Downton, about six miles away) the pursuit of pleasure was portrayed as evil and a cult of chastity was promoted. The language which Milton used drew on the ancient rivalry between the Epicureans and the Stoics. Knight subscribed to a version of Epicureanism, the philosophy promoted by Lucretius, which saw happiness to lie in the pursuit of very moderate pleasures but it was portrayed by its opponents, especially the Stoics, as a form of very unphilosophical self-indulgence. Milton's sympathies were entirely Stoic and he

Fig. 10.11   Sir Thomas Lawrence, Homer Reciting his Verses. *Tate Gallery, London.*

sought to reconcile the Stoic virtues of chastity and abstinence with Christianity – that it led him into heresy need not detain us here.[37] The argument of the Ludlow masque answers that of Ben Jonson's *Pleasure Reconcild to Vertue* (1618) which portrayed Comus, the god of revelry, as its hero. Jonson's Comus was introduced to the stage riding in triumph to the song:

> Roome, roome, make roome for yᵉ bouncing belly,
> first father of Sauce, & deuiser of gelly.[38]

Milton portrayed Comus in this way, but instead of following Jonson and showing that virtue might result from pleasurable well-being, Milton's Comus was a character of wanton appetite, and the reckless indulgence of his followers turned them into animals. Milton not only made Comus present his own (Comus') views in the language of Epicurus *as misunderstood by the Stoics,* he also made Comus denigrate those who favoured chastity by calling them Stoics:

Fig. 10.12   Richard Westall, The Bard. *National Trust, Attingham Park.*

> O foolishness of men! that lend their ears
> To those budge doctors of the Stoick fur,
> And fetch their precepts from the Cynick tub,
> Praising the lean and sallow Abstinence.
> Wherefore did Nature powre her bounties forth
> With such a full and unwithdrawing hand,
> Covering the earth with odours, fruits, and flocks,
> Thronging the seas with spawn innumerable,
> But all to please and sate the curious taste?[39]

In *Paradise Lost* Satan's great crime was that he saw no reason why he should be subject to God's rule and so set himself against Him. There is much to be admired in Milton's Satan; he had, after all, been an angel – albeit one who had forgotten where he owed his loyalty. Milton chose to diabolize human reason, reason unguided by God, which was precisely the type of reason which found favour with

*Fig. 10.13   Richard
Westall,* Comus. *Courtauld
Institute of Art, Witt
Library.*

Knight, who, like many another intellectual inspired by Enlightenment ideas,
would have identified with the villains in both *Paradise Lost* and *Comus*. Whereas
Milton saw the pursuit of pleasure as an evil, and sensuality as the characteristic
trait of the fallen, Knight saw in it the very point of existence.[40]

'Milton is said,' said Sir George Cumberland, 'to have planned his *Comus* in
the wooded valley at Downton',[41] but by whom it was said he left unclear. It is
most likely that the story was started by Knight, who was the first educated
person to live there and who could imaginatively have populated his gorge with
Comus and his followers, feeling them as a benign presence there. In Westall's
illustrations for the masque a predatory Pan-like Comus lurks in the forest's
secret places (fig. 10.13) and acts as the exact anti-type of Westall's Orpheus: one
civilized the animals, the other brought out the bestial in men. A comparison of
the images (pl. 19 and fig. 10.13) can be made by seeing the pale, vulnerable figure
in each to be set against the threatening forces of the ancient forest, held in

abeyance for the time being. The maiden in the forest substitutes for Orpheus, and Comus substitutes for the wild animals. A line stretches between these two tendencies and one can travel along it in either direction: either becoming animal, or becoming human; becoming barbaric, or becoming civilized; becoming instinctive, or becoming rational. If Knight imagined Comus' followers running wild in his woods, then he imagined Orpheus bringing them under control again, restoring harmonious relations through the influence of music. The monkish chastity which Milton's masque advocated would have been anathema to Knight, whereas Comus and his band would have seemed healthily in touch with their instincts.

If we now look back again at the contrasting illustrations for *The Landscape*, we can see that the overgrown picturesque landscape includes great thickets with shadows and hiding places which the nymphs and dryads can haunt, whereas the controlled clumps and spaced planting of the Brown-inspired landscape has no secrets. The political content of Knight's poem made it a sensation in its day but the more enduring aspect of the work is Knight's attempt to reinvest the landscape with a sense of the spiritual. His proposals for the reform of landscape design and his own garden at Downton show that he could manage this but his poetry let him down. Wordsworth managed to inspire not only his contemporaries but generations since then with a sense of the sublimity of the scenery of the Lake District and the heroism involved in the everyday lives of the people who lived there. If Knight did not have Wordsworth's genius, then his poetry need not be condemned as completely as it has been, because on such a scale of judgement very few indeed would not stand condemned.[42] If we take Knight's symbolism seriously and treat his verse indulgently, then we can begin to see what it was that he said and be moved by it. The ancient forest was for Knight a sacred space in which to commune with nature and be restored to a state of primitive grace; it is unfortunate for his lasting reputation that the language he chose – the language of polite accomplishment in his day – should now look like a rather ludicrous pagan fancy dress. However, as so often when we look at the past, we must learn the language, which is more carefully modulated than at first it might appear, if we are not to lose what is of value in Knight's thought.

Notes

Preface

1. This study focuses on the period 1700–1840 but not to the exclusion of material on either side of these dates. The terms 'Georgian' and the 'long eighteenth century' are used interchangeably to describe this period.
2. For a fuller discussion of this point see D. Arnold, 'Wittgenstein and the Country House', *Society of Architectural Historians GB Newsletter*, 58 (1996).
3. Arnold, 'Wittgenstein'.

Chapter 1

1. These include J. Summerson, *Architecture in Britain 1530–1830*, Pelican History of Art (Harmondsworth, many editions, firs published 1953), M. Girouard, *Life in the English Country House* (New Haven and London, Yale University Press, 1978), James Lees Milne, *Earls of Creation* (London, Century Classics, 1986) and C. Hussey, *The English Country House: Georgian*, vols 1–3 (Woodbridge, Antique Collectors' Club, 1984–5). For a fuller résumé of texts which chronicle the architectural developments of the country house see Bibliography pp. 205–6.
2. Six noble houses and the Deputy Ranger's Lodge in Green Park were illustrated by Adam. Only three of these were country houses: Syon, Kenwood and Luton Hoo.
3. For a full discussion of Adam at Kedleston see L. Harris Gervase Jackson-Stops, *Robert Adam and Kedleston: The Making of a Neoclassical Masterpiece* (London, National Trust, 1987)
4. Paine's role at Kedleston and his relationship with Adam is discussed in C. Webster 'Architectural illustration as revenge: James Paine's designs for Kedleston' in *The Image of the Building:*

Papers from the Annual Symposium of the Society of Architectural Historians of Great Britain, 1995, M Howard (ed.) (London, Society of Architectural Historians, 1996) pp. 83–92 and P. Leach, *James Paine* (London, Zwemmer, 1988) and 'James Paine's design for the south front at Kedleston Hall', *Architectural History*, 40 (1997) pp. 159–70.

5. Richardson went on to exhibit one of his designs 'The Ceiling executed in the Grecian Hall at Keddlestone' at the Royal Academy in 1776.
6. For instance, work had been carried out on the west side of the house, including the gallery, by Sir Francis Child before his death in 1761. For a fuller discussion of Osterley see J. Hardy and M. Tomlin, *Osterley Park House* (London, Victoria & Albert Museum, 1985).
7. Wanstead was demolished in 1824.
8. Campbell produced three designs for Wanstead. The first two are illustrated in *Vitruvius Britannicus*, vol. I plates 21–6 and the second design was more or less that executed. The third design showing unexecuted additions appears in vol. III plates 39–41. Gibbs' involvement is discussed by J. Harris, 'Who Designed Houghton?', *Country Life*, (2 March 1989).
9. Burlington's activities at Londesborough are discussed by L. Boynton, 'Lord Burlington at Home' in D. Arnold (ed.), *Belov'd by Evr'y Muse: Richard Boyle 3rd Earl of Burlington and 4th Earl of Cork (1694–1753)* (London, The Georgian Group, 1994), pp. 21–8.
10. According to Matthew Brettingham the younger, 'The general ideas . . . were first struck out by the Earls of Burlington and Leicester, assisted by Mr William Kent.' *The Plans and Elevations of the late Earl of Leicester's House at Holkham*, 2nd edn (1773).

Burlington and Coke are also identified with designs for chimney stacks at Coleshill House, Berkshire. H. Colvin, *A Biographical Dictionary of British Architects, 1600–1840* 3rd edn, (New Haven and London, Yale University Press 1995), pp. 151.

11. On this point see L. Schmidt, 'Holkham Hall', *Country Life*, (24 and 31 January 1980), 214–17 and 298–301 and more recently C. Hiskey, 'The Building of Holkham Hall: Newly Discovered Letters', *Architectural History*, 40 (1997), 144–58.

12. See C. Saumarez Smith, *The Building of Castle Howard* (London, Faber, 1990).

13. These historical questions are discussed in F. Braudel, *Écrits sur L'Histoire* (Paris, Flammarion, 1969), part II, pp. 41–238.

14. For a detailed discussion of the relationship between style and class ideology see N. Hadjinicolao, *Art History and Class Struggle*.

15. Part four, chapter 21, 'The Individual Contribution of James Gibbs'.

16. Summerson, *Architecture in Britain* (1977 edn), p. 403.

17. For a discussion of the nature of the architectural profession at this time see S. Kostoff (ed.), *The Architect: Chapters in the History of the Profession*, and Colvin *Biographical Dictionary of British Architects*, pp. 29–45.

18. '. . . the whole output of English building [from the period 1710–50], has long ago become labelled "Palladian", a description not wholly accurate (as no such labels can be), but accurate enough and secure in acceptance.' Summerson, *Architecture in Britain*, p. 317.

19. Summerson, *Architecture in Britain* (1977 edn), p. 320.

20. For a fuller discussion of trends in the writing of architectural history see D. Watkin, *The Rise of Architectural History* (London, The Architectural Press, 1980).

21. For instance, brief sections on 'Palladianism in Scotland' and 'Palladianism in Ireland' appear in Summerson, *Architecture in Britain* (1977 edn), pp. 376–80.

22. For a fuller discussion of the work of William Adam see J. Gifford, *William Adam* (Edinburgh, Edinburgh University Press, 1989) and *Architectural Heritage*, i.

23. H. Walpole, *Journals of Visits to Country Seats &c*, ed. P. Toynbee, The Walpole Society, vol. XVI (1928), p. 41

24. On this point see Summerson, *Architecture in Britain*, part 4, chapter 20, p. 317 and R. Wittkower, *Palladio and English Palladianism* (London, Thames & Hudson, 1974).

25. *Essay on Design*, 1712.

26. Campbell, *Vitruvius Britannicus* (1717), vol. I, introduction. Mr Wren is not listed in Colvin, *Biographical Dictionary of British Architects*.

27. Jean Bernard le Blanc (1706–81), known as Abbé le Blanc, was appointed Historiographer of the King's Buildings in 1749 after his anti-rococo views brought him to the attention of Mme de Pompadour. He travelled to Italy with Soufflot and C.N. Cochin and shortly after published letters as Jean Bernard le Blanc, *Lettres de Monsieur l'Abbé le Blanc concernant le gouvernment, la politique et les moeurs des Anglois et des François* (Paris, 1747, translations published the same year in London and Dublin). This extract is from a letter to the noted antiquarian and collector le Comte de Caylus (1692–1765).

28. The historical background to British imperialism and mercantilism, which underpinned the choice of Augustan Rome as an imperialistic and cultural model, is discussed in C. Hill, *The Century of Revolution, 1603–1714* (London, Oxford University Press, 1966) and W. Speck, *Stability and Strife in England, 1714–1760* (Cambridge, Mass., Harvard University Press, 1977).

29. Alongside the obvious examples of Chiswick Villa and Mereworth, Nostell Priory was based on Villa Mocenigo and other Palladian villas. See Leach, *James Paine*, p. 29. Moreover, it has been argued that Lord Burlington quickly moved away from Palladio to other expressions of classical form. On this point see J. Harris 'Lord Burlington The Modern Vitruvius' in D. Arnold (ed.) *The Georgian Villa* (Stroud, Sutton Publishing, 1996) and C. Sicca, 'The Architecture of the Wall: Astylism in the Architecture of Lord Burlington', *Architectural History*, 33 (1990).

30. A useful discussion of the writings of Alexander Pope in this context can be found in L. Brown, *Alexander Pope*, (Oxford and New York, Blackwell, 1985).

31. C. Anne Wilson, *The Country House Kitchen Garden* (Stroud, Sutton Publishing, 1998).

32. E.P. Thompson, 'Patrician Society, Plebeian Culture', *Journal of Social History*, vol. 7, no. 4 (summer 1974), pp. 382–405.

33. I follow Thompson's 'Patrician Society' argument, in these paragraphs.

34. R. Williams, *Marxism and Literature* (Oxford, Oxford University Press, 1978), p. 112.

35. See H. Clemenson in *English Country Houses and Landed Estates*, (London, Croom, Helm, 1982) chapter 1 especially. Clemenson discusses the problem of identifying different land owning groups. See also G.E. Mingay, 'The Size of Farms in the Eighteenth Century', *Economic History Review*, 2nd series, vol. XIV, no. 3 (1962), 469–88 and F.M.L. Thompson, 'The Social Distribution of Landed Property in England since the sixteenth century', *Economic History Review*, 2nd series, vol. XIX, no. 3 (December 1966), 505–17. This question is discussed more fully in Chapter 9, 'Living off the Land'.

36. British Parliamentary Papers, LXXII (1875).

37. Mingay, 'Farms in the Eighteenth Century'.

38. *Spectator* (4 March 1876).

39. C.B. Macpherson (ed.), *Property: mainstream and critical positions* (Toronto, University of Toronto Press, 1978), p. 8.

40. C. Fabricant, 'The Literature of Domestic Tourism and the Public Consumption of Private Property' in F. Nussbaum and L. Brown (eds), *The New Eighteenth Century: Theory, Politics and English Literature* (New York and London, Methuen, 1987), p. 261.

41. On this point see N. Mackendrick, J. Brewer and J.H. Plumb, *The Birth of a Consumer Society: The Commercialization of Eighteenth-century England* (London, Europa, 1982).

Chapter 2

1. This phrase is used by C. Fabricant, 'The Literature of Domestic Tourism', pp. 254–75.

2. Of particular note here are E. Moir, *The Discovery of Britain: The English Tourists 1540–1840*, (London, Routledge, 1964) and A. Tinniswood, *A History of Country House Visiting* (Oxford and London, Blackwell and The National Trust, 1989).

3. C. Morris (ed.), *The Illustrated Journeys of Celia Fiennes 1685–c. 1712*, (London, Macdonald, 1982).

4. For instance as an abridged version D. Defoe, *A Tour Through the Whole Island of Great Britain* (Harmondsworth, Penguin, 1971 and 1986) and many editions of the complete volumes.

5. Domestic tourism and its social and political significance are both discussed by L. Colley in *Britons: Forging the nation 1707–1837* (New Haven and London, Yale University Press, 1992).

6. Moir, *The Discovery of Britain*.

7. D. MacCannell, *The Tourist: A New Theory of the Leisure Class* (New York, Schocken, 1976), p. 14.

8. See Girouard, *Life in the English Country House*, pp. 189–90 especially.

9. See D. Solkin, *Richard Wilson: The Landscape of Reaction* (London, Tate Gallery, 1982), pp. 103–5 especially.

10. As quoted in P. Langford, *Public Life and the Propertied Englishman 1689–1798* (Oxford, Clarendon Press, 1991), pp. 378–9.

11. I am very grateful to Dr Mary Cosh who kindly brought the writings of Byrd, Silliman and Colman to my attention.

12. William Byrd of Virginia, *The London Diary 1717–1721 and other writings*, (ed.) L.B. Wright and M. Tinling, (New York, Oxford University Press, 1958).

13. Byrd, London Diary, 30 May 1718.

14. B. Silliman, *Journal of Travels in England, Holland and Scotland and of two passages over the Atlantic in the years 1805–1806*, (3 vols, New Haven, Yale College, 1820). Silliman was more interested in topography but makes some interesting comments about the country house.

15. Ibid., vol. II, pp. 217

16. H. Colman, *European Life and Manners in Familiar Letters to Friends* (2 vols, Boston and London, 1850)

17. Ibid., Letter X, 16 June 1843.

18. Ibid.

19. *A Regency Visitor: The English Tour of Prince Pückler-Muskau Described in his Letters 1826–28* ed. E.M. Butler, (London, Collins, 1957), p. 61.

20. le Blanc, *Lettres*.

21. See J. Harris, 'English Country House Guides 1740–1840', in J. Summerson (ed.) *Concerning Architecture*, (London, Allen Lane, 1968), pp. 63–74.

22. Byrd, *London Diary*, 30 July 1718.

23. A. Young, *A Six Month Tour through the North of England*, (4 vols, London, 1770), vol. II p. 186.

24. Walpole, *Journals*.
25. Ibid., p. 41.
26. Ibid., p. 64.
27. Ibid., p. 54. Boughton was owned by the Dukes of Montagu.
28. Dr G. Waagen, *Treasures of Art in Great Britain*, 3 vols (London, John Murray, 1854, reprinted Cornmarket Press, London, 1970). Gustav Friedrich Waagen was the Director of the Royal Gallery of Pictures in Berlin.
29. Ibid., p. 336.
30. Ibid., p. 337.
31. Ibid., p. 334.
32. Ibid., p. 337.
33. H. Walpole, *Correspondence*, ed. W.S. Lewis, (42 vols, Oxford, Oxford University Press, 1937), vol. XXV, p. 423.
34. Ibid., vol. XII, pp. 219–20.
35. *The Torrington Diaries, containing A Tour Through England and Wales by the Honourable John Byng Later Fifth Viscount Torrington between the years 1781–1794*, ed. C. Bruyn Andrews, (4 vols, London, Eyre and Spottiswoode, 1934), vol. I, p. 237.
36. Colman, *European Life and Manners*, Letter LVIII, 11 May 1844.
37. For a discussion of the debates around the terms of admission and the social relationships between landowner and tourist in the latter part of the century see also Chapter 4.
38. For a full discussion of Stourhead see K. Woodbridge, *Landscape and Antiquity: Aspects of English Culture at Stourhead 1718–1838* (Oxford, Oxford University Press, 1970).
39. See L. Whistler et al, *Stowe: a Guide to the Gardens* (1968).
40. Henry Flitcroft had also designed a similar tower at Wentworth Woodhouse some years earlier in 1748.
41. For a fuller discussion of the significance of landscape see T. Williamson, *Polite Landscapes* (Stroud, Sutton Publishing, 1994).
42. On this point see M. Andrews, *The Search for the Picturesque* (Aldershot, Scolar, 1989) and M. Andrews, 'A Picturesque Template: The Tourists and their Guidebooks' in D. Arnold (ed.), *The Picturesque in late Georgian England*, Proceedings of the 1994 Georgian Group Symposium (London, The Georgian Group, 1995), pp. 3–9.
43. Of particular interest here are the writings of William Stukeley.
44. An excellent list of these appears as an appendix in Moir, *Discovery of Britain*.
45. A concise bibliography of guides to country houses, with some catalogues of collections, appears at the end of Harris, 'Country House Guides'.
46. Young's writings are discussed in chapter 4 and chapter 9. For a fuller discussion of Defoe see T.S. Ashton, *Economic History of England in the Eighteenth Century* (London, Methuen, 1955), pp. 32–3.
47. Further texts of relevance can be found in 'Travel and Topography in C18 England. A bibliography of sources for Economic Historians', *Transactions of the Bibliographic Society*, (2nd series, 1930), pp. 84–103. Also, a select bibliography of manuscript and published tours of Britain in the latter half of the eighteenth century appears in Andrews, *Search for the Picturesque*.
48. *Torrington Diaries*, vol. I, p. 47.
49. The relationship between literature, morality and aesthetics is discussed with references to Jane Austen's attitudes towards the country house and its occupants in Chapter 8.
50. See Harris, 'Country House Guides' for a fuller discussion of the tradition of representing the country house in its landscape setting.
51. An overview of the evolution of portraits of country houses including views of their landscape is given in J. Harris, *The Artist and the Country House* (London, Sotheby Parke Burnet, 1979). The significance of the representation of the landscapes is discussed in D. Solkin, *Richard Wilson*, (London, Tate Gallery, 1982).
52. Inigo Jones's annotated copy of *I Quattro Libri* is at Worcester College, Oxford, Lord Burlington's is held at the Chatsworth archive and Robert Adam's is at the Sir John Soane's Museum.
53. See E. Harris and N. Savage, *Architectural Books and Writers 1556–1795*, (Cambridge, Cambridge University Press, 1990), pp. 496–8 especially.
54. Ibid., pp. 387–90.
55. Volume III does contain some views with a landscape setting. This is discussed in chapter 3.
56. le Blanc, *Lettres*.
57. These are discussed in S. Blutman, 'Books of designs for country houses, 1780-1815', *Architectural History*, 11 (1968), 25–32.

58. A more general survey of architecture books 1790 to 1835 and the influence of new techniques of production and aesthetic taste appears in M. McMordie, 'Picturesque pattern books and pre-Victorian designers', *Architectural History*, 18 (1975), 43–59.

Chapter 3

1. Harris, *Artist and the Country House*, discussed some prints but concentrated on paintings. His interpretation was hampered by the lack of reliable catalogues and he was sometimes misled by dates on prints that were dates of republication rather than first publication (for instance, the prints listed under Thomas Smith on p. 248 are nearly all dated twenty years or more too late). D. Watkin's statement that few prints appeared between 1740 and 1780 (*The English Vision*, 1979, p. 31) is also misleading. Prints were barely mentioned by Tinniswood, *Country House Visiting*, I. Ousby, *The Englishman's England: Taste, Travel and the Rise of Tourism* (Cambridge, Cambridge University Press, 1990), Girouard, *English Country House*, D. Jacques, *Georgian Gardens: the Reign of Nature* (London, Batsford, 1983) or Williamson, *Polite Landscapes*, all of whom, conventionally enough, use literary sources without considering the potential influence of printed pictorial material.

2. P. Monier, *The History of Painting, Architecture, Sculpture, Graving*, translation (London, 1699), p. 182.

3. Williamson, *Polite Landscapes*, p. 18.

4. For an introduction see Harris, *Artist and the Country House*, pp. 3–7. Falda's *Li Giardini di Roma* is usually dated 1683 but was first listed in G.G. de Rossi's 1676 catalogue. On Dutch gardens see J. Dixon Hunt and E. de Jong (eds), 'The Anglo-Dutch Garden in the Age of William and Mary', *Journal of Garden History*, VIII, nos 2 and 3 (1988) and D. Jacques and A.J. van der Horst, *The Gardens of William and Mary* (Chelmsford, Batsford, 1988).

5. Switzer, for instance, wished to surpass 'France our great Competitor' and 'to excel the so-much boasted Gardens of France' (*Ichonographia Rustica*, p. 274; see James Turner, 'Stephen Switzer and the Political Fallacy in Landscape Gardening History', *Eighteenth-Century Studies*, XI (1978), 489–96 and Williamson, *Polite Landscapes*, p. 50).

6. Harris, *British Architectural Books*, pp. 144–5. About the same time Robert Thacker drew and published a series of views of Longford House (Harris, *Artist and the Country House*, p. 104).

7. Joseph Smith in his preface to *Ecclesiarum Angliae et Valliae Prospectus* (1719).

8. Harris, *Artist and the Country House*, p. 103, illustrates the advertisement together with other views etched by Winstanley. See also A. Griffiths, *The Print in Stuart Britain 1603–1688* (London, British Museum Press, 1998), pp. 245, 149–51.

9. See J. Harris and G. Jackson-Stops (eds), *Britannia Illustrata* (Bungay, National Trust, 1984), pp. 5–8; Harris, *British Architectural Books*, pp. 140 and 145; T. Clayton, *The English Print 1688–1802* (London and New Haven, Yale University Press, 1997), pp. 52–4, 75–6.

10. Clarke Print Collection, Worcester College, Oxford. Salisbury was visiting Oxford for his installation as Chancellor.

11. These vary in content. In the Bodleian Library, Oxford, a volume dated 1717 has seventy-three plates with sixty-four of country houses. A 1724 edition contains seventy plates with views of Oxford colleges and others removed and further houses added.

12. See Harris, *British Architectural Books*, pp. 139–46. The dedications to Tories give offices that were held only until early 1715. The Jones designs are dedicated to Tories including George Clarke. Two of the leading figures at Oxford University, William Lancaster and George Clarke, were dedicatees and Harris possibly underestimates the influence of the University's building programme.

13. Ibid., p. 145 n. 27.

14. Ibid., pp. 496–8.

15. Proposals in Richard Gough's collection, Bodleian Library, Oxford, Gough Gen. Top. Collinson conditions p. 3; Shaw p. 2; Suffolk 365, pp. 186–7.

16. Proposal in Richard Gough's collection, Bodleian Library, Oxford, Gough Gen. Top. 363, f. 126.

17. See Clayton, *The English Print*, pp. 73–4. Bernard Baron published *The Pembroke Family* (*London Evening Post*, 18 March 1740) and *The Earl of Carnarvon*. For reviews of later publications of paintings at

Wilton see *Neue Bibliothek der schönen Wissenschaften und der freyen Künste*, VI (1768), 160; XXXIII (1787), p. 154.

18. *Spectator*, 17 March 1711; there is an incomplete set at Worcester College, Oxford.

19. 'At last I have seen Stowe . . . this little modern miracle and the most enchanted place in all England! Not a single traveller, however lacking in connoisseurship and curiosity, comes to London without seeing Blenheim and, above all, Stowe, as being the most brilliant and magnificent sights that this country can show' . . . 'one must see this enchanted place in order to judge it' from *Les Charmes de Stow* (1748), p. 5, reprinted in G.B. Clarke (ed.), *Descriptions of Lord Cobham's Gardens at Stowe (1700–1750)*, Buckinghamshire Record Society no. 26 (1990), p. 159. J.B. Naudin, *Plan General des Ville et Château de Versailles*, published by Nicolas Langlois (Worcester College, Oxford, Clarke Print Collection, vol. 60, no. 113).

20. *General Advertiser*, 22 February 1746; reissue: *General Advertiser*, 22 April 1752.

21. *London Evening Post*, 25 August; *General Advertiser*, 28 September 1750; *Public Advertiser*, 11 May 1753; Bickham's *A List of Books, Prints, Metzotinto, &c.*, includes no. 11, 'Six new Views of the above Gardens larger' at 1 guinea. This catalogue lists guides to Blenheim and Ditchley and to Kensington, Hampton Court and Windsor as well as *The Beauties of Stowe* (5s), 'Stowe, a Poem, with a Description of the House' (1s 6d) and 'A Head of the late Lord Cobham'. *Public Advertiser*, 17 March 1759.

22. See Clayton, *The English Print*, pp. 155–6.

23. For further detail and discussion of the pictures at Foots Cray see Clayton, *The English Print*, pp. 163–7.

24. The house itself had been included in *Vitruvius Britannicus*. Published paintings included Poussin's *Judgement of Hercules*, a Claude, two Rembrandts and a Kauffman (for reviews see *Bibliothek der schönen Wissenschaften und der freyen Künste*, V (1759), 185; *Neue Bibliothek*, VII (1768), 372; XVI (1774), 146; XVIII (1775), 167; XXXI (1785), 339).

25. *Morning Chronicle*, 5 June 1772.

26. Printed leaflets sent by Watts to Richard Gough in Bodleian Library, Oxford, Gough Maps 178.

27. Harris, *Artist and the Country House*, p. 282.

28. *The World*, 9 January 1787. Bodleian Library, Oxford, Gough Gen. Top. 363, f. 146. Stephen Clarke, whose conversation and notes have guided me through these sets and others I have not had space to describe, owns a volume with sixty-three plates, the last of which is dated 1815.

29. *An Alphabetical catalogue of Plates . . . which compose the stock of John and Josiah Boydell*, (London, 1803), p. v. The hundred large plates of the Shakespeare Gallery cost £63 but most of these were in the cheaper medium of stipple.

30. Tinniswood, *Country House Visiting*, p. 89. He notes that about 300 people visited Strawberry Hill each year between May and September.

31. *Public Advertiser*, 5 June 1755.

32. Girouard, *Life in the English Country House*, p. 217.

33. On deer see Williamson, *Polite Landscapes*, pp. 93–4 and 119–30; Girouard, *Life in the English Country House*, p. 217.

34. Francis Norton Mason, *John Norton & Sons: Merchants of London and Virginia* (Newton Abbot, 1937), p. 249.

35. *London Evening Post*, 26 May 1747.

Chapter 4

1. For an impressive survey of socio-economic pressures in the creation of the landscape garden, see Williamson, *Polite Landscapes*. Williamson largely avoids the polite literature with which the present chapter is concerned.

2. John Barrell, *The Political Theory of Painting from Reynolds to Hazlitt* (London, Yale University Press, 1986).

3. Notably, see J. Dixon Hunt, 'Emblem and Expressionism in the Eighteenth-Century Landscape Garden', *Eighteenth Century Studies*, 3 (1971), pp. 294–317, and '"Ut Pictura Poesis, Ut Pictura Hortus", and the Picturesque', *Word and Image*, 1 (1985), pp. 87–107; and Ronald Paulson, *Emblem and Expression; meaning in English art of the eighteenth century* (London, Thames and Hudson, 1975); the implications of this argument are also explored in Solkin, *Richard Wilson: the landscape of Reaction*

(London, Tate Gallery, 1982), John Barrell, 'The public figure and the private eye: William Collins' "Ode to Evening"', in *Teaching the Text*, ed. Susanne Kappeler and Norman Bryson (London, Routledge, 1983), pp. 1–17 and Ann Bermingham, *Landscape and Ideology: The English Rustic Tradition, 1740–1860* (London, California University Press, 1987).

4. Notably, see Williamson, *Polite Landscapes*; and Edward Harwood, 'Personal Identity and the Eighteenth-Century Garden', *Journal of Garden History*, 13:1 and 2 (1993), 36–48.

5. Harwood, 'Personal Identity', p. 43.

6. For an impressive analysis of such ways of seeing, see Peter de Bolla, 'The charm'd eye' in Veronica Kelly and Dorothea E. Von Mücke (ed.). *Body and Text in the Eighteenth Century*, (Stanford, Stanford, University Press, 1994), pp. 89–111.

7. Important work concentrating on the earlier century has been seeking to complicate Barrell's model, but the basic narrative outline is still largely accepted. For a summary, see Stephen Copley's discussion of the debate in 'The Fine Arts in Eighteenth-Century Polite Culture', in John Barrell ed. *Painting and the Politics of Culture: New Essays on British Art 1700–1850* (Oxford, Oxford University Press, 1992), pp. 13–37.

8. Edward Daniel Clarke, *A Tour through the South of England, Wales, and part of Ireland, made during the Summer of 1791* (London, 1793).

9. Paul Langford, *A Polite and Commercial People: England 1727–1783* (Oxford, Oxford University Press, 1992), p. 71. For other recent discussion of polite culture early in the century, see also Copley, 'The Fine Arts', Michael G. Ketcham, *Transparent Designs: Reading, Performance and Form in the Spectator Papers* (Athens, Georgia, University of Georgia Press, 1985), and Lawrence Klein, *The Rise of Politeness in England, 1660–1715* (Ann Arbor, Michigan, 1985).

10. In particular see G.J. Barker-Benfield, *The Culture of Sensibility: Sex and Society in Eighteenth-Century Britain* (Chicago, Chicago University Press, 1992); John Mullan, *Sentiment and Sociability: The Language of Feeling in the Eighteenth Century* (Oxford, Clarendon Press, 1988);

and Ann Jessie Van Sant, *Eighteenth-Century Sensibility and the Novel: The Senses in a Social Context* (Cambridge, Cambridge University Press, 1993).

11. Ann Bermingham, 'The Picturesque and ready-to-wear femininity' in Stephen Copley and Peter Garside ed. *The Politics of the Picturesque: Literature, landscape and aesthetics since 1770* (Cambridge, Cambridge University Press, 1994), pp. 81–119 (p. 87).

12. Huntington Library MS, ST vol. 359. The diary entry begins 8 September 1791. Lady Anne (Grenville) Hadaway, 'Travel & Tour Guide for England' (incomplete), 1791.

13. *The Original New Bath Guide; or, Useful Pocket Companion . . .* (Bath, 1804).

14. Bodleian Library, MS.Eng. misc.180(1), f. 11; and MS.Eng. misc. f. 179(2) 'Particular Parts. Hagley & Leasowes', ff. 44–54.

15. *Selected Letters between the late Duchess of Somerset, Lady Luxborough, Mr. Whistler, Miss Dolman, Mr. R. Dodsley, William Shenstone, Esq. and others; including a Sketch of the Manners, Laws, &c. of the Republic of Venice, and some Poetical Pieces; the whole now first published from Original Copies, By Mr. Hull* (2 vols, London 1778), pp. 285–93.

16. Elizabeth A. Bohls in her *Women Travel Writers and the Language of Aesthetics, 1716–1818* (Cambridge, Cambridge University Press, 1995), has recently argued for a female aesthetic set in opposition to what she terms the 'mainstream' masculine aesthetic of disinterestedness. However, confidence in the influence of this 'mainstream' masculine aesthetic becomes extremely difficult to maintain in the context of the vast and socially varied output of polite travel writing in the period.

17. Dodsley to Shenstone, 12 October 1759, *Selected Letters between the late Duchess of Somerset . . .*, pp. 265–7.

18. *Journal of a Three Week Tour, in 1797, Through Derbyshire to the Lakes. By a Gentleman of the University of Oxford*, vol. 5 in William Mavor (ed.) *The British Tourist; or Traveller's Pocket Companion, through England, Wales, Scotland, and Ireland. Comprehending the most celebrated Tours in the British Islands*, ed. William Mavor 6 vols, London, (1798–1800).

19. *The Autobiography of Arthur Young with selections from his correspondence*, ed. M. Betham-Edwards (London, 1898). For Young's life see also John G. Gazley, *The Life of Arthur Young, 1741–1820*, Memoirs of the American Philosophical Society, vol. 97 (Philadelphia, 1973).

20. See Langford, who points to the appearance of the term 'gentleman farmer', a term which 'had come into being to describe a new breed of tenants whose wealth made them genteel, but who lacked the proprietorial standing of the squirearchy. It had exactly the ambiguity to match the pretensions of the former with the condescension of the latter', *Public Life and the Propertied Englishman* (Oxford, Clarendon Press, 1991), p. 560.
    Here I am at odds with Beth Fowkes Tobin's account of Young. In her desire to create of Young a 'new economic man' in opposition to aristocratic masculinity, Tobin places him together with the likes of William Marshall, ignores his claims to gentry status, and takes little account of the polite context in which his tours are written. See Beth Fowkes Tobin, 'Arthur Young, Agriculture, and the Construction of the New Economic Man' in Beth Fowkes Tobin (ed.), *History, Gender and Eighteenth-Century Literature* (Athens, Georgia, University of Georgia, 1994), pp. 179–97.

21. Arthur Young, *A Six Week Tour, through the Southern Counties of England and Wales* . . . (London, 1768), pp. 130–45.

22. *Six Week Tour*, Young, pp. 6–7.

23. *Six Week Tour*, Young, p. 197.

24. See especially, Henry Home, Lord Kames, *Elements of Criticism* (2 vols, Edinburgh, 1762).

25. Young, *Southern Tour*, pp. 131–2.

26. Ibid., pp. 139–40, my emphasis.

27. Young, *Northern Tour*, vol. III, pp. 355–6

28. For the rival gardening programmes at the two estates see Michael Charlesworth, 'Elevation and Succession: The representation of Jacobite and Hanoverian politics in the landscape gardens of Wentworth Castle and Wentworth Woodhouse', *New Arcadian Journal*, 31/32 (summer/autumn 1991), pp. 7–65.

29. Young, *Northern Tour*, vol. 1, 147–8.

30. Young, *Southern Tour*, pp. 96–7.

31. Arthur Young, *Travels, during the Years 1787, 1788, and 1789. Undertaken more particularly with a View of ascertaining the Cultivation, Wealth, Resources, and National Prosperity, of the Kingdom of France* (2 vols, Bury St Edmund's, 1792), vol. 1, p. 189.

32. Ibid., pp. 107–8.

Chapter 5

1. See for instance T. Lummis and J. Marsh, *A Woman's Domaine* (London, Viking 1990)and R. Parker, *The Subversive Stitch* (London, Women's Press, 1984).

2. Here the study of architectural history and the country house *per se* lags behind other disciplines. The role and import-ance of women has featured prominently, for instance, in the scholarship con-cerning art history and cultural studies. See, for instance, G. Pollock and R. Parker, *Old Mistresses* (London, Routledge, 1984)

3. See M.W. McCahill, 'Peerage creations and the changing character of the British nobility 1750–1830', *English Historical Review*, 96 (1981, 259–84.

4. For a more general discussion see D. Large, 'The Wealth of the greater Irish landowners, 1750–1815', *Irish Historical Studies*, XV (1966).

5. On this point see Boynton, 'Lord Burlington at Home' in Arnold (ed.), *Belov'd by Ev'ry Muse*, p. 21 especially.

6. See Clemenson, *English Country House*, pp. 7–31 and more specifically, H.J. Habakkuk, 'Marriage and Ownership of Land' in R.R. Davies et al. (eds), *Welsh Society and nationhood: Historical essays presented to Glamor Williams*, (Cardiff, University of Wales Press, 1984). See also n. 9.

7. E. Burke, *Reflections on the Revolution in France*, (ed.) C.C. O'Brien (Harmondsworth, Penguin, 1968), pp. 194–5.

8. On this point see my essay, 'It's a wonderful life, Richard Boyle 3rd Earl of Burlington and 4th Earl of Cork (1694–1753)' in Arnold (ed.) *Belov'd by Ev'ry Muse*, p. 13 especially.

9. For a fuller discussion of the Lascelles family and their Yorkshire estate see M. Mauchline, *Harewood House* 2nd edn, (Ashbourne, Moreland Publishing, 1992), chapter 1, pp. 7–41.

10. On this point see *inter alia* H.J. Habakkuk, 'Marriage settlements in the Eighteenth century', *Transactions of the Royal Historical Society*, 4th series, 32 (1950), 15–30 and L. Bonfield, 'Marriage Settlements and the "Rise of the Great Estates": the demographic aspect', *Economic History Review*, 2nd series, 32 (1979), 483–93.

11. On this point see J.B. Burke, *The Rise of Great Families*, 2nd edn, (London, Longman, 1873).

12. On the issues raised here see Parker, *Subversive Stitch*, p. 118 especially.

13. On this point see P. Brown, *In Praise of Hot Liquors* (York, York Civic Trust, 1996).

14. See R. Roth, 'Tea-Drinking in Eighteenth-Century America: its etiquette and equipage' in R. Blair St George (ed.), *Material Life in America 1600–1860* (Boston, Northwestern University Press, 1988), pp. 439–62.

15. Parker, *Subversive Stitch*, p. 114.

16. For a fuller discussion of these episodes see P. Somerville-Large, *The Irish Country House: a social history* (London, Sinclair Stevenson, 1995), chapter 16 especially.

17. See *Letters Written by the late Right Honourable Lady Luxborough to William Shenstone Esq.* (ed) John Hodgetts (Dublin, 1776). The correspondence took place in the 1740s.

18. See Emily, Countess of Cork and Orrery, *The Orrery Papers*, vols I and II, 1903.

19. See L. Walker, 'Women and Architecture' in J. Attfield and P. Kirkham (eds), *A View from the Interior* (London, The Womens' Press, 1989 and revised 1995), chapter 7, p. 92 especially.

20. This is discussed by C. Hussey in *Country Life*, 98 (9 November 1945), p. 819.

21. I. Eller, *The History of Belvoir Castle* (1841), p. 136.

22. Soane's designs for garden seats can be seen in the Victoria & Albert Museum, V&A, 3306.162 recto and V&A, 3306.161.

23. On this point see C. Cunningham, ' "An Italian House is my Lady", Some aspects of the definition of women's role in the architecture of Robert Adam' in G. Perry and M. Rossington (eds), *Femininity and Masculinity in Eighteenth-century Art and Culture* (Manchester and New York,

Manchester University Press, 1994), pp. 63–77, p. 70 especially.

24. For a full discussion of Mrs Coade see A. Kelly, *Mrs Coade's Stone*, (Upton-upon-Severn, Self Publishing Association, 1990)

25. This is fully discussed throughout Girouard, *Life in the English Country House*.

26. Ibid., pp. 144 ff.

27. As quoted in Hussey, *Country Houses: Early Georgian*, p. 196.

28. *Letters Written by . . . Lady Luxborough.*

29. *The Correspondence of Emily Duchess of Leinster* (London 1949) and *Lady Louisa Connolly*, (London, 1957), ed. B. Fitzgerald.

30. Parker, *Subversive Stitch*, chapter 6 especially.

31. This is discussed more fully in ibid., p. 114.

32. Ibid., p. 110.

33. See A. Wells-Cole, *Historic Paper Hangings* (Leeds, Leeds City Art Galleries, 1983), pp. 14–15 especially.

34. *Leinster Correspondence.*

35. On this point see C. Calloway, *Country Life* (18 April 1991), pp. 102–3 and S. Lambert, *The Image Multiplied*, Victoria & Albert Museum Exhibition Catalogue, (1987), p. 183 especially.

36. For a discussion of the frames see Leeds Art Calendar, no. 89, 1981.

37. Wells-Cole, *Historic Paper Hangings*, pp. 34–5 especially.

38. Walpole, *Journals*, xxxiii

39. As quoted in M.R. Rahl and H. Koone (eds), *The Female Spectator: English Women Writers Before 1800* (Bloomington and London, University of Indiana Press, 1977), p. 234.

40. *The Correspondence of Mary Granville – Mrs Delany* (ed.) Lady Llanover (London, 1861).

41. See P. Du Prey, *John Soane, the Making of an Architect* (London and Chicago, University of Chicago Press, 1982), p. 245.

42. See M. Jourdain, 'Shellwork Rooms and Grottoes', *Country Life*, 95 (February 1944), pp. 241–3.

Chapter 6

1. The most recent studies include: A. Wilton and I. Bignamini, *The Grand Tour, The Lure of Italy in the Eighteenth Century, The*

Tate Gallery, Exhibition catalogue 1996; J. Ingamells (ed.), *A Dictionary of British and Irish travellers to Italy 1701–1800* (London and New Haven, Yale University Press, 1997).

2. One of the most interesting recent studies on the reinterpreation and reuse of antique architecture appears in W. Macdonald and J. Pinto, *Hadrian's Villa and its Legacy*, (New Haven and London, Yale University Press, 1995).

3. For full discussion of the evolution and implementation of Adam's gallery design for Harewood see Mauchline, *Harewood House*, chapter 3 especially.

4. For a fuller discussion of the Grand Tour see J. Black, *The Grand Tour in the Eighteenth Century* (Stroud and New York, Sutton Publishing, 1992); R. Shackleton, 'The Grand Tour in the Eighteenth Century' in L.T. Milic (ed.), *Studies in Eighteenth-century Culture* (1971), vol. I.

5. A definition of what did and did not constitute either a Grand Tour or a Grand Tourist and the anachronistic use of the notion of tourism is presented by B. Redford, *Venice and the Grand Tour* (New Haven and London, Yale University Press, 1996), chapter 1 especially. This chapter uses the terms Grand Tour and tourism as taxonomic tools to refer a diverse range of travellers and journeys alongside the specificity of Redford's definitions.

6. Later in the century the Grand Tour developed to include Naples, Sicily and Greece, but Rome still remained an essential part of the itinerary.

7. E. Gibbon, *Memoirs of my life*, ed. G.A. Bonnard (London, Nelson, 1966).

8. L. Sterne, *A Sentimental Journey Through France and Italy* (London, 1768), vol. I.

9. See N. Hardwick, *The Grand Tour; William and John Blathwayt of Dyrham Park 1705–1707* (Saltford, 1985).

10. The fashion for this kind of travel literature endures today as seen in the continued publication of the letters of Grand Tourists and their tutors. Joseph Spence's letters home to his mother are now published as *Joseph Spence, Letters from the Grand Tour*, ed. S. Klima (Montreal, 1975).

11. Only around one-third of the nobility attended Oxford or Cambridge when the Grand Tour was at its height between about 1700 and 1760. See J. Cannon, *Aristocratic Century: The Peerage of Eighteenth-century England* (Cambridge, Cambridge University Press, 1984), p. 48 especially.

12. Sterne, *Sentimental Journey*.

13. This anthropological aspect of the Grand Tour is discussed in Redford, *Venice and the Grand Tour*, chapter 1 especially.

14. Sterne, *Sentimental Journey*.

15. *The Letters of Lady Mary Wortley Montagu*, ed. R. Halsband (Oxford, Oxford University Press, 1966), ii, p. 177.

16. The term British is used here as the Grand Tour was common to the élite of all parts of the British Isles. Moreover, the Act of Union, 1707 introduced the term to refer to the whole nation.

17. See G. Newman, *The Rise of English Nationalism: A Cultural History 1740–1830* (New York, Weidenfeld & Nicolson, 1987).

18. See particularly J. Macpherson, *The Works of Ossian, the Son of Fingal, Translated from the Gaelic language* (1765). There was also a Welsh version of the Ossianic legend.

19. These sentiments are forcibly expressed by Lord Shaftesbury *A Letter concerning the Art or Science of Design* (1712).

20. Hamilton, Naples and d'Hancarville are fully discussed in I Jenkins and K. Sloan *Vases and Volcanoes*, British Museum, Exhibition Catalogue, 1996.

21. These are fully discussed in *Captain Cook*, The National Maritime Museum, Exhibition Catalogue, 1988.

22. Lord Burlington's Grand Tours are discussed in J. Wilton Ely, 'Lord Burlington and Italy' in Arnold (ed.) *Belov'd by Ev'ry Muse*, pp. 15–20.

23. See T. Connor, 'The Fruits of the Grand Tour: Edward Wright and Lord Parker in Italy, 1720–22', *Apollo*, vol. CXLVIII, (July 1998) 23–30.

24. See *The Genius of Wedgwood*, Victoria and Albert Museum, Exhibition catalogue 1995.

25. On this point see W. Benjamin, 'The Work of Art in the Age of Mechanical Reproduction' in *Illuminations*. (London, Fontana, 1992)

26. For a fuller discussion of the response of different European nations to Rome see N. Hampson, *The Enlightenment* (Harmondsworth, Penguin, 1968).

27. S. Freud, 'Civilization and its Discontents' in A. Dickson (ed.) *Civilization, Society*

4

and *Religion*, The Penguin Freud Library, vol. 12 (Harmondsworth, Penguin, 1991), pp. 251–340.

28. Freud, 'Civilization and its Discontents', p. 257.
29. Freud, 'Civilization and its Discontents', pp. 257–8.
30. Walpole, *Correspondence*, xiii, p. 231.
31. For a discussion of the influence these maps had on garden design see D. Arnold, 'Literature and Landscape', *Landscape Design*, February 1993.
32. A. Palladio, *I Quattro Libri dell'Architettura*, IV, ch.XX.
33. The scientific investigation of antiquity began in earnest with the excavations at Pompeii and Herculaeneum but knowledge about these sites was disseminated very slowly. See C. Parslow, *Re-Discovering Antiquity The Excavations at Pompeii, Herculaeneum and Stabiae* (Cambridge, Cambridge University Press, 1996).
34. For a discussion of the philosophy of association and its relationship to architectural aesthetics see D. Watkin, 'Soane and the Picturesque: the Philsophy of Association' in Arnold (ed.) *The Picturesque in late Georgian England*.
35. Reynolds's fifteen discourses delivered at the Royal Academy were published individually from 1769 to 1791. They are reprinted in Sir Joshua Reynolds, *Discourses on Art*, ed. Robert R. Wark (San marino, Huntingdon Library, 1959).
36. David Hume, *Enquiry into the Human Understanding* (1748). This drew on the ideas of Hume's *Treatise* (1739, 1740) which had not been well received.

Chapter 7

1. For example, L. and J.C.F. Stone, *An Open Elite? England 1540–1880* (Oxford, Oxford University Press, 1984), pp. 252–4, 326, 365; H.J. Habakkuk, *Marriage, Debt, and the Estates System. English Landownership 1650–1950* (Oxford, Clarendon Press, 1994), pp. 290–1.
2. E.A. Wrigley, 'A Simple Model of London's Importance in Changing English Society and Economy, 1650–1750', *Past and Present*, XXXVII (1967), 44–70.
3. Quoted, Habakkuk, *Marriage, Debt, and the Estates System*, p. 296.

4. *Torrington Diaries*, II (1935) pp. 75–6, 87–8.
5. Habakkuk, *Marriage, Debt, and the Estates System*, p. 291.
6. *Torrington Diaries*, III (1936), p. 7.
7. In 1771, the 3rd Duke of Portland had to obtain a private act to sell his Hampshire estates, Habakkuk, *Marriage, Debt, and the Estates System*, p. 385; in 1756 the 3rd Duke of Marlborough obtained a private act to amend his grandmother's will, A.L. Rowse *The Later Churchills* (Harmondsworth, Penguin, 1971), p. 91, and the 4th Duke similarly in 1772, 12 Geo.III, private acts, c. 120.
8. Whether for ministerial office, or professional advancement, or a place of profit, whether for themselves or their dependents see Sir Lewis Namier and John Brooke, *The House of Commons, 1754–1790* (London, Secker & Warburg, 1964), *passim*.
9. As witness the Leveson-Gowers: in the 1670s Sir William took lodgings for the London season; his son, the 1st Lord Gower, made politics his whole life, and bought a house in Dover Street; this 'functional' house was not to the taste of his son, the 2nd Baron, who rented instead Lord Coningsby's house in Albemarle Street, let by the executors of the Duke of Queensberry. J.R. Wordie, *Estate Management in Eighteenth-Century England. The Building of the Leveson-Gower Fortune* (1982), pp. 26, 77 and 79.
10. *Torrington Diaries*, IV (1938), p. 9.
11. W. Blake, *An Irish Beauty of the Regency* (1911), p. 241.
12. *Leinster Correspondence*, I (1949), 20 September 1764, p. 413.
13. A.S. Turberville, *Welbeck and its Owners*, II, 1755–1879 (1939), pp. 52, 317–19.
14. *Leinster Correspondence*, I, p. 354.
15. R.A. Kelch, *Newcastle. A Duke without Money* (London, Routledge, 1974), pp. 17–18.
16. Ibid., pp. 10–13, 52, 115–16, 149–50.
17. *Torrington Diaries*, II, p. 14.
18. Data from the *Survey of London*, XXXIX, i, pp. 90–4.
19. Departures not being as fully reported as arrivals, the *Survey* has multiplied departures by a factor of 1.6 (p. 91).
20. *Leinster Correspondence*, I, p. 219.
21. 'Don't let Louisa forget the Indian paper, and if you see any more you like buy it at

once . . . you know we have four [rooms] to do' – Lady Kildare to the Earl in London, ibid, I, 80, 10 May [1759]. 'I have got ten pieces of taffeta . . . they cost sixty-five guineas . . . I have got you two bottles of Ward's scurvy drops' – Earl of Kildare to wife in Ireland, ibid, I, p. 89, 19 May 1759. 'We want small tablecloths for a table of six . . . no bird's-eye pattern to be got, nor has there been any they say in Dublin these eight years; I fancy you cou'd get them in London' – Lady Kildare to Marquess of Kildare, ibid, I, 139, [20 November 1762].
22. *Torrington Diaries*, IV (1938), p. 107. And, twenty years earlier, 'You can't conceive how provoked I feel at anybody's having a notion Ciss came to England to get married' – Lady Holland in London to Dss of Leinster in Ireland about the arrival of their sister, *Leinster Correspondence* I, p. 556, 10 December [1768].
23. Habakkuk, *Marriage, Debt, and the Estates System*, p. 291.
24. *Survey of London*, XL, p. 132, the 2nd Earl of Rockingham, 1736.
25. *Survey of London*, XXXIX, p. 85.
26. *Leinster Correspondence*, I, p. 235.
27. *Survey of London*, XXXIX, 175–9.
28. M.H. Port, 'West End Palaces: The Aristocratic Town House in London 1730–1830', *London Journal*, XX (1995), pp. 17–46.
29. *Survey of London*, XL, pp. 119–21, 142–4.
30. Blake, *An Irish Beauty*, p. 55.
31. *Leinster Correspondence*, I, p. 217.
32. Habakkuk, *Marriage, Debt, and the Estates System*, p. 370.
33. G.E. Mingay, *English Landed Society in the Eighteenth Century* (London, Routledge, 1963), p. 159.
34. Roebuck, *Yorkshire Baronets*, p. 319, cited Habakkuk, *Marriage, Debt, and the Estates System*, p. 290.
35. Thus Lord Spencer in the summer of 1779, passed predominantly at Althorp, spent 6–8 June at Spencer House in order to attend Speeches at Harrow School on the 7th: British Library, Spencer Papers, Lord Spencer's Diary.
36. *Leinster Correspondence*, I, p. 184.
37. Ibid., I, p. 212.
38. Ibid., I, p. 255–6.
39. Blake, *Irish Beauty*, p. 13.
40. *Leinster Correspondence*, I, p. 283.
41. Ibid., II, pp. 201–2.
42. Ibid., I, p. 362, 21 March 1763.
43. Ibid., I, pp. 69, 73, 74, 77–8, 80–2, 85, 88, 91.
44. Ibid., I, pp. 119, 122, 154, 156, 158, 162.
45. Ibid., II, pp. 78–9, 92, 98; III, pp. 9–10, 15, 17, 50.
46. *Torrington Diaries*, II, p. 8.
47. J. Grieg (ed.), *Diaries of a Duchess*, pp. 206–7.
48. Jane Austen, *Sense and Sensibility* (1811), chapter 20.
49. *Leinster Correspondence*, I, p. 314, 9 February 1762.
50. Ibid., I, p. 321, 9 March 1762.
51. Leach, *James Paine*, pp. 178–9.
52. Chatsworth MSS. All figures to the nearest pound. I am grateful to the Trustees of the Chatsworth Settlement for permission to work on their papers and to Mr Peter Day, the Chatsworth archivist, for supplying this information.
53. Ibid.
54. *Torrington Diaries*, II, p. 37.
55. Chatsworth MSS.
56. Ibid.
57. Ibid., C 165 c.
58. Chatsworth MSS.
59. Chatsworth MS C 171, p. 109.
60. Chatsworth MSS, 1820s accounts.
61. *Syon Park* (1996), p. 9.
62. Alnwick MSS. U.I, 58 (1) and 61 (2), by kind permission of the Duke of Northumberland.
63. Alnwick MS. U.I, 58 (2).
64. Ibid.
65. BL, Spencer MSS, D. 49.
66. Household book, pp. 27, 29. I am grateful to Dr Toby Barnard for this reference and the next.
67. Household book, p. 86.
68. In the seventeenth century, when the Bedfords migrated from Woburn to Bedford House (usually from February to June), quantities of provisions (including fowls, turkeys and eggs) were sent 'for the use of the family while they were in town', G. Scott Thomson, *Life in a Noble Household* (1965 edn), pp. 210, 215. In George II's time, the Duke of Newcastle's gardens and farm at Claremont (sixteen miles from London) supplied him and his friends with melons and pineapples, and grain, hay and meat for his establishment. Newcastle's Sussex and Nottinghamshire estates also supplied food for London and

Claremont. Kelch, *Newcastle*, pp. 24, 171, citing BL, Add. MSS 33325–31.

69. *Leinster Correspondence*, I, p. 322, 8 April 1762; pp. 326–7, 23 May 1762.

70. Ibid., p. 339, 5 September 1762.

71. *Creevey Papers*, ed. Sir H. Maxwell (1904), I, pp. 65–6, 148.

72. M. Girouard, *The English Town* (New Haven and London, Yale University Press, 1990), pp. 113–19; Stone, *Open Elite*, p. 113.

73. Habakkuk, *Marriage, Debt, and the Estates System*, p. 281; Stone, *Landed Elite*, pp. 254, 313.

74. J.K. Walton, *The English Seaside Resort. A Social History 1750–1914* (Leicester, Leicester University Press, 1983).

Chapter 8

1. See *Jane Austen's Letters*, ed. R.W. Chapman (London, Oxford University Press, 2nd edn repr. 1969), nos. 95, 98, 100, 101, 107.

2. Jane Austen's eldest brother, James, succeeded his father as rector of Steventon in 1801. Anna was James's daughter by his first marriage.

3. The one exception in the completed novels is Lady Dalrymple in *Persuasion*, a dowager viscountess whose title appears to be Irish, and whose standing is therefore no higher than a baronet's in England.

4. The dating of the first three novels has been much debated. I have adopted the chronology suggested by A. Walton Litz, 'Chronology of Composition', *The Jane Austen Handbook*, ed. J. David Grey (London, Athlone Press, 1986), pp. 47–52. *Sense and Sensibility*, begun in epistolary form as *Elinor and Marianne*, c. 1795, was rewritten as narrative in 1797, and again revised 1809–11 before publication in November 1811. *Pride and Prejudice* was begun as *First Impressions*, 1796–7, radically revised 1811 to 1812, and published in 1813. *Northanger Abbey* was drafted 1798 to 1799, sold as *Susan* to Crosby and Co. in 1803 but never published; the MS was repurchased from them in 1815, and Jane Austen wrote an advertisement for it as *Catherine* in 1817; it was published posthumously with *Persuasion*, 1817–18, and may or may not have been rewritten since 1803.

5. Litz, 'Chronology of Composition' in Grey (ed.) *Jane Austen Handbook* suggests that *Mansfield Park* (1814) was written 1811 to 1813; *Emma* (1815–16) from 1814 to 1815; *Persuasion*, drafted 1815 to 1816, was posthumously published 1818.

6. Excursions apart, locations are as follows: *SS*, Sussex and Devonshire; *PP*, Hertfordshire; *NA*, Gloucestershire; *MP*, Northamptonshire; *E*, Surrey; *P*, Somerset.

7. Edward Austen, Jane Austen's third brother, was adopted by his father's childless relatives, the Knights of Godmersham in Kent, and took their surname in 1812, after both had died. Goodnestone Park belonged to his father-in-law, Sir Brook Bridges.

8. Page references given in brackets to Jane Austen's novels relate to *The Oxford Illustrated Jane Austen*, ed. R.W. Chapman, 3rd edn (5 vols, London, Oxford University Press, 1932–34). References to unfinished novels relate to vol. VI, *Minor Works*, repr. with revisions by B.C. Southam.

9. Wellesley, Lord Gerald, later Duke of Wellington, 'Houses in Jane Austen's Novels' (1926), repr. in *Collected Papers of the Jane Austen Society, 1949–1965* (London, 1967), pp. 185–8.

10. Quoted by T.C. Duncan Eaves and Ben D. Kimpel, *Samuel Richardson: a Biography* (London, Oxford University Press, 1971), pp. 405–6.

11. Samuel Richardson, *The History of Sir Charles Grandison* (1754), ed. Jocelyn Harris, 3 parts (London, Oxford University Press, Oxford English Novels, 1972), part III, p. 285.

12. Godmersham Park was illustrated by Edward Hasted in 1790, *The History and Topographical Survey of Kent*, vol. III.

13. Matching Priory in Trollope's Palliser novels (1864–80) and Monk's Topping in George Eliot's *Daniel Deronda* (1876) are idealized examples; the 'lay abbots' of Marney Abbey in Disraeli's *Sybil* (1845) fail in their duty.

14. *Letters*, ed. Chapman, p. 315. See also Alistair Duckworth, *The Improvement of the Estate*, revised edn, (Baltimore and London, Johns Hopkins University Press, 1994).

15. Cobbett distinguishes between 'yeoman', a freeholder, and 'farmer', a tenant, but Jane Austen applies both words to tenants.

16. Henry Fielding, *Joseph Andrews* (1742), book II, chapter XIV.

17. Sir Francis Austen became Admiral of the Fleet at the age of eighty-nine; Charles Austen was a rear-admiral and CB when he died of cholera, aged seventy-three, during a naval expedition against Burma.

18. *Persuasion* is the only novel where actual dates are given from the *Baronetage* which date the action from the late summer of 1814 to late February or early March 1815. See *Handbook*, ed. Grey, p. 38.

19. *PP*, p. 310. The Great House was leased when Jane Austen first arrived at Chawton.

20. For example, *Dombey & Son* (1848), *David Copperfield* (1849–50), *Great Expectations* (1860–2), and Dickens' last, unfinished novel, *The Mystery of Edwin Drood*, all contain delightful descriptions of nautical interiors, expressive of the virtues of their owners.

21. William Cobbett, *Rural Rides*, 30 September 1826.

22. See particularly *SS*, pp. 28–30, 72–4, 96–8, 107–9, 251–2.

23. Samuel Taylor Coleridge and Robert Southey, 'The Devil's Thoughts', 1.24, on 'a cottage of gentility'.

24. See Beaumanoir in *Coningsby* (1844) book III, chapter 2.

25. The only significant exception is in *Mansfield Park* where Sir Thomas orders that a fire be lit for Fanny in her retreat, the former schoolroom.

26. Examples in *Barnaby Rudge* (1841), *Tale of Two Cities* (1859), *Great Expectations* (1860–1). Dickens's most important great house, Chesney Wold, is desolate and mostly closed at the end of *Bleak House* (1852–3).

Chapter 9

1. This is discussed more fully in S. Daniels and C. Watkins, 'Picturesque landscaping and estate management: Uvedale Price and Nathaniel Kent at Foxley' in S. Daniels and P. Garside (eds), *The Politics of the Picturesque* (Cambridge, Cambridge University Press, 1994), pp. 13–41 and C. Watkins, 'Picturesque Woodland

Management: The Prices at Foxley' in Arnold (ed.), *Picturesque in late Georgian England*.

2. See Andrews, *Search for the Picturesque*, and Andrews, 'Picturesque Template' in Arnold (ed.), *Picturesque in late Georgian England*.

3. This is discussed by Thompson, 'Patrician Society', pp. 382–405 and I reiterate some of his arguments in these paragraphs.

4. On this point see Mingay, 'Size of Farms', p. 470.

5. See Thompson, 'Social Distribution of Landed Property'.

6. On this point see McCahill, 'Peerage creations', pp. 259–84.

7. Ibid. also identifies the freeholder class which comprised a variety of farmers of small holdings. Both Thompson and Mingay, loc. cit., agree that these small farms, whether freehold or leasehold, endured into the nineteenth century.

8. This is discussed in J. Martin Robinson 'Model Farm Buildings of the Age of Improvement', *Architectural History*, 19 (1976), pp. 17–23 and gazeteer and Model Farms (Oxford, Zwemmer, 1983.

9. This is discussed by J. Martin Robinson, 'Estate Buildings at Holkham', *Country Life*, (21 and 28 November 1974).

10. Martin Robinson, 'Modern Farm Buildings' and J. Loch, *Improvements on the Estates of the Marquess of Stafford* (1820).

11. This is fully explored in Langford, *Public Life and the Propertied Englishman*.

12. Ibid., pp. 192–6 and 360–1.

13. Mingay, 'Size of Farms', p. 469.

14. Colman, *European Life and Manners*, Letter XXXII, October 1843.

15. A. Young, *General Report on Enclosures* (1808) pp. 32–3.

16. Langford, *Public Life and the Propertied Englishman*, p. 370.

17. See G.E. Fussell and C. Goodman, 'The Housing of the Rural Population in the eighteenth century', *Economic History Review*, ii (1930–33), 63–90; N. Cooper, 'The Myth of Cottage Life', *Country Life*, 141 (1967), 1290–3.

18. See G. Darley, *Villages of Vision* (London, Architectural Press, 1975) and 'In Keeping with the Mansion: The making of a model village', *Country Life*, 153 (1975), 1080–82.

19. The level of contribution of Brown and Chambers is not known. See A. Oswald,

'Market Town into Model Village', *Country Life*, 140, (29 September 1966), 762–6.

20. Young, *Northern Tour*, pp. 100–1.
21. This is discussed in W. Pitt, *Topographical History of Staffordshire* (1817), pp. 90–91.
22. Mingay, 'Size of Farms', p. 473.
23. The addition of marl – a soil consisting of lime and clay – to the ground as a fertilizer.
24. The addition of manure to the land.
25. Colman, *European Life and Manners*, Letter XXXII, October 1843.
26. Ibid., Letter LXXXIX, 7 February 1845.
27. Waagen, *Treasures of Art*, vol. III, Letter XXXIII.
28. Langford, *Public Life and the Propertied Englishman*, p. 308.
29. Colman, *European Life and Manners*, Letter XXXII, October 1843
30. See *The Particulars and Inventories of the Estates of the Late . . . Directors of the South-Sea Company*, 1721.
31. Young, *Southern Tour*, pp. 3–4.
32. Silliman, *Journal*, vol. III, pp. 147–8.
33. Young, *Northern Tour*, II, p. 476.
34. Young, *Northern Tour*, I pp. 334–5.
35. For a discussion of Palladio's villa and farm designs see H. Burns (ed.), *Andrea Palladio (1508–80): The Portico and the Farmyard*, Arts Council, Exhibition Catalogue (London, 1975).
36. The layout of model farms is discussed in Martin Robinson, 'Model Farm Buildings'.
37. This was part of Adam's scheme to replace Cullen House with Findlater Castle. This design was probably based on the Villa Lante at Bagnaia or the Villa Pia in the Vatican. See A.A. Tait, *Robert Adam, The Creative Mind: from sketch to finished drawing* (London, The Soane Gallery, 1996), p. 29 especially.
38. Ibid.
39. For a full discussion of Soane's approach to architectural theory and design see D. Watkin, *Sir John Soane and Enlightenment Thought: The Royal Academy Lectures* (Cambridge, Cambridge University Press, 1996).
40. This is discussed by P. du Prey in *Country Life*, 159 (8 January 1976), 84.
41. On this point see J. Rykwert, *On Adam's House in Paradise: The idea of the primitive hut in architectural history* (New York, 1972).
42. On this point see E. Kaufman, *Architecture in the Age of Reason* (Cambridge, Mass. and London, Harvard University Press, 1955).

Chapter 10

1. Horace Walpole, *History of the Modern Taste in Gardening*, printed 1771 (but not published until 1780). Winckelmann: see Alex Potts, *Flesh and the Ideal: Winckelmann and the Origins of Art History* (New Haven, Yale University Press, 1994).
2 John Milton, *Paradise Lost* (London, 1667), book IV, lines 223–63.
3. J. Dixon Hunt, ' "Palladian" Gardening' in *Garden and Grove: the Italian Renaissance Garden in the English Imagination, 1600–1750* (London, Dent, 1986), pp. 180–222.
4. *The Yale Edition of Horace Walpole's Correspondence*, ed. W.S. Lewis, 48 vols. (New Haven: Yale University Press, 1937–83), vol. XXIV, p. 193, Walpole to Sir Joseph Banks, 31 March 1787. The book was Richard Payne Knight, *A Discourse on the Worship of Priapus* (London, Society of Dilettanti, 1786). See also Peter Funnell, 'The Symbolical Language of Antiquity' in Michael Clarke and Nicholas Penny (eds), *Arrogant Connoisseur* (Manchester, Manchester University Press, 1982).
5. *Feltham's Picture of London for 1808*, quoted Margaret Goldsmith, *Soho Square* (London, Sampson Low, 1947), p. 145. Coleridge visited Knight to look over his collection and described the experience in a letter to Sir George Beaumont, Thursday 8 March 1804, in *Memorials of Coleorton*, 2 vols., vol. II, p. 55.
6. Joseph Farington, *Diary*, 24 July 1796, Walpole's *Correspondence*, vol. XXIX, p. 338, Walpole to William Mason, 22 March 1796.
7. Uvedale Price, *Essay on the Picturesque* (Hereford, 1794), preface, pp. iii–v.
8. Richard Payne Knight, *The Landscape, a didactic poem*, 2nd edn (London, 1795), preface, p. vi.
9. Knight, *The Landscape*, p. 43n.
10. Uvedale Price, *Essays on the Picturesque* 3 vols (London, 1805), vol. II, pp. 118–20.
11. e.g. Humphry Repton, *Letter to Mr Price* (1794), in Price, *Essays*, vol. III, pp. 10–13.
12. Jay Appleton: 'Richard Payne Knight and *The Georgics*' in *The Picturesque*, no. 5 (Hereford, The Picturesque Society, 1993), pp. 1–8; Andrew Ballantyne, 'Bloodshed and Rankling Passion: Lucretius in *The*

Landscape', in *The Picturesque*, no. 7 (Hereford, The Picturesque Society, 1994), pp. 1–6; Andrew Ballantyne, 'The Didactic Poem as a *Ferme Ornée*' in *The Picturesque*, no. 8 (Hereford, The Picturesque Society, 1994), p. 6.

13. Knight, *The Landscape*, III, 377–400.
14. Alexander Pope, 'Windsor-Forest' (1713). Marilyn Butler, *Burke, Paine, Godwin, and the Revolution Controversy* (Cambridge, Cambridge University Press, 1984) p. 108.
15. William Mason, *Epitaph: On Lancelot Brown, Esq.* in *The Works of William Mason M.A.*, (4 vols, London, Cadell and Davies, 1811), vol. I, p. 143.
16. Knight, *The Landscape*, preface, pp. ix–xii.
17. Walpole, *Correspondence*, vol. XXIX, p. 334, William Mason to Horace Walpole, 15 March 1796.
18. Walpole, *Correspondence*, vol. XXIX, p. 338, Horace Walpole to William Mason, 22 March 1796.
19. Knight, *The Worship of Priapus* and Richard Payne Knight, *The Symbolical Language of Ancient Art and Mythology* (London, 1818).
20. William Wordsworth, from 'Lines written a few miles above Tintern Abbey, on revisiting the banks of the Wye during a tour, July 13, 1798'.
21. Knight, *Symbolical Language*, ed. Alexander Wilder (New York, 1876), p. 141, section 189.
22. Farington, *Diary*, 17 April 1803.
23. Knight, *Symbolical Language*, p. 48, p. 141.
24. Farington, *Diary*, 5 September 1806.
25. Illustrating Isaiah, chapter 11, verse 6. Eleanore Price Mather, 'A Quaker Icon: The Inner Kingdom of Edward Hicks' in *The Art Quarterly* (London, spring/summer 1973), 84–99.
26. Knight, *Symbolical Language*, p. 11, sections 21–2.
27. Giambattista Vico, *Scienza nuova* (3rd edn, Naples, 1744), paragraph 659; trans. Thomas Goddard Bergin and Max Harold Fisch, *The New Science of Giambattista Vico* (Ithaca and London, Cornell University Press, 1968).
28. Vico, *Scienza nuova*, paragraph 615.
29. Gilles Deleuze, *Périclès et Verdi: la philosophie de François Châtelet* (Paris, Editions de Minuit, 1988).

30. I have not traced the whereabouts of Westall's portrait of Lady Oxford, but there is a printed image of it in the Witt Library of the Courtauld Institute, London, from a German-language source.
31. George Cumberland, *An Attempt to Describe Hafod, and the neighbouring scenes about the bridge over the Funack, commonly called the Devil's Bridge, in the county of Cardigan* (London, 1796) includes a plan which shows a 'Druid Temple'. However, it seems never to have been built. Cumberland says in his text that 'if a druid's temple never stood [there], a druid's temple is unquestionably called for; and, I cannot help expressing a hope, that a rude imitation will one day there be placed' (p. 11), a remark which he footnoted with the observation that he had since found this to be Johnes's intention. The intention seems, however, not to have been acted upon in the manner envisaged by Cumberland, though the planting of trees here might have made a Druid grove of the place. 'Ossian' is quoted on p. 31.
32. Richard Payne Knight, *Alfred; a Romance in Rhyme* (London, 1823), pp. 38–43; Plato, *Timaeus*, trans. Desmond Lee (Harmondsworth, Penguin, 1965 rev. 1977), p. 58.
33. Knight, *The Landscape*, p. 3n.
34. Richard Payne Knight, *An Analytical Inquiry into the Principles of Taste* (4th edn, London, 1808) pp. 125, 405.
35. Ibid., p. 50.
36. Ibid., pp. 363–4.
37. George N. Conklin, *Biblical Criticism and Heresy in Milton* (New York, King's Crown Press, 1949).
38. Ben Jonson, *Pleasure Reconcild to Vertue* (1618), lines 13–14.
39. John Milton, *A Maske Presented at Ludlow Castle, 1634* (London, 1637), lines 705–13.
40. Denis Saurat, *Milton: Man and Thinker* (London, Dent, 1944), p. 127.
41. Cumberland, *Hafod*, p. 4.
42. Pevsner said that Knight wrote bad verse, and this has often been taken to be the definitive judgement. Nikolaus Pevsner, *The Buildings of England, Herefordshire* (Harmondsworth, Penguin, 1963), p. 117.

Select Bibliography

This select bibliography serves to highlight works of general relevance to the country house and the Georgian period. Full references to the books and articles referred to in the text can be found in the notes.

Contemporary Sources

Bruyn Andrews, C. (ed.), *The Torrington Diaries*, 4 vols, London, Eyre and Spottiswoode, 1934.

Byrd, William, *The London Diary 1717–1721 and other writings* (ed.) L.B. Wright and M. Tinling, New York, Oxford University Press, 1958.

Campbell, C., *Vitruvius Britannicus*, 3 vols, 1715, 1717 and 1725.

Colman, H., *European Life and Manners in Familiar Letters to Friends*, 2 vols, Boston and London, 1850.

Defoe, D., *A Tour Through the Whole Island of Great Britain*, Harmondsworth, Penguin, 1971 and 1986.

The Correspondence of Mary Granville – Mrs Delany, ed. Lady Llanover, London, 1861.

The Illustrated Journeys of Celia Fiennes 1685–c. 1712, London, Macdonald, 1982.

Gilpin, Revd W., *Observations on the River Wye, and Several parts of South Wales, etc. relative chiefly to Picturesque Beauty; made in the Summer of the Year 1770*, 1782.

Payne Knight, R., *The Landscape, a didactic poem*, 2nd edn, London, 1795.

Price, U., *Essay on the Picturesque*, Hereford, 1794.

A Regency Visitor: The English Tour of Prince Pückler-Muskau Described in his Letters 1826–28 ed. Silliman, B., *Journal of Travels in England, Holland and Scotland and of two passages over the Atlantic in the years 1805–1806*, 3 vols, New Haven, Yale College, 1820.

Waagen, Dr G., *Treasures of Art in Great Britain*, 3 vols, London, John Murray, 1854, reprinted Cornmarket Press, London, 1970.

Walpole, H., *Journals of Visits to Country Seats &c*, ed. P. Toynbee, The Walpole Society, vol. XVI 1928.

The Letters of Lady Mary Wortley Montagu, ed. R. Halsband, Oxford, Oxford University Press, 1966.

Young, A., *A Six Month Tour through the North of England*, 4 vols, London, 1770.

Books

Andrews, M., *The Search for the Picturesque* Aldershot, Scolar, 1989.

Arnold, D., (ed.) *The Georgian Villa*, Stroud, Sutton Publishing, 1996.

——. (ed.) *The Picturesque in late Georgian England*, London, The Georgian Society.

——. (ed.) *Belov'd by Evr'y Muse: Richard Boyle 3rd Earl of Burlington and 4th Earl of Cork (1694–1753)*, London, The Georgian Group, 1994.

Ballantyne, A. *Architecture, Landscape and Liberty: Richard Payne Knight and the Picturesque*, Cambridge, Cambridge University Press, 1997.

Beckett, J.V., *The Aristocracy in England 1660–1914*, Oxford, 1986.

Black, J., *The Grand Tour in the Eighteenth Century*, Stroud and New York, Sutton Publishing, 1992.

Clayton, T., *The English Print 1688–1802*, London and New Haven, Yale University Press, 1997.

Clemenson, H., *English Country Houses and Landed Estates*, London, Croom Helm, 1982.

Duckworth, A., *The Improvement of the Estate*, revised edn, Baltimore and London, Johns Hopkins University Press, 1994.

Girouard, M., *Life in the English Country House*, New Haven and London, Yale University Press, 1978.

Habakkuk, H.J., *Marriage, Debt, and the Estates System. English Landownership 1650–1950*, Oxford, Clarendon Press, 1994.

The Jane Austen Handbook, ed. J. David Grey, London, Athlone Press, 1986.

Harris, J., *The Artist and the Country House*, London, Sotheby Parke Burnet, 1979.

Hussey, *The English Country House: Georgian*, vols 1–3.

Kelsall, M. *The Great Good Place: The Country House and English Literature*, 1993.

Langford, P., *Public Life and the Propertied Englishman 1689–1798*, Oxford, Clarendon Press, 1991.

——. *A Polite and Commercial People: England 1727–1783*, Oxford, Oxford University Press, 1992.

Leavis, Q.D., *Collected Essays*, ed. G. Singh, 2 vols., Cambridge Paperback Library, London, Cambridge University Press, 1983.

Lees Milne, J., *Earls of Creation*, London, Century Classics, 1986.

Mingay, G.E., *English Landed Society in the Eighteenth Century*, London, Routledge, 1963.

Porter, R., *English Society in the Eighteenth Century*, Penguin, Harmondsworth, 1982.

Somerville-Large, P., *The Irish Country House, a Social History*, London, Sinclair Stevenson, 1995.

Stone, L. and Fawtier Stone, J.C., *An Open Elite? England 1540–1880*, Oxford, Oxford University Press, 1984.

Summerson, J., *Architecture in Britain, 1530–1830*, Pelican History of Art, Harmondsworth, many editions, first published 1953.

Tinniswood, A., *A History of Country House Visiting*, Oxford and London, Blackwell and The National Trust, 1989.

Thompson, F.M.L., *English Landed Society in the Nineteenth Century*.

Tristram, P., *Living Space in Fact and Fiction*, Routledge, London, 1989.

Williamson, T., *Polite Landscapes*, Stroud, Sutton Publishing, 1994.

Index